The Victory of Zionism

*Reclaiming the Narrative about
Israel's Domestic, Regional,
and International Challenges*

Emmanuel Navon

ISBN: 1502327945
ISBN 13: 9781502327949

To Sima, Yonah, Eitan,
Noam and Gilead,
with love.

"Memory is necessary for all the operations of reason."

Blaise Pascal, *Pensées* (« Les philosophes, » Art. 369).

"No son of Allah, who calls for the punishment of the 'infidel bitch,' will ever manage to scare me, to make me give up. Never. Even if I am at the twilight of my life, and even though I no longer have the energy of my youth. I intend to live that twilight and to drink it till its last drop."

Oriana Fallaci, *The Force of Reason*

Table of Content

Introduction

This book is a collection of articles on Israeli politics, the Arab-Israeli conflict, and Israel's foreign policy. It covers four eventful years, from October 2010 to October 2014.

During those years, a massive rebellion (the ill-named "Arab Spring") shook the Arab world; Syria sank into an endless civil war; US troops left Iraq, and radical Islamists took over the northern part of the country; Israel experienced an unprecedented yet short-lived social protest; President Obama defeated his Republican contender, and Prime Minister Netanyahu was reelected with a narrow majority; US secretary of state John Kerry attempted, and failed, to broker a peace agreement between Israel and the Palestinian Authority (PA); two wars were fought between Israel and the Hamas-controlled Gaza Strip; the Jewish people were the target of horrendous terror attacks both in Israel and abroad; and diplomatic tensions worsened between Israel and Turkey as well as between the United States and Russia.

I challenge the conventional wisdom and offer a different reading of Israeli politics, of the Arab-Israeli conflict, and of Israel's foreign policy. By "conventional wisdom" I mean three basic ideas typically expressed by government officials and Middle East commentators: a) Israel will lose altogether its Jewish majority, its democratic regime, and its international support if a Palestinian state is not established in the near future; b) Solving the Israeli-Palestinian conflict depends mostly on Israel being willing to make concessions; c) Israeli democracy and the Israel-Jewish Diaspora relationship are threatened by the shifting of Israeli politics to the right.

On Israeli politics, I argue the following:

a. Israel's ideological contests and competing political agendas are not settled at the polls but rather by a power struggle between politicians on the one hand and between judges, journalists, and academics on the other hand. Over the past three decades, Israel's Supreme Court has unilaterally expanded its powers by opening its gates to petitioners without the requirement of standing, by making political decisions "justiciable," and by granting itself the right to repeal laws and government decisions not only for being allegedly "unconstitutional" (despite the fact that Israel does not have a constitution) but also for being "unreasonable" (an arcane concept whose interpretation belongs to the judges alone). Among the petitioners who try (often successfully) to repeal government decisions and Knesset (Israel's parliament) laws are non-governmental organizations (NGOs) that are funded by the ultra-liberal New Israel Fund as well as by European governments and the European Union (EU). The agenda of these NGOs is shared and supported by influential Israeli academics and journalists whose worldviews do not convince enough voters to foster political majorities in the Knesset. Instead of a separation of powers between the three branches of government, Israel's political system is therefore characterized by a power struggle between elected officials and unelected ones.

b. Israel's mainstream intelligentsia has lost its credibility by preventing intellectual pluralism in academia, by stubbornly refusing to reassess failed ideas and policies such as socialism and "peace for our time," and by circling wagons around indefensible causes (such as siding with French journalist Charles Enderlin in the "al-Durrah affair").

c. The very idea of a Jewish nation-state is under assault both at home and abroad. This idea, therefore, must be defended in the realm of ideas and entrenched by legislation.

On the Arab-Israeli conflict, I make three main points:

a. The idea that Israel can reach peace with the Palestine Liberation Organization (PLO) by reverting to its pre-1967 boundaries is delusional. For the Arabs of the former British Mandate on Palestine, the historical scar and humiliation (what they call *Naqba*) is 1948, not 1967. Hence was there no peace with them before 1967, and hence have they rejected all peace proposals that would have settled the 1967 issue but not the 1948 one. This is why there is no solution to the Arab-Israeli conflict. This lack of solution, while unfortunate, is sustainable. Israel has thrived and will continue to thrive despite this protracted and unsolvable conflict.

b. Because the idea that an Israeli withdrawal to the pre-1967 boundaries will bring peace has lost its credibility, advocates of withdrawal base their case on demographics (Israel, according to their argument, will cease to be a Jewish state if it does not withdraw from the West Bank). Actual demographic trends, however, point to a stable and even growing two-thirds Jewish majority between the Mediterranean Sea and the Jordan River (excluding the Gaza Strip). Hence the "demographic threat" is a sham that certainly does not justify establishing a failed, hostile, and armed (how would it be demilitarized?) state surrounding Jerusalem, overlooking Tel-Aviv, and controlling the fate of Ben-Gurion airport.

c. The concept of a "Palestinian people" is a fraud and the "two-state solution" is a deception inspired by the Vietnam precedent. There is an Arab nation divided into twenty-two dysfunctional states, many of which have been falling apart for the past three years, and most of which are threatened by Islamist movements that deny the very legitimacy of the artificial Arab states established by European powers after World War I. The idea of establishing a twenty-third failed Arab state (a so-called Palestinian state) in such a context defies logic. The claim that such a state would grant freedom, dignity, and economic opportunity to its inhabitants begs disbelief, since no Arab state provides freedom, dignity, and economic opportunity to its subjects.

Finally, on Israel's foreign policy, my ideas may be summarized as follows:

a. Israel can and must be more vocal and assertive on the EU's double standards and hypocrisy, when compared to other conflicts around the world, on the Arab-Israeli conflict. Israel is a technology powerhouse, and it is emerging as a major natural gas exporter. Its economic relationship with the EU is based on common interests. Israel can now afford to challenge the EU's double standards. It is for the EU to explain, for example, why it imposes economic sanctions on certain disputed territories (such as Judea and Samaria) but not on others (such as Northern Cyprus, Western Sahara, and Abkhazia).

b. The Obama administration's mishaps and blunders in the Middle East have affected Israel's interests, deterrence, and international standing by forcing Israel to free terrorists, by demanding from Israel a pointless apology to Turkey, by backing down from the threat to intervene in Syria, and by falling into the trap of Iran's charm offensive. While Israel's strategic relationship with the United States remains of utmost importance, Israel must rethink the terms of this relationship so as to limit the side effects of America's mistakes and miscalculations.

c. The Islamic threat in Africa and the proxy war between Israel and Iran on that continent create new diplomatic opportunities for Israel. Israel's antiterrorist expertise and its positive image among African Christians must be fully leveraged to restore and expand the strategic and economic ties between Israel and Africa, which were initiated in the late 1950s by Golda Meir.

In the pages below, I elaborate on the above ideas with a historical and factual background.

● ● ●

Israeli Politics

Israel's pre-state Jewish population (the *Yishuv* in Hebrew) was made up of the "old Yishuv" (i.e., the small number of Jews who had remained in the Land of Israel since the exile imposed by the Roman Empire in AD 135) and the "new Yishuv" (i.e., Jews mostly from eastern Europe, Russia, and Yemen, who had immigrated to the Land of Israel in the nineteenth century). While the first waves of immigration (*aliyah* in Hebrew) from 1881 onward were mostly composed of eastern European and Yemenite Jews, the fifth aliyah (1930–1939) included many German Jews fleeing Nazi Germany. Thus the country's economic infrastructure and political institutions were mostly built by eastern European and Russian Jews, while German Jews formed the bulk of the country's intellectual elite.

Both Russian and German Jews were mostly secular, but the former oscillated between nationalism and socialism, while the latter were staunchly liberal. German émigrés founded the liberal *Haaretz* newspaper and became key figures at the Hebrew University and, later, at the Supreme Court. Both Israel's first justice minister, Pinhas Rozen, and Israel's first president of the Supreme Court, Moshe Smoira, were *Yekim* (the Hebrew word for German Jews).

Even though the Yekim dominated academia and the judiciary, and even though they considered themselves "the enlightened ones" in a society mostly dominated by nationalism and socialism, the Supreme Court did respect the principle of the separation of powers during the first decades of Israel's independence. For example, the High Court of Justice was petitioned in 1969 by an aspiring politician who claimed that the law on political parties was unfair because it did not enable new political parties to obtain state funding. In its decision, the court agreed that the law was unfair and discriminating, but ruled that there was nothing the court could do. Only the Knesset, the judges wrote in their ruling, had the legislative power to pass a new law, and the court could not infringe upon that power.

The High Court of Justice also used to be of the opinion that not everything is justiciable and that it should therefore not be asked to get involved in political matters. When Israel established diplomatic relations with the Federal Republic of Germany in 1965, for instance, the court was petitioned to prevent the appointment of the first German ambassador, who had been an officer in the Wehrmacht. The court dismissed the petitioners and explained, "The Government decided what it decided. The Knesset endorsed the Government's decision. The considerations were not legal ones, but matters of foreign policy and of the suitability of the designated ambassador. The Court is not entitled to get involved in those matters."

This traditional stance of the court changed under the leadership of Justice Aharon Barak. Barak served as justice at the Supreme Court between 1978 and 1995 and as the court's president between 1995 and 2006. In 1992, Barak proclaimed, unilaterally, a "constitutional revolution" based on two basic laws passed that year —Basic Law: Human Dignity and Liberty, and Basic Law: Freedom of Occupation—even though these two laws had gone nearly unnoticed when they were passed: Human Dignity and Liberty only gathered thirty-two votes out of 120.

When the two above basic laws were voted on, the Knesset had no intention of granting the court the power to repeal regular laws that allegedly contradict basic laws. Indeed, Aharon Barak was criticized for unilaterally declaring a "constitutional revolution" that had not been intended by the Knesset. Thus did former justice Moshe Landau declare that "this would be the first constitution in history produced by a mere declaration from the court," and thus did former Knesset member Michael Eitan quip that "this is the first revolution in history that happened without the people's knowledge."

In truth, Barak had started his "revolution" before the passing of the two above basic laws, and before he became president of the Supreme Court. He had canceled the principle of "standing" (i.e., the requirement that a petitioner must prove that he is directly affected by the government decision or law against which he is petitioning the court) in 1986. Back in 1970, the High Court of Justice had established the precedent for standing when it rejected a petition about the drafting of ultra-orthodox Jews to the army, arguing that the petitioner was not directly and personally affected by the military service exemption enjoyed by *yeshiva* (Talmudic academy) students, and therefore that he had no standing. In 1986, Barak ruled otherwise in a petition submitted on the same issue: standing, he decided, was no longer required.

Thus did Barak open the gates of the High Court of Justice to everyone. The fact that the court could now be petitioned by anyone, however, did not mean that it could be petitioned for everything. Yet this also Barak changed by declaring that "everything is justiciable." While in the past the court had declared that it could not interfere with political issues (such as the government's decision to accept the credentials of a German ambassador, for instance), Barak declared that, from now on, nothing would be beyond the court's reach.

But how could the court interfere with government decisions that were clearly not illegal? For a government decision to be justiciable, it must first be potentially illegal. Barak solved that problem too, by declaring that the court could interfere not only based on the alleged illegality of a government decision, but also based on its alleged "unreasonableness."

Citizens today are now entitled to petition the court not only if they are convinced that a government decision is illegal, but also if they feel that the decision is "unreasonable." And who shall decide whether or not a government decision is "reasonable"? Well, the court, of course.

Barak's constitutional revolution replaced the separation of powers with a hierarchy of powers dominated by the judiciary. This constitutional revolution enables political parties that lose elections to promote and even to impose their agendas, via the court, on elected governments.

Not only did Barak unilaterally extend the powers of the court, but he also extended the powers of the government's attorney general. In 1962, the Agranat Commission had determined what the powers of the attorney general should be. The report of the commission concluded that, while the government should take into account the opinion of the attorney general, his opinion was not binding. Barak decided otherwise, however, and ruled in a 1993 court decision that the attorney general's opinion was binding. The government had once been free to follow or not follow the non-binding opinions of the attorney general, but from now on, it would have to follow his instructions.

The three elements of Barak's constitutional revolution—canceling standing, making everything justiciable, and making the opinions of the attorney general legally binding—became fully palpable in the *Pinhassi* ruling of 1993.

Raphael Pinhassi was a cabinet member who had been indicted for financial wrongdoings. According to the law, only convicted ministers must resign in such circumstances. Pinhassi had not been convicted yet (his trial had not even begun), and Prime Minister Yitzhak Rabin did not want to fire him. But some Israeli politicians and NGOs decided that Pinhassi should be fired anyway.

Since there was no standing requirement anymore, those NGOs were able to petition the court. By law, Pinhassi didn't have to resign, and the prime minister didn't have to fire him, and so there was nothing illegal with keeping him in his job. But the petitioners claimed that it was "unreasonable" for Pinhassi to stay. The prime minister's opinion was that Pinhassi should neither resign nor be fired, but the attorney general thought otherwise.

In his ruling, Aharon Barak made full use of his new arsenal. The NGOs that petitioned the court were obviously entitled to do so even without having to prove that they would suffer some direct and irreparable damage were Pinhassi to keep his job. There was nothing illegal in the prime minister's decision not to fire Pinhassi, but Barak ruled that it was "unreasonable." As for the prime minister's position that Pinhassi should keep his job, Barak ruled that it did not matter, because only the binding opinion of the attorney general should be taken into account in court, and not the personal (and irrelevant) opinion of the prime minister.

Barak went a step further in 1995 by repealing a Knesset law. In his *Bank Mizrahi* ruling, Barak ruled that the court could repeal regular laws deemed inconsistent with basic laws—though as mentioned before, the Knesset itself had never meant to grant the court the power to repeal laws because of their alleged "unconstitutionality."

At that point, legislators and government ministers decided that the court had gone too far. No justice minister, however, has so far been able to introduce reforms aimed at reining in the constitutional revolution. In fact, all justice ministers who have tried to question the unilateral extension of the judiciary's powers have ended up being investigated by the police and indicted. All have had to resign from their jobs. The list includes Yaacov Neeman in 1996, Reuven Rivlin in 2001, and Haim Ramon in 2006. Former justice minister Daniel Friedman, a respected law professor, was spared despite his determination to undo Barak's "revolution," but the prime minister who appointed him, Ehud Olmert, was indicted and had to resign.

Trying to challenge the enormous powers of the attorney general is a nonstarter as well. The attorney general is a legal advisor whose "advice" now constitutes a binding instruction. He is also the government's lawyer when the state is petitioned at the High Court of Justice. Last but not least, he is the state prosecutor. This means that he is in charge of prosecuting elected officials and government ministers who are suspected of wrongdoings. Considering these powers, no government minister in his right mind would want to antagonize the attorney general by curtailing his authority. Former justice minister Yaacov Neeman, who served from 2009 to 2013, tried to limit the powers of the attorney general, but he faced strong resistance from the legal establishment and so decided to drop the idea. Former attorney general Menny Mazuz once complained that "we've had some confrontational justice ministers lately." Yaacov Neeman concluded that it would be unwise to be confrontational vis-à-vis his subordinates.

Attempts to significantly reform the mechanism by which judges are appointed to the Supreme Court have also failed so far. In the current system, Supreme Court justices are nominated by a commission composed of judges, MKs, and other representatives, but in practice judges have veto power over who will replace them, and thus did Aharon Barak veto Ruth Gavison because she was critical of his constitutional revolution. Former justice minister Daniel Friedman tried to reform the appointment mechanism but was unable to carry out his project, as early elections brought down the government in which he was serving.

As explained by law professor Menachem Mautner in his book *Law and Culture in Israel at the Threshold of the Twenty-First Century* (2008), the constitutional revolution enabled the Israeli left to partially regain the power it had lost at the polls in 1977, when the Labor Party, in power since Israel's independence in 1948, was trumped by Likud's electoral victory. The "former hegemons," as Mautner calls them (and with whom he fully identifies), thus lost their political hegemony but jealously kept—and expanded—their unchallenged power in the judiciary, academia, and the media.

The constitutional revolution in fact opened a Pandora's Box, because it enabled individuals and groups with radical agendas to challenge the legal principles that define Israel as a Jewish state. In 2000, for example, the High Court of Justice ruled in the *Kaadan* case that Arab citizens should be allowed to purchase a plot on land bought by the Jewish Agency with the specific purpose of settling Jews in Israel. On the face of it, the court's ruling looked like an anti-discriminatory measure favoring equal civil rights, even at the expense of the Jewish Agency's commitment to its donors. But the same court ruled in 1989 in the *Avitan* case that a Jew should not be allowed to purchase a plot on land designated by the state for the settling of Bedouins in Israel. So an Arab is allowed to buy a house in a village established for Jews, but a Jew is not allowed to buy a house in a village established for Arabs.

Likewise, the High Court of Justice was petitioned twice, in 2006 and in 2012, to cancel Israel's citizenship law because the law prevents family reunification between Israeli Arabs and Arabs from the West Bank. The true purpose of the petitioners, however, was to impose upon Israel, via the back door, the Palestinian "right of return" by way of fictitious marriages. The High Court rejected the petition both times, but with a very short majority. Had the petition been accepted, Israel's demographic makeup would have been dramatically transformed.

Thus is Israel's self-definition as a Jewish state being challenged via the High Court of Justice as a result of the constitutional revolution. Israel did define itself as a Jewish state in its declaration of independence: "We... hereby declare the establishment of a Jewish state in the land of Israel, to be known as the State of Israel." But the legal status of the Declaration of Independence is that of a declaratory document with no constitutional value (as a result of the High Court of Justice's 1948 *Ziv v. Governik* ruling).

So Israel's declaratory self-definition as a Jewish state is not legally binding, which means that Israel is not a Jewish state de jure.

There are, potentially, far-reaching consequences to the fact that Israel is a Jewish state de facto but not de jure. De facto, Israel's symbols and national anthem express the historical legacy and culture of the Jewish people; the law of return grants automatic immigration rights to Jews; Hebrew is the official language, and national holidays are based on the Jewish calendar; the IDF protects all Jews, not only Israelis (as it did during the 1976 rescue of hostages in Entebbe); and taxpayer money was used in the past to airlift Jews in distress, as it is used today to fund Jewish education in the Diaspora.

Instead of a constitution, Israel passed basic laws defining the powers of the three branches of government (such as the Knesset law) and protecting human rights (such as the Human Dignity and Liberty law). No basic law, however, defines the state's Jewish identity. The consequence of this legal void is that the laws, policies and practices that characterize Israel as a Jewish state can be challenged in court thanks to the constitutional revolution of Aharon Barak. It is therefore time to pass a basic law defining Israel as a Jewish state.

• • •

The Arab-Israeli Conflict

Albert Einstein defined insanity as "doing the same thing over and over again and expecting different results." According to this definition, it is clearly insane to believe in the "two-state solution." Yet expressing disbelief at that "solution" is what is commonly considered insane.

There was no "Palestine" under the Ottoman Empire, but administrative districts called Sanjaks (such as the Sanjaks of Jerusalem, Nablus, and Acre). When the British conquered the Ottoman Empire and divided it with the French, they recreated the Roman "Palestina" (named after the Philistines, Israel's eternal enemies), which became "Palestine" in English. In 1922, Britain was mandated by the League of Nations to establish a Jewish "national home" in Palestine, but the British government cut off nearly 80 percent of the territory (east of the Jordan River) to give a country to Abdullah after the French conquered Damascus.

What was left of Palestine west of the Jordan River became hotly disputed between Jewish and Arab nationalists, with the British using their usual divide-and-rule method and making incompatible commitments to both sides.

Two of the dominant Zionist leaders at the time were David Ben-Gurion and Vladimir (Ze'ev) Jabotinsky. Ben-Gurion had left his native Poland in 1906 for the land of Israel, where he wanted to build a socialist Jewish state. Jabotinsky arrived a decade later as an officer in the Jewish Legion, which he had established within the British army to help evict the Turks during World War I. Jabotinsky rejected socialism, and his political outlook was more hawkish and conservative than Ben-Gurion's. In pre-state Zionist politics, Ben-Gurion was the leader of the left, and Jabotinsky the leader of the right.

As opposed to Ben-Gurion, who did not want to break the Jews' allegiance to the Ottoman Empire, Jabotinsky realized that Palestine would be freed only under the auspices of Great Britain. Jabotinsky convinced the British to form the Jewish Legion, which fought under the Union Jack to drive out the Turks with Jabotinsky himself serving as an officer. The land of Israel was freed from the Turks by the British and by the Jews. In 1917, the British Government issued the "Balfour Declaration" in which it committed itself to the establishment of a "Jewish National Home" in Palestine. The 1922 League of Nations mandate turned the Balfour Declaration into an internationally binding legal document.

Even though the Arabs had inherited the Ottomans' large Middle East empire, they wanted Palestine as well, and so they rejected the

League of Nations mandate. Socialist Zionists such as Ben-Gurion origi-nally believed that the Arabs, realizing the material benefits of Zionism, would welcome it. Jabotinsky, by contrast, rejected this hope as delu-sional. In his 1923 article "The Iron Wall," Jabotinsky argued that natives never willingly accept newcomers (even if the original natives were Jews, in the case of Palestine) and that it was absurd to expect a different at-titude from the Arabs. Zionism had to be imposed by force, and only an allegorical "Iron Wall" of Jewish deterrence might eventually convince the Arabs to accept a reality they disliked.

Ben-Gurion ended up adopting Jabotinsky's Iron Wall strategy, though he never openly admitted it. Arab violence and British duplicity eventually convinced him that no amount of material benefits would convince the Arabs to cooperate with the Zionist project. In the 1930s, Ben-Gurion's hawkishness (or realism?) became nearly undistinguishable from Jabotinsky's.

There were both good and tragic reasons for Ben-Gurion to aban-don his hopes. In April 1920, Arab rioters killed six defenseless Jews and injured 200 in the old city of Jerusalem. Had it not been for Jabotinsky's self-defense forces, the number of victims would have been much high-er. These riots were incited by Arab leader Hadj Amin al-Husseini, who was tried in absentia and sentenced to ten years in jail. As for Jabotinsky, he was sentenced to fifteen years for having organized the Jewish de-fense. Because of the international outcry caused by Jabotinsky's sen-tence, however, the British decided to pardon him—though in order to be perceived as "fair," they also pardoned al-Husseini. The new high commissioner for Palestine, Sir Herbert Samuel, hoping to further pla-cate al-Husseini, also decided to appoint him grand mufti of Jerusalem as well as leader of the Supreme Muslim Council. Motivated by a policy of appeasement, this appointment was a fatal mistake.

It was a fatal mistake because al-Husseini, a radical Islamist and rabid anti-Semite, used his power to create a pattern that kept repeating itself until the British left Palestine: he would incite terrorism against Jews, and, as a result of the violence, the British would appease him by meeting his demands. Al-Husseini, however, was never appeased by British concessions, which he pocketed nevertheless. He wasn't looking for accommodation but for the elimination of Zionism. Indeed, opposition to Zionism was the defining element of the Palestinian ethos he invented. Seeing that his strategy worked, he repeated it. In May 1921, al-Husseini organized a pogrom that killed 43 Jews. There was another wave of Arab violence in 1924, in which 133 Jews perished. In 1929, al-Husseini instigated a major onslaught against the Jewish communities of Jerusalem, Hebron, and Safed, in which 135 Jews were murdered and 300 wounded. Instead of protecting the Jews, the British forced them out of Hebron.

The British later responded to the 1929 pogrom with more appeasement toward al-Husseini, establishing the Shaw Commission with the purpose of finding a solution to the conflict in Palestine. In 1930, the Shaw Commission recommended limiting Jewish immigration. Three years later, Adolf Hitler became chancellor of Germany. With European Jews now in clear danger, allowing their immigration to Palestine was more urgent than ever. Al-Husseini, however, did not see it that way. He cleverly saw in the rise of Nazism an excellent opportunity to blackmail Britain: as war with Germany became inevitable, Britain was anxious to secure the loyalty of its colonies. Al-Husseini threatened to side with Germany were Britain not to meet his demands (which included the cessation of Jewish immigration), though in reality he sided with Nazi Germany regardless of Britain's concessions. His threats bore fruit: by 1935, the British high commissioner to Palestine, Sir Arthur Wauchope, recommended the establishment of an elected council that would have ensured a majority to the Arabs. This was precisely what al-Husseini had been asking for. And yet he rejected Wauchope's plan because it did not include the total cessation of Jewish immigration.

One year later, in 1936, al-Husseini launched a new wave of terror against the Jews. This terrorist campaign lasted for three years and produced 547 Jewish victims. The British, in turn, first tried to appease al-Husseini by agreeing to the 1937 Peel Commission Plan, a partition plan that would have left about 70 percent of western Palestine to the Arabs. Not only did al-Husseini reject the proposal, however, but he redoubled his violence against the Jews and again openly threatened to side with Nazi Germany. This threat convinced the British to publish the White Paper in May 1939, an official document approved by the British government, which accepted all the Arab demands of the time. With this Britain reneged the League of Nations mandate by declaring that it had no intention of establishing a Jewish state in Palestine. Jewish immigration was limited to 75,000 over the coming five years, and further Jewish immigration after that would have to be approved by the Arabs. Just as the Jews were now trapped in Hitler's claws, Britain sealed the gates of Palestine to Jewish immigration. This is what ultimately convinced Menachem Begin, Jabotinsky's successor, to lead the revolt against Britain. Yet even the White Paper was not good enough for al-Husseini: he protested at the fact that 75,000 Jews would be allowed to immigrate over five years.

Al-Husseini's rejection of Britain's ultimate capitulation and betrayal of the Jews was not surprising. He was only extorting England. He would have supported Hitler regardless of British concessions—and, indeed, so he did. Far from thanking the British for their capitulation, al-Husseini deepened his ties and cooperation with Adolf Hitler.

British appeasement was as counterproductive and ill advised toward Hitler as it was toward al-Husseini. Instead of seeing those fanatic and insatiable ideologues for what they were, British appeasers tried to justify and rationalize their enemies' hatred: Hitler had a point, since the Versailles agreements had humiliated Germany; Al-Husseini was not to be blamed, since the Jews were taking over Palestine.

Al-Husseini had created a lethal fusion between Islamic anti-Jewish themes and European anti-Semitism. In 1922 he had initiated the Arabic translation and dissemination of the *Protocols of the Elders of Zion*, and in 1933 he welcomed the election of Adolf Hitler. It took until 1937, however, for Hitler to provide funds and weapons to al-Husseini. It was then, as war with Britain looked inevitable, that Hitler sought to weaken the British Empire in the Middle East by building an alliance between Nazi Germany and Arab leaders such as al-Husseini.

The British in turn tried to arrest al-Husseini, who fled to Beirut and then to Baghdad, where he was instrumental in the anti-British and pro-Nazi coup executed by Rashid Ali al-Gaylani in Iraq in 1941. After Britain defeated al-Gaylani and retook control of Iraq, al-Husseini and al-Gaylani had to flee again, but not before organizing a pogrom against the Jews of Baghdad, killing 120, wounding over 1,000, and destroying Jewish homes and businesses.

Al-Husseini then found political asylum in Germany, where he met with Hitler in November 1941. He committed to helping Hitler fight Britain in the Middle East, and Hitler committed to helping al-Husseini exterminate the Jews of the Middle East. This cooperation was translated into actions, with al-Husseini establishing, in 1943, an SS division composed of Bosnian Muslims who murdered 90 percent of Bosnia's 14,000 Jews. In addition, al-Husseini convinced Heinrich Himmler to send 5,000 Hungarian Jews to Auschwitz rather than to Mandatory Palestine after he heard that Britain and Germany were negotiating the exchange of German war prisoners.

Yet despite the fact that al-Husseini had sided with the Nazis during the war and had actively participated in the Holocaust, he was never tried for war crimes. He settled in Egypt after the war but was still considered the leader of Palestine's Arabs. And although they had bet on the wrong horse during World War II, Palestine's Arabs were nevertheless offered a state alongside a Jewish one within the British Mandate. Such was the proposal of the United Nations Special Committee on Palestine (UNSCOP), which was endorsed as a nonbinding recommendation by the United Nations General Assembly on November 29, 1947. Even though the borders proposed by UNSCOP were unworkable, and even though they left Jerusalem outside the proposed Jewish state, the Zionist leadership accepted the plan. Al-Husseini and the Arab League rejected it.

Arab armies launched a war of extermination against the nascent Jewish state, and Arab countries expelled their Jewish communities. Yet even invaded by five Arab armies (Egypt, Jordan, Iraq, Syria, and Lebanon), Israel was still able not only to secure its existence but also to expand its territory beyond the lines proposed by UNSCOP. The war and its aftermath created a double refugee phenomenon of 600,000 Arabs and 900,000 Jews. The Arab aggressors (except Iraq) accepted a ceasefire that was signed in Rhodes in 1949.

The demarcation line between Israeli and Jordanian forces was drawn with a green marker on the map of the armistice agreement by Ralph Bunch, the UN mediator (hence the expression "green line"). It was defined as a "temporary ceasefire line," not a border, upon Jordan's insistence. In 1948, Jordan had conquered, by attaching Israel, a territory (known today as the West Bank) that had been attributed to Jewish self-determination by the 1922 League of Nations mandate—a mandate that was not canceled by the General Assembly vote of November 29, 1947, since this vote was a nonbinding recommendation that had become moot the moment it was rejected by the Arabs. Jordan not only conquered the West Bank but also annexed it. With the exception of Britain and Pakistan, however, the international community did not recognize Jordan's annexation of the West Bank.

Israel hoped to turn the armistice agreement into a peace agreement, but that never happened. The Arab states' rulers, especially Egyptian leader Gamal Abdel Nasser, were determined to take revenge against the "humiliation" of Israel's war of independence and to win the next round. Hence did Egypt and Jordan encourage endless and lethal terrorist infiltrations against Israel from the Gaza Strip and from the West Bank in the 1950s, and hence did Nasser sign a military agreement with the Soviet Union in 1955, thus making Egypt a new Soviet satellite in the Middle East.

The 1955 Soviet-Egyptian deal was a game changer. Israel's prime minister at the time, David Ben-Gurion, hoped that the United States would react with a similar deal with Israel in order to counter Soviet influence. But that was not the policy of the Eisenhower administration. Like the British in the 1930s, the United States reacted to Arab threats with cajoling and appeasement. In 1955, the Eisenhower administration came up with the Alpha Plan. The idea was to demand an Israeli withdrawal from territories Israel had conquered during its war of independence, in order to convince Nasser to make peace with Israel. But Nasser was not interested. Emboldened by his new alliance with the Soviet Union, he wanted to defy the West and was confident that he could win his next war against Israel—so confident indeed that he decided in 1956 to nationalize the Suez Canal (thus taking it away from the joint French-British ownership) and to close the Straits of Tiran to Israeli shipping (thus barring Israel from accessing Asia via the Red Sea). Nasser's double provocation triggered a joint Israeli-French-British military operation known as the Suez War.

The Suez War was a military success and a diplomatic disaster. Britain and France had not fully realized that the nineteenth century was over and that they were no longer world powers. Hence, they had expected a strong condemnation from the Soviet Union, but not from the United States. As the United States was busy wooing the Arab world away from the Soviet Union, however, the last thing it needed was to be perceived as a backer of Britain and France, the two bêtes noires of the Arab world at the time. This is why Eisenhower ordered the humiliated French and British out of the Suez Canal. As for Ben-Gurion, he agreed to pull out of the Sinai Peninsula only after obtaining the guarantee that Sinai would be demilitarized and that the Tiran Straits would be open to Israeli shipping.

Having humiliated the British and the French, Nasser became the hero of the Arab world. But he had not delivered on his promise to defeat Israel. In 1964, he created the Palestine Liberation Organization (PLO) and the United Arab Command under Egypt's aegis. In May 1967, he remilitarized the Sinai Peninsula and closed again the Tiran Straits, thus creating a casus belli against Israel. His threats to destroy Israel and to throw the Jews into the sea were explicit. The Soviets, for their part, were confident that an Egyptian victory was not only feasible but also necessary to boost their standing in the Middle East. Against all expectations, however, Israel defeated the combined armies of Egypt, Syria, and Jordan within six days in June 1967.

Despite his War of Attrition following the 1967 Six-Day War, Nasser failed to push Israel out of Sinai. So did his successor, Anwar Sadat, who launched a surprise attack against Israel on October 6, 1973.

The 1973 Yom Kippur War proved to the Arab world that it had no military option against Israel. Sadat realized that he would only be able to recuperate Sinai via diplomacy: if he would offer to trade Egypt's allegiance from the Soviet Union to the United States, America would surely twist Israel's arm out of Sinai. This is exactly what happened. President Gerald Ford forced Prime Minister Yitzhak Rabin to withdraw from about 20 percent of the Sinai Peninsula in 1975, and Jimmy Carter coerced Menachem Begin into abandoning Sinai altogether with the 1979 Camp David agreements.

The PLO, however, reached a different conclusion. Sadat was interested in recuperating Sinai. By contrast, the PLO's raison d'être, as its name unmistakably indicates, is the "liberation of Palestine." Created three years before Israel took control of the West Bank and Gaza in

1967, the PLO's aim was never to limit its struggle to those two territories previously controlled by Jordan and Egypt, respectively.

Soon after Yasser Arafat had taken over the PLO's leadership in 1969, he had gone to North Vietnam to study the strategy and tactics of guerrilla warfare waged by Communist leader Ho Chi Minh. This was also when the PLO started translating the writings of North Vietnam's General Nguyen Giap into Arabic. Arafat was particularly impressed by Ho Chi Minh's success in mobilizing sympathizers in Europe and the United States. Giap explained to Arafat that in order to succeed, he too had to conceal his real goal and use the right vocabulary: "Stop talking about annihilating Israel and instead turn your terror war into a struggle for human rights," Giap told Arafat. "Then you will have the American people eating out of your hand."

What Giap taught Arafat was that, in asymmetric struggles, the militarily weaker side can win thanks to what became an integral part of warfare in the twentieth century: the media. Ultimately, Vietnam defeated both France and the United States because Giap knew how to manipulate the media in order to convince the French and the Americans that they were sacrificing their sons for an unjust and hopeless war. This is how Giap summarized his strategy: "In 1968 I realized that I could not defeat 500,000 American troops who were deployed in Vietnam. I could not defeat the 7th Fleet, with its hundreds of aircraft, but I could bring pictures home to the Americans which would cause them to want to stop the war." It worked.

But Giap did not only teach Arafat the wonders of propaganda in the age of modern media; he also introduced him to the idea of "phased strategy." What the Communist Vietnamese meant by "two-state solution" was the conquest of the south in phases: first signing a two-state agreement with the United States, and then repealing it unilaterally by invading the south after the withdrawal of US forces.

In January 1973, the Paris Peace Accord had officially partitioned Vietnam into two states: North Vietnam and South Vietnam. The agreement was immediately violated by the Communists, who attacked South Vietnam and conquered it within two years. Embattled in the Watergate scandal and driven from office in 1974, President Richard Nixon abandoned the south to its fate. At least 1 million South Vietnamese were sent to "reeducation camps," an estimated 200,000 were executed, and millions fled their country on boats, with hundreds of thousands dying at sea.

If Communist Vietnam could achieve a "two-state solution" in Vietnam, thus defeating and deceiving the world's greatest power, was it far-fetched for the PLO to corner Israel despite its military power?

This is how Arafat endorsed his own phased two-state strategy. In June 1974, the PLO adopted the Phased Plan, in light of the Arab failure in the 1973 Yom Kippur War and in light of the success of the two-state strategy in Vietnam. It called for the establishment of the Palestinian National Authority in the West Bank and Gaza as a first step toward the "liberation of Palestine."

By thus inventing a "Palestinian people" and by rebranding his genocidal terrorism as a liberation movement, Arafat gained the sympathy of both Third World leaders and Western liberals. Even in Israel itself, a younger generation of Israelis traumatized by the Yom Kippur War bought into Arafat's "two-state" deceit. As former Israeli politician Yossi Beilin wrote in his semiautobiographical book, *Touching Peace,* the Yom Kippur War had shaken his confidence in Israel's ultimate victory, and it had convinced him to pursue peace via a two-state solution. Twenty years after the Yom Kippur War, Yossi Beilin saved Arafat from political death by initiating the 1993 Oslo agreements.

The PLO made progress in world public opinion in the 1970s, but not in Israel. Having openly declared with its 1974 Phased Plan that the only point of negotiating with Israel was to destroy it from the inside via the Trojan horse strategy, Israelis were not about to negotiate the terms of their suicide. Besides, the PLO at the time was engaged in horrendous terrorist attacks against Israelis.

On February 21, 1970, the Popular Front for the Liberation of Palestine (FPLP), affiliated with the PLO, blew up in midflight a Swiss Air flight, killing 47 people. On May 8, 1970, PLO terrorists murdered 9 Israeli children from the Avivim village in northern Israel. In May 1972, the FPLP dispatched the Japanese Red Army to Ben-Gurion Airport, killing 27 people. On September 5, 1972, the PLO murdered 11 Israeli athletes at the Munich Olympic Games. On April 11, 1974, 11 Israelis were killed by Palestinian terrorists in the northern city of Kiriat Shmona. On May 15, 1974, PLO terrorists, infiltrating from Lebanon, killed 26 residents (including 21 children) of the Maalot kibbutz. In March 1978, PLO terrorists took over a bus on the Tel-Aviv–Haifa road, killing 21 Israelis. On October 7, 1985, PLO terrorists hijacked Italian cruise ship *Achile Lauro*, shooting and throwing overboard the wheelchair-bound and elderly passenger Leon Klinghoffer. Between 1969 and 1985, the PLO murdered over 650 Israelis in total.

Despite those horrendous murders, and despite the declared objective of the 1974 Phased Plan, the PLO did gain some momentum in international public opinion. Arafat was invited to address the United Nations General Assembly in November 1974. During the 1982 Lebanon War, Arafat deployed the "media war" strategy he had learned from his Vietnamese comrades. He rebranded PLO terrorists as Jews fighting for their freedom in the Warsaw ghetto and the IDF as the Wehrmacht.

In 1988, however, when King Hussein of Jordan announced that he was severing all ties with the West Bank, a void was created. The PLO tried to fill that void, but the United States was not going to recognize the PLO as a legitimate actor without the PLO renouncing terrorism. On December 13, 1988, Arafat made an ambiguous statement about terrorism and about Israel's right to exist, and this was considered good enough by the Reagan administration ("The intifada will come to an end only when practical and tangible steps have been taken towards the achievement of our national aims" Arafat said).

The PLO, however, never ended its terrorist activities, and many of its leaders clarified that Arafat's declaration was purely tactical. In that declaration, Arafat had praised Abu Jihad, who was responsible for the PLO's terrorist attacks of 1974, 1978, and 1985. Ten days after Arafat's declaration, on December 23, Salim Zanoun, spokesman for the Palestinian National Council, said that the struggle against the "Zionist enemy" was not over. FPLP leader Nayef Hawatmeh added on April 19, 1989, that the PLO's strategy was still to "liberate Palestine" from the Mediterranean Sea to the Jordan River. And in January 1990, Arafat declared that the State of Israel was a remnant of the Second World War and should disappear just like the Berlin Wall. Finally, on May 30, 1990, a PLO terrorist attack on an Israeli beach was foiled by the IDF. So much for the "condemnation" of terrorism.

Yet the United States ignored Arafat's doublespeak and continued terrorist activities. It took the first Gulf War in 1991 and Arafat's support for Saddam Hussein for the United States to finally abandon Arafat. Once the Gulf War was over, the Bush administration was determined to handle and solve the Arab-Israeli conflict while sidelining the PLO. Indeed, even Martin Indyk, who at the time was serving as executive director of the Washington Institute for Near East Policy, published an article called "Peace without the PLO" in the summer 1991 edition of *Foreign Policy*. The PLO had lost not only the trust of the United States, but also the financial support of Saudi Arabia and Kuwait (Kuwait had been invaded by Saddam Hussein and Saudi Arabia was thought to be next in line). Exiled in Tunis, financially bankrupt, and diplomatically isolated, the PLO was on the verge of collapse. With hundreds of thousands of Jews meanwhile immigrating to Israel from the former Soviet Union, Arafat realized that the clock was ticking against him.

And yet precisely when Arafat was finished and desperate, Israel decided to save him. The idea was that a weak and desperate Arafat would be amendable to signing anything. The problem with this theory was that Arafat understood it in his own way: for him, meeting Israel's demands was a temporary and tactical move. On May 23, 1994, he declared in a Johannesburg mosque that the Oslo agreements he signed with Israel were a modern version of the Hudaibiya Treaty signed in AD 628 between Prophet Muhammad and the Quraish tribe of Mecca—a temporary agreement signed for lack of better options, and with the sole purpose of defeating the enemy once conditions changed. Arafat also confirmed, time and again, that the purpose of the Palestinian Authority was to implement the PLO's Phased Plan adopted in 1974. This strategy was not Arafat's alone. Former PA representative for Jerusalem affairs Faisal Husseini admitted that Oslo was a "Trojan horse," and that, had the United States and Israel realized this, "they would never have opened their fortified gates to let it inside their wall," for "the Oslo agreement, or any other agreement, is just a temporary procedure, or just a step towards something bigger…We distinguish the strategic, long-term goals from the political phased goals, which we are compelled to temporarily accept due to international pressure…[Palestine] according to the higher strategy [is] from the river to the sea."[1] Othman Abu Gharbia, a senior Fatah ideologue, was no less explicit: "Every Palestinian must know clearly and unequivocally that the independent Palestinian state, with Jerusalem as its capital is not the end of the road. The Palestinian state is a stage after which there will be another stage, and that is the democratic state of all of Palestine."[2]

And, indeed, Arafat was quick to prove that his strategy was to merely deceive Israel and implement the Phased Plan of 1974. On July 1, 1994,

---

[1] *Al Arabi*, 24 June 2001.

[2] *Al Hayat al-Jadidah*, 25 November 1999.

twenty years after the adoption of the Phased Plan and shortly after the signing of the Gaza-Jericho agreement with Israel in May 1994, Arafat entered the Gaza Strip in a black Mercedes. In the trunk of his car were four PLO terrorists, whose entry to the Gaza Strip had been barred by Israel. Arafat immediately proceeded with implementing the Phased Plan by turning the territories under his jurisdiction into terrorist enclaves and by coordinating his moves with Hamas. In addition, Arafat infused the school system and the media with the message that Jews were evil and that all of Palestine would be liberated. It took Arafat seven years, until September 2000, to officially launch his terrorist war against Israel. During those seven years, 269 Israelis were murdered by PLO and Hamas terrorists.

Besides believing that signing an agreement with a bankrupt and desperate Arafat was clever, the Israeli left had also believed that Arafat would not be foolish enough to reject a final peace agreement with Israel once convinced of the objective benefits of peace. This was obviously a grave misreading of Arafat's intentions. At the Camp David Conference in July 2000, Arafat was offered by Israeli Prime Minister Ehud Barak a Palestinian state on 100 percent of the Gaza Strip and 92 percent of the West Bank, as well as Palestinian sovereignty over Jerusalem's Arab neighborhoods. Arafat rejected the offer because he refused to commit to the end of the conflict with Israel, and because he refused to give up on the so-called right of return whose purpose is to undo Israel's Jewish majority. His "reply" to Barak's offer was the launching of the war that had been prepared for seven years.

Even though Israeli citizens were being murdered by PLO and Hamas terrorists, Israel and the United States decided to try to appease Arafat. On December 23, 2000, President Clinton presented Arafat with a more generous offer yet: instead of 92 percent of the West Bank, he could have between 94 and 96 percent, together with a 1 to 3 percent land swap with Israel; Palestinian sovereignty in Jerusalem not only over the Arab neighborhoods but also in the Old City and over the Temple Mount; and Israeli recognition of the right of return, but no Israeli commitment to actually accept the refugees and their descendants. Clinton made it clear to both sides that accepting his proposal (which came to be known as the Clinton Parameters) meant the end of claims and the end of the conflict. The Israeli government accepted the Clinton Parameters. Arafat rejected them.

As former Middle East coordinator Dennis Ross wrote in his book *The Missing Peace*, "How many times did Arafat have to tell us no before we heard 'no'? How many times could excuses be made for him? Those who argue that we just ran out of time ignore the many opportunities Arafat had refused. They ignore that with the Clinton ideas practically on the table at the end of September, Arafat either let the Intifada begin or, as some argue, actually gave orders for it." Ross adds that "Rabin and Peres had made a historic choice; Arafat only made a tactical move. He might say Oslo represented a strategic choice; in reality, for him it represented a strategic necessity. Arafat went to Oslo after the first Gulf War not because he made a choice but because he had no choice…Oslo was his salvation. As such, it represented less a transformation than a transaction." Ross concludes, "Yasir Arafat had definitely demonstrated that he could not end the conflict…Anwar Nusseibeh decried the Mufti of Jerusalem as someone who succeeded as a symbol and failed as a leader. Tragically, for Palestinians and Israelis alike, these words captured the essence of Arafat fifty-three years later."

Arafat's successor, Mahmoud Abbas, was no better. Abbas had claimed in his PhD thesis that Zionists collaborated with the Nazis to perpetuate the Holocaust in order to attract international sympathy and support for the establishment of a Jewish state. All his life, he was closely associated with Arafat, and he was personally involved in the murder of the Jewish athletes in Munich in 1972. Like Arafat, he praised terrorists as heroes, maintained the anti-Israeli incitement in Palestinian media and schoolbooks, and played a double game with Hamas.

Abbas proved that he was no different from al-Husseini and Arafat when faced with the choice between peace and mythology. In September 2008, Prime Minister Ehud Olmert offered Abbas 99.5 percent of the West Bank, with land swaps (Israel was to annex 6.3 percent of the West Bank, and the Palestinian state was to annex 5.8 percent of pre-1967 Israel). Olmert also accepted the partition of Jerusalem, with Israel relinquishing its sovereignty over the Temple Mount and the Holy Basin to an international trusteeship composed of the United States, Saudi Arabia, Jordan, Israel, and the proposed Palestinian state, and further agreed to absorb thousands of Palestinian refugees and create a safe passage (which did not exist before 1967) between the West Bank and the Gaza Strip. Abbas didn't pocket Olmert's offer, saying he would get back to him. He never did.

Olmert's original proposal was actually submitted to Abbas via US secretary of state Condoleezza Rice back in May 2008, long before Olmert was considered a political lame duck. When Abbas justified his rejection of the proposal, first to Rice and then to American journalist Jackson Diehl, he did not mention Olmert's legal troubles, nor did he complain about being offered 99.5 percent of the West Bank instead of 100 percent. Abbas instead clearly stated that he could not relinquish the "right of return" of "millions" of Palestinian refugees.

The "right of return" is a catchy expression for the demographic demise of Israel. The PLO and Hamas talk about a "right" that has no basis in international law and no precedent in international relations. According to Hamas and the PLO, United Nations General Assembly (UNGA) Resolution 194 grants a legal right to the Palestinian refugees and their descendants to settle in Israel and to reclaim the real estate and land they lost in 1948. But General Assembly resolutions are mere recommendations; as opposed to Security Council resolutions, they are not binding in international law. UNGA Resolution 194 is no exception: it is a nonbinding recommendation, and so even if this resolution recognized the right of Palestinian refugees and their descendants to return to Israel (which it doesn't), such recognition would be neither binding nor enforceable.

Article 11 of Resolution 194 says inter alia that "the refugees wishing to return to their homes and live at peace with their neighbors should be permitted to do so at the earliest practicable date, and...compensation should be paid for the property of those choosing not to return." The resolution doesn't talk about "Palestinian refugees" but about "refugees" as the word refers to both Arabs and Jews displaced as a result of war in the former British Mandate. It mentions both return and compensation as possible solutions. More significantly, the resolution only refers to the refugees themselves and not to their future descendants. This central point touches to the core of the refugee problem: the Palestinians claim that the refugee status and the right of return allegedly recognized by the UN applies not only to the 1948 refugees but also to their descendants. This claim is groundless in international law and has no precedent in international relations.

In the twentieth century, refugees were unfortunately a common phenomenon in international relations. There was a population transfer of 2 million between Greece and Turkey in 1923. In 1937, the Peel Commission proposed a population exchange between Jews and Arabs in the framework of a territorial partition of British Palestine. After World War II, some 14 million Germans were expelled from Eastern Europe and became refugees. The partition of India in 1947 created a double refugee problem: over 7 million Hindu refugees and over 7 million Muslim refugees (and with the breakup of Pakistan in 1971, some 10 million Bangladeshi refugees as well). So did the partition of British Palestine, though with different proportions: some 600,000 Arab refugees from the newly established State of Israel, and some 900,000 Jewish refugees expelled from Arab and Muslim countries in the wake of the first three Arab-Israeli wars (1948, 1956, and 1967). All in all, there were about 60 million refugees in the world in 1948, and the Palestinian Arab refugees represented 1 percent of the world's refugee population.

These Palestinian refugees could have been integrated in Arab countries with which they shared a common ethnicity, culture, language, and religion. Instead, they were kept in camps and discriminated against by Arab leaders who cynically used them as pawns against Israel. Rather than trying to solve the Palestinian refugee problem, Arab leaders did everything to maintain it. While the United Nations High Commissioner for Refugees (UNHCR) was established to solve the global refugee problem, the United Nations Relief and Works Agency for Palestine Refugees in the Near East (UNRWA) was created to maintain and perpetuate the Palestinian refugee problem.

Even though Palestinian refugees only represented 1 percent of the world refugee population in 1949, they were the only refugees for whom a special UN agency was established. The rest of the world's refugees were (and still are) dealt with by UNHCR. This unjustified institutional inconsistency has far-reaching implications because of how UNHCR and UNRWA define refugees. While UNHCR defines refugees as forcibly displaced persons, UNRWA applies this definition to the refugees' descendants too. Hence the world's global refugee population has decreased from 60 million in 1948 to about 17 million today, while the Palestinian "refugee" population has increased from 600,000 in 1948 to 5 million today.

It is time to put an end to this absurd and unjustified double standard. There is no reason why UNHCR's definition and jurisdiction should not apply to Palestinian refugees. Doing so, incidentally, would "reduce" the actual number of Palestinian refugees to about 50,000 (most of them elderly by now). Alternatively, were the world to universalize the UNRWA algorithm, Poland would have to reintegrate the descendants of German refugees, and millions of Hindus and Muslims would have to re-cross the border between India and Pakistan.

In 2000 and 2008, the PLO rejected a two-state compromise because of the so-called right of return. Between 2009 and 2013, Abbas refused to even meet with Netanyahu, despite the latter's acquiescence to a settlement freeze as a goodwill gesture. Yet in August 2013, US secretary John Kerry decided to give it another try by renewing the "peace process" between Israel and the Palestinian Authority. He declared that his target was to reach a final peace deal within nine months. After nine months, in April 2014, John Kerry publicly admitted that he had failed. Shortly after that, Mahmoud Abbas joined forces with Hamas, bringing it into his government. In June 2014, three Israeli teenagers (Eyal Ifrah, Gilead Shaar, and Naftali Frankel) were kidnapped and murdered by Hamas terrorists. As the IDF cracked down on Hamas's terror network in Judea and Samaria, Hamas started shooting rockets at Israel from Gaza. Israel responded with Operation Protective Edge in July 2014. Dozens of tunnels dug by Hamas over the years were discovered. Israel's 2005 unilateral withdrawal from Gaza had turned that territory into a major terror base, threatening Israeli citizens from above with thousands of missiles and from below with tunnels. Hamas had planned on carrying out a mega terror attack against Israel, via those tunnels, in September 2014. The Gaza Strip proved to be more lethal from without than from within.

Meanwhile, in the Middle East, radical Islam is today gaining ground, and Arab states are imploding. Syria's civil war has produced over 200,000 victims, as well as millions of refugees. In Iraq, the Islamic State of Iraq and Syria is tearing the country and the region into pieces. Libya, an Italian colonial creation, has been imploding since the demise of Muammar Gaddafi. Lebanon is under the de facto control of the pro-Iranian Shia militia of Hezbollah. Iran is approaching the nuclear threshold. And finally, Israel is fighting for its life in a toxic and psychotic region. It is a democracy threatened by fanatic Islamists, a success story surrounded by failed states. The so-called two-state solution means creating a twenty-third failed Arab state ruled by the successors of Hadj Amin al-Husseini—a state that could at any point be taken over by the most radical Islamists, and whose borders would surround Jerusalem and overlook Tel-Aviv. This is sheer madness, a madness that surpasses Albert Einstein's definition of insanity. As for unilateral withdrawal from Judea and Samaria, recent events have confirmed the folly of such a plan.

Opponents of the so-called two-state solution have been vindicated by reality, especially in recent years. But do they have a credible alternative to this failed idea? I shall address this question in the book's conclusion.

• • •

Israel's Foreign Policy

Theodore Herzl, the founder of modern Zionism, had a dream: to restore Jewish statehood in the Land of Israel. He was also a realist in the sense that he presented Zionism to world powers as a national movement that would serve their interests. As for the Jewish settlers of the late nineteenth century, they realized that facts had to be established on the ground for Zionism to gain credence. Most Zionist settlers were influenced by Marxism, and therefore there was something very ideological in their reading of world politics. Many thought that Arab and Hebrew workers shared the same struggle against British imperialism, and that class struggle was stronger than competing national claims. Also because of their Marxist ideology, many Zionist leaders felt that the Jewish national home should align with the Soviet Union. With the rise of Nazism in Europe, aligning with the "antifascist" Socialist Big Brother seemed even more natural.

The 1930s shattered the Marxist outlook of many Zionist leaders— first and foremost of David Ben-Gurion himself. The Arab Revolt of

1936 to 1939 convinced him that the conflict with the Arabs was indeed a national one. Talk about a common class struggle against British imperialism had come to sound completely out of touch with reality. The year 1939 was a particularly bleak one: Britain officially betrayed the Zionist movement with the White Paper, and the Soviet Union officially betrayed its "comrades" around the world by signing the Ribbentrop-Molotov Pact with Nazi Germany. While some leftist Zionist ideologues were still debating the merits of aligning with the Soviet Union, Ben-Gurion had no more time for philosophy. As far as world politics were concerned, his only ideology was Realpolitik.

It was out of realism, not ideology, that the Soviet Union supported the UN partition plan in November 1947, recognized Israel immediately after it declared its independence in May 1948, and provided Israel (via Czechoslovakia) with the weaponry that played a critical role in Israel's victory in its war of independence. Stalin wanted Britain out of Palestine and the Middle East altogether, and supporting Israel's independence served that objective. Whereas in the early 1940s, Britain's hegemony in the Middle East was threatened by Nazi Germany, by the late 1940s, it was threatened by the Soviet Union.

As for the United States, meanwhile, the Washington establishment shared Britain's concerns in the Middle East. Neither the State Department nor the Pentagon supported the establishment of a Jewish state. Had it not been for Harry Truman's personal decision (admittedly under the influence of his Jewish friend Edward Jacobson), the United States would not have voted in favor of partition, and the United States would not have recognized Israel upon its independence.

With the election of Dwight Eisenhower in December 1952, the new US administration took its distances from what it perceived and defined as Truman's "irresponsible policies," which were allegedly throwing the Arab states into Soviet arms. Eisenhower's secretary of state, John Foster Dulles, went out of his way to convince the Arab states that the United States was not their foe. In 1953, the Eisenhower administration sided with Syria in its water dispute with Israel. In 1955, together with Britain, the United States came up with its Alpha Plan, which called for an Israeli withdrawal, more or less, to the proposed borders of the 1947 UN Partition Plan. That same year, Egyptian president Abdel Nasser announced his new military alliance with the Soviet Union. Ben-Gurion hoped that the United States would respond by arming Israel, but the Eisenhower administration was convinced that what had caused the Soviet-Egyptian alliance was the United States' perceived closeness to Israel. Rather than selling weapons to Israel in order to contain the new Soviet-Egyptian alliance, the Eisenhower administration tried to convince the Arab and Muslim states that the United States was on their side. In 1955, the United States together with the United Kingdom created the Baghdad Pact, a military alliance with Turkey, Iraq, Iran, and Pakistan. In 1956, when Israel, France, and Britain attacked Egypt following Nasser's nationalization of the Suez Canal, the Eisenhower administration sided with the Soviet Union by demanding an immediate withdrawal of British, French, and Israeli troops. As it was competing with the Soviet Union over the allegiance of Arab states, the last thing the United States needed was to be perceived as siding with the three bêtes noires of the Arab world.

As for the Soviet Union, its support of Israel was short lived. As soon as Britain lost an important foothold in the Middle East with the establishment of Israel, the Soviets lost the common interest they had briefly shared with Zionism. Realizing the popularity of Zionism among Soviet Jews (Israel's first ambassador to the Soviet Union, Golda Meir, received a hero's welcome by Moscow's Jewish community), the Soviet regime started adopting both a negative rhetoric and a hostile policy toward Israel. With the 1955 Soviet-Egypt alliance, it was clear that the Soviet Union was instead trying to build alliances in the Arab world. The Soviet support for Israel from 1947 to 1948 was no longer a Soviet interest by the early 1950s.

As the United States and the Soviet Union were then competing over the Arab world, Israel found itself alone in the international order of the Cold War. Its only ally was France. The alliance between Israel and France was, of course, the outcome of common interests. That allegiance was formed when the Algerian War broke out in 1954, and Egyptian president Nasser actively supported the Algerians, thus giving France and Israel a common enemy. The French and Israeli nuclear programs were a joint venture between the two countries. France sold Israel its *Mystère* and *Rafale* fighter aircrafts from the mid-1950s onward.

Ben-Gurion, however, was aware of the fact that the military alliance with France would vanish with the end of the war in Algeria. With the return of de Gaulle to power in 1958, Ben-Gurion's concerns began to prove justified. De Gaulle immediately downgraded France's military cooperation with Israel.

Feeling that this was the beginning of the end of Israel's special relationship with France, and as the United States was still not interested in developing a strategic relationship with Israel, Ben-Gurion thought of a diplomatic plan B. He came up with the "periphery strategy," which consisted of developing strategic ties with the Middle East's non-Arab and anti-Soviet regimes: Iran, Turkey, and Ethiopia, as well as the Christians of South Sudan and Lebanon, and the Kurds of northern Iraq. This policy was successful until the fall of Ethiopian emperor Haile Selassie in 1974 and the Islamic revolution in Iran in 1979 (Ethiopia having become Marxist and Iran Islamist, they could no longer be relied upon as regional partners). In addition to the periphery strategy, Israel developed close ties with the newly independent countries of Africa, actively providing them with agricultural, medical, and military expertise. This pro-active policy toward Africa was initiated by then foreign minister Golda Meir.

With regard to France, the end of the war in Algeria in 1962 put an end to the common interests that had engendered the French-Israeli alliance in the first place. At the same time, the new Kennedy administration

(1961–63) started rethinking the US policy in the Middle East. Obviously, the strategy of the Eisenhower administration had not convinced the Arab states not to join the Soviet camp. In 1958, a pro-Soviet military coup had taken power in Iraq, and Egypt had created a political union with Syria. In 1964, Nasser created the Palestine Liberation Organization and the United Arab Command. His moves were coordinated with the Soviet Union. It was clear at that point that the Middle East was polarized around Cold War enmities and that the US policy of rebuffing Israel had been counterproductive.

In 1964, Israeli Prime Minister Levy Eshkol paid an official visit to the United States. It was the first such visit by an Israeli prime minister. This was the beginning of a strategic relationship between the two nations, a relationship that deepened following the 1967 Six-Day War. This new relationship also created a dependency that was highlighted by the 1973 Yom Kippur War, wherein US secretary of state Henry Kissinger used his leverage with Israel to prevent the destruction and humiliation of the Egyptian army, and coercing Israel in 1975 into withdrawing from about 20 percent of the Sinai Peninsula in order to convince Egyptian President Anwar al-Sadat that America could deliver.

The Yom Kippur War created an international environment that gravely isolated Israel on the world scene. The oil embargo imposed by the Organization of Petroleum Exporting Countries (OPEC) was devastatingly efficient, while Western Europe aligned with the positions of the Arab League, and all but four African countries severed their diplomatic relations with Israel. The Arab states meanwhile used their automatic majority at the UN General Assembly to wage a diplomatic war against Israel, which culminated in the 1975 vote of the General Assembly to condemn Zionism as a racist movement.

Faced with such international isolation, Israel pushed Realpolitik to its limits by developing military ties with the anti-Soviet and unsavory regimes of Latin America and South Africa. Israel's anti-Soviet policy also created unexpected common interests with Communist China. At first Mao Zedong's attitude and policy toward Israel was deeply hostile, as he was competing with the Soviet Union to be the leader of the Third World against "the imperialists." It was the diplomatic rupture and tension between the Soviet Union and China in the 1960s that played to Israel's advantage. Having lost its only arms supplier, China was stuck with outdated Soviet weaponry. Israel was meanwhile known for its expertise at upgrading Soviet tanks and weapons, having captured many of those in the 1956, 1967, and 1973 wars. Hence the Chinese interest in Israel, an interest that was translated into a behind-the-scenes rapprochement after Mao's death in 1976 and his replacement in 1979 by the pragmatic Deng Xiaoping. China by this time had more animosity toward the Soviet Union than toward Israel, and Israel was the Soviet Union's main target and opponent in the Middle East.

The end of the Cold War, however, dramatically improved Israel's international standing. In 1991, the Soviet Union renewed its diplomatic ties with Israel, and the UN resolution defining Zionism as racist was repealed. In 1992, both China and India (more than half of the world's population) established diplomatic relations with Israel. Meanwhile the Oslo process, started in 1993, initially improved relations with Europe and paved the way for diplomatic relations with the Vatican. With the collapse of the Oslo process at the Camp David Conference of July 2000, however, relations with Europe started souring again. Instead of being commended for its generous peace offer at the Camp David Conference, Israel was blamed for the war launched by Arafat in September 2000.

Worse, Israel became the target of a vicious defamation campaign. Once again, the UN was hijacked by the PLO and by political NGOs determined to demonize Israel. The first manifestation of this campaign was the Durban Conference in August and September 2001, which was dominated by hate speeches against Israel. It ended on September 8,

2001. Three days later, on September 11, al-Qaeda flattened the World Trade Center and almost destroyed the Pentagon. As Israel was being demonized as the enemy of humanity, the same humanity was cruelly reminded about who its real enemies were.

The same al-Qaida beheaded US journalist Daniel Pearl in February 2001. Thirteen years later, in August 2014, two other American journalists, James Foley and Steven Sotloff, were also beheaded, this time by the Islamic State of the Levant. The civilized world is currently facing a fanatic and barbaric ideology of which Israel is the first, but not the last, target. President Obama thought he could appease the Muslim world by pulling out of Iraq, by being tough on Israel, and by making praising speeches. Rather than being appeased, however, the Middle East is imploding, with civil wars raging in Libya, Syria, and Iraq. The one-time free elections that were held following the 2011 revolts in the Arab world have all brought anti-American Islamists to power. Only the military coup of General al-Sissi in Egypt temporarily saved that country from the rule of the Muslim Brotherhood. Meanwhile, Iran is moving ahead with its nuclear program.

In such a context, Israel must and can capitalize on the countries and peoples that are threatened by radical Islam and that understand the nature of that threat. More and more political and intellectual leaders in Europe are now talking openly in defense of Israel because they understand that, for radical Islam, the road to Rome goes through Jerusalem. In sub-Saharan Africa, Israel is now recognized as a country that is an indispensable partner in the fight against radical Islam and the deleterious influence of Iran. In Kenya, Nigeria, Côte d'Ivoire, and other African countries, the Islamist threat is palpable, and cooperation with Israel is growing. India's tensions with Pakistan also play to Israel's advantage, especially since the electoral victory of the nationalist Hindu party in 2014.

The fact that Israel is a technological powerhouse and that it is emerging as a major energy exporter will also influence its relations with Europe and with China. As America has significantly reduced its dependency on Middle Eastern oil, OPEC's "oil weapon" has become almost inefficient, as will be further explained in the book's conclusion.

International relations are governed by interests, not by feelings. In the twenty-first century, economic interests play a central role in the international system. From that point of view, the prospects for Israel's international stance are good. Yet Israel must be proactive and always initiate—just as Ben-Gurion did in the late 1950s with his periphery strategy.

•   •   •

It is my hope that this book will contribute to the debates surrounding Israeli politics, the Arab-Israel conflict, and Israel's foreign policy. Many of the ideas developed here go against the tide of conventional wisdom. If the reader is willing to look at Israel and at the Middle East from a different angle after reading this book, this alone will have justified the time I spent writing it.

Part One:

Domestic Challenges – What Actually
Threatens Israel's Democracy and Jewishness

Chapter 1:

If You Will It, It is No Nightmare - On Academic and Judicial Nepotism in Israel

"If you will it, it is no dream," wrote Theodore Herzl in his book *Altneuland.* The dream came true, but so did the nightmarish sight of an intellectual tyranny.

Ever since Israel's first Minister of Justice Pinhas Rosen called his law partner Moshe Zmora to appoint him President of the Supreme Court, the country's ruling elites have mastered a type of nepotism that favors and reproduces intellectual uniformity. Former Chief Justice Aaron Barak made sure that Law Professor Ruth Gavison wouldn't get his job because she had dared to question his judicial activism ("She has an agenda" Barak explained –as if Barak himself didn't have one). Similarly, Barak declared in January 2008 that the Minister of Justice's attempts to reform the appointment of Israel's Supreme Court could turn Israel into a third world country.

Really? Actually, Israel is the only Western democracy whose Supreme Court is not appointed by politicians. Our judges are selected by a nine-member committee comprised of two cabinet ministers (chosen by the government), one coalition and one opposition Member of Knesset (MK), three sitting justices (chosen by the Supreme Court President), and two lawyers (chosen by the Bar Association). So politicians occupy only four out of the nine seats. The legal establishment, with five seats, dominates the panel.

What Minister of Justice Daniel Friedmann wanted to do in 2007 was to grant the Executive a majority in the appointing committee. He proposed an eleven member panel with two ministers, two MKs and two Bar Association representatives (just like today), but only two Supreme Court justices rather than three. The remaining three members would be a retired district court judge (chosen by the government), a public figure from any field except law (also chosen by the government), and an academic from a field other than law (appointed by the council of university presidents).

Aaron Barak claimed that Friedmann's proposal would politicize the court and "set Israeli democracy back several years." Given Barak's knowledge of other legal systems, his statement was sheer hypocrisy. In most Western democracies, the government dominates the process of nominating judges. In the United States, the President appoints justices and the Senate confirms them. In Germany, Parliament's upper and lower houses each select half the justices. In Austria, the Government and Parliament each appoint half. In France, the President appoints nine of the fifteen justices, while the heads of the two houses of Parliament appoint three each. In Switzerland, Parliament selects the justices; in Sweden, the Government does. In Australia, Canada, Belgium and Norway, justices are appointed by the monarch but either nominated or approved by the Government. In Japan, the Government appoints the justices and voters must ratify its choices in the next election.

Are these third world countries? No, those are democracies, meaning polities whose fundamental premise is that the people should choose their rulers, and since supreme courts must occasionally rule on major political and social issues, this includes justices. Moreover, since judges interpret the law differently (which is why many verdicts are split decisions), supreme courts should properly reflect a wide spectrum of opinions. Democratic selection processes achieve this goal, since governments change frequently, and different governments tend to appoint candidates with different judicial worldviews.

A process dominated by the judiciary, by contrast, perpetuates ideological uniformity, because sitting judges prefer candidates who share their own views. This is why Barak blocked Gavison, and this is why Israel's Supreme Court is not representative of the country's social fabric.

The same intellectual nepotism rules in Academia. In 2010, Dr. Ran Baratz lost his job at the Hebrew University's philosophy department because of his politics (he lives beyond the "Green Line," is a fellow at the conservative Shalem Center,[3] and is involved with the unapologetically Zionist grassroots movement Im Tirzu[4]). While he received his doctorate with honors and was consistently rated the department's best lecturer by students, he committed the "crime" of not toeing the party line.

It is precisely against this intellectual tyranny that Im Tirzu is struggling. Recently, for instance, it made public the fact that Ben-Gurion University's political science department is basically an indoctrination machine that leaves no place for critical thinking, let alone dissent.

The reaction of Israel's academic establishment to Im Tirzu's resistance has been hysterical. Last in date is a recent op-ed by Prof. Zeev

---

[3] The "Shalem Center" was an Israeli conservative think-tank that became in 2013 the "Shalem College," Israel's first Liberal Arts College.

[4] "Im Tirtzu" is a student movement that was established to challenge the lack of pluralism is Israeli academia.

Sternhell's in *Haaretz*.[5] The Left, explains Sternhell, has been dominating academia for the past six decades, and this should remain so. Why? Because the Left promotes peace, while the Right promotes war.

So being from the Right means being a warmonger. Talk about a lazy and demagogical way of trying to embarrass and intimidate your opponents. Then Sternhell goes to explain why there are new think-tanks and movements in Israel who "dare" to challenge intelligent, saintly, and well-meaning people such as himself: It is because, you see, those Israeli right-wingers never managed to produce a true intellectual. So because there is no Israeli equivalent of Raymond Aron or Milton Friedman, the Israeli Right is trying to intimidate the country's academics via the Shalem Center and Im Tirzu.

The fact that there is hardly an Israeli equivalent of Raymond Aron or Milton Friedman is mostly true. And there is a reason for it, too: Israel's Social Sciences and Humanities departments would never let such people emerge in the first place. Ask Ran Baratz about it: you cannot get a tenured position if you are a "dissident." Zeev Sternhell is part of the intellectual cartel that prevents people like Ran Baratz from having an academic career in the Humanities and in the Social Sciences. And then, Sternhell complains about the fact that dissidents, because they are barred from academia, have the nerve to try and express themselves elsewhere.

So dissidents must be prevented from expressing themselves even outside of academia, and Sternhell knows just how to do that: by using force, he suggests. He threatens to encourage the international boycott of Israeli universities that will try to put an end to the intellectual monopoly of Sternhell and his peers. And then comes the ultimate threat to Education Minister Gideon Saar and to Finance Minister Yuval Steinitz. Incidentally, both men aspire to one day become Prime Minister –which

---

[5] *Haaretz* is Israel's leading liberal newspaper.

means that they need the "approval" of the Branja.[6] If you want that approval, warns Sternhell, say loud and clear that Im Tirzu is the enemy.

Strong will, perseverance and determination, is what will enable true pluralism to finally emerge in our Humanities and Social Science departments. If you will it, the nightmare will soon be over.

---

[6] "Branja" is the word commonly used in Israel to describe the country's clique of secular and urban intellectuals.

Chapter 2:

Which Part of "Jewish State" Do You Not Understand?

The new citizenship law recently proposed by the Government once again raises the question of why Israel should define itself as a Jewish state and what this definition means in the first place.

According to the proposed law, naturalized citizens will have to pledge their allegiance to Israel as a "Jewish and democratic state." Imagine if France would pass a law stating that France is a French state, if Japan would pass a law stating that Japan is a Japanese state, or if Sweden would pass a law stating that Sweden is a Swedish state. This would sound both silly and unnecessary. Far from being ridiculed for stating the obvious, however, Israel is being taken to task for stating the odious.

When the United Nations Special Committee on Palestine (UNSCOP) recommended in September 1947 that the British Mandate in Palestine be divided between a Jewish state for the Jews and an Arab state for the Arabs, everyone understood that this meant each nation would have its own nation-state (though many opposed the idea). In May 1948, Israel's Declaration of Independence clearly proclaimed the establishment of a "Jewish state" and specified that this state would both be the nation-state of the Jewish people and respect the civil rights of the country's non-Jewish minorities.

In recent years, the very legitimacy of Israel as the nation-state of the Jewish people has been under attack. Sophisticated people realize that they cannot logically question the legitimacy of the Jewish nation-state without doing the same for every nation-state (indeed, most countries in the world today are nation-states). Hence their claim (itself stated in the PLO charter and recently popularized by Prof. Shlomo Sand[7]), that the Jews do not constitute a nation but only a religion, and thus that a Jewish state is not a nation-state but a religious state. Therefore, its legitimacy can be challenged without questioning the principle of self-determination.

But who are those people to decide whether or not the Jews constitute a nation? Scholars have been debating for at least a couple of centuries about what makes a nation a nation (Ernest Renan called it "a soul, a spiritual principle"). In recent years, many attempts have been made to "deconstruct" the very concept of national identity (Benedict Anderson comes to mind). But the bottom line is that if people define themselves as a nation and are ready to fight in order to preserve their national independence or identity (whether this identity is real or "imagined" as Anderson would put it), then they obviously do constitute a nation.

How people define their national identity is also their own business. Japan's definition is ethnic, while America's is ideological, and France's is

---

[7] In his book *The Invention of the Jewish People* (Verso, 2009).

cultural (though this is a hotly debated issue in France). Moreover, religion is central to the national identity of many nations. Catholicism is intrinsically linked to the national identity of Poland, Ireland, and Italy. The Shinto religion is part of Japan's national identity. The Queen of England is both Head of State and Head of the Anglican Church. Armenian identity mixes nation and religion. Afghanistan, Iran, Mauritania and Pakistan, are all "Islamic Republics." Surely, the fact that there is a religious dimension to the Jewish definition of national identity is no exception.

Instead of saying that Judaism does indeed constitute part of Jewish identity and that there is nothing wrong with that, many Israelis feel the need to be apologetic about the religious component of Jewish national identity and therefore suggest redefining this identity in purely secular terms. Such is the essence of Amnon Rubinstein's article in *Azure* ("The Curious Case of Jewish Democracy," *Azure* 41, Summer 2010).[8] He suggests a purely "national-cultural reinterpretation" of Jewish identity.

Though a professed liberal, Rubinstein is suggesting something illiberal: that the state should choose, institutionalize and favor one specific definition of national identity despite the will of many citizens. A true liberal, however, would say that it is not the state's business to define and impose a definition of its national identity over all its citizens.

Rubinstein, however, has the merit of addressing the core issue: can and should the Jews keep their national identity and rights while abandoning the traditional Jewish definition of nationhood? In the Biblical narrative, Jewish faith is intrinsically related to Jewish identity and nationhood. Until Emancipation, Jews defined their identity in religious terms. Zionism tried to undo that link by redefining Jewish identity based on territory, language, and history. The problem is that it is the non-Jews who won't take it.

---

[8] Prof. Amnon Rubinstein is one of Israel's leading legal scholars.

The same way that Jews, as individuals, were not left alone in Europe after assimilating, Israel as a state was never left alone when it was established as a secular nation-state. No matter how hard the Jews tried to stop being Jewish in Europe, they were still perceived and reviled as such by the gentiles. And no matter how secular Israel was when it was established, it was opposed by the Vatican and by the Muslim world on religious grounds. Jewish "rationality" won't rid the world of its irrationality. Even if Israel were to officially declare itself a purely secular nation-state and retreat to the armistice lines of 1949, it would still be reviled and hated (as it was before 1967) by a plethora of zealots –from devout Muslims to European radicals.

This is a point that Rubinstein, with all his brilliance, does not seem to get.

It says in the Book of *Deuteronomy*: "And among those peoples, you shall not find any rest for the sole of your foot." Rabbi Yitzhak Arama[9] writes in his book *Akedat Yitzhak* that this verse teaches us that the Jews will never be able to completely assimilate among the nations, and will never be able to forget who they are. No matter how hard Jews try to forget and to be forgotten, the nations will always remind them that they are Jewish. The Midrash[10] (*Bereshit Rabah*) says there is a connection between the above verse and the one in the Book of *Genesis* describing the return of the dove to Noah's Arch ("And the dove did not find any rest for the sole of her foot, so she came back to the ark").

The Midrash teaches us that we can turn the curse of "There shall be no rest for the sole of your foot" into a blessing. For if the Jews had found a rest for the sole of their foot in Exile, they would never

---

[9] A 15th century Jewish commentator of the Hebrew Bible.

[10] The body of homiletic stories told by Jewish rabbinic sages to explain passages in the Hebrew Bible.

have come back to the Ark (i.e. the Land of Israel), both physically and spiritually.

The Jews came back to the ark physically. Only when they do so spiritually as well will they not only be left alone, but also be respected and admired.

Chapter 3:

Mount Scopus or Mount Olympus?
On Zionism and Israeli Academia

On November 2nd, 2010, the Knesset's Education Commission hosted a special hearing under the title: "The Exclusion of Zionistic Positions from Academia." The event was chaired by Member of Knesset (MK) Zevulun Orlev and attended, among others, by Education Minister Gideon Saar, by members of Knesset from various political parties, by high-ranking representatives of Israeli universities, by Israeli NGOs, and by ordinary citizens.

Two Israeli NGOs, the Institute for Zionist Strategies (IZS) and *Im Tirtzu*, were asked to present the main conclusions of their study on what they claim to be the growingly post-Zionistic narratives of Israel's political science and sociology departments. In October 2010, the IZS published a 122-page document called "Post-Zionism in Academia." *Im Tirtzu*, for its part, published in May 2010 a 64-page document called

"Anti-Zionistic Incitement and Bias in Universities." Both publications include an extensive review of syllabi, and both reach the conclusion that students are mostly taught a one-sided and derogatory description of nationalism in general and of Zionism in particular. *Im Tirtzu*'s report also includes testimonies of students about what they claim to be the one-sidedness and political intolerance of their professors, as well as a review of the political petitions signed by Israeli academics.

Instead of addressing the issues raised by the IZS and by *Im Tirtzu*, Israel's academic establishment has reacted with scorn and arrogance. At the Knesset hearing, the Rector of Ben-Gurion University (BGU), Prof. Zvi Hacohen, interrupted the IZS's presentation, calling it "nonsense" and claiming (without proving it) that the IZS's paper does not meet the most basic criteria of academic research. Tel-Aviv University Rector Prof. Aharon Shai also claimed that the IZS's paper is not a research paper (without explaining why) and added that adopting an academic ethical code (as proposed by Education Minister Gideon Saar at the beginning of the hearing) would "destroy Israeli Academia."

Members of Knesset, for their part, were divided. Meretz MKs Haim Oron and Nitzav Horowitz claimed that the alleged political bias of Israel's political science departments should be discussed at the Higher Education Committee (HEC) and not at the Knesset. To which Kadima MK Ronit Tirosh replied that expecting the HEC to discuss the issue is naïve at best and hypocritical at worst: since the HEC is mostly composed of University professors, it automatically circles the wagons around its peers. Tirosh, of course, could have added that, as the body that represents tax-paying citizens, the Knesset is entitled to check if the tax money it levies from citizens to fund universities is used to pay the salaries of professors who call for the international boycott of Israel.

Two days after the Knesset hearing, *Haaretz* came out to the defense of the universities by claiming that adopting an ethical code would harm academic freedom. *Haaretz* wrote that Gideon Saar proposed such a code as a result of the lobbying of *Im Tirtzu*. But, in fact, the idea of an academic ethical code for Israel was first proposed by Prof. Amnon Rubinstein, himself a renowned Israeli academic with impeccable liberal credentials. Moreover, BGU does have an ethical code (it is the only Israeli university to have one). Did BGU adopt an ethical code to "destroy Israeli Academia?"

Amnon Rubinstein advocates the adoption of an ethical code for Israeli universities. He addresses, among other things, the question as to whether calls from certain Israeli academics to boycott Israel are part of academic freedom of expression.

Rubinstein argues that professors enjoy a special status because their students have to listen to them and take their exams in order to succeed (certainly for mandatory classes). So professors have obligations precisely because they have privileges. Rubinstein is of the opinion that there is no appropriate legal mechanism in Israel to ensure that professors do not abuse their freedom of expression and respect the obligations that stem from their privileges.

Thus does Rubinstein recommend the adoption of an academic ethical code in Israel in order to clearly define what constitutes and what does not constitute academic freedom of expression. In the United States, such a code was adopted in 1940 by the American Association of University Professors (AAUP) and it has been revised and updated ever since. The AAUP's code states, among other things, that professors "should at all times be accurate, should exercise appropriate restraint, should show respect for the opinions of others."

Those in Israel who oppose the adoption of an academic ethical code would do a favor to public debate by presenting sound arguments instead of claiming that such a code would "destroy Israeli Academia" and that Gideon Saar is a pawn of *Im Tirtzu*. Until they do, one will have reasonable reasons to assume that they have a problem with accuracy, restraint, and respect for the opinions of others.

Chapter 4:

The Meaning of Jewish Brotherhood: On Jewish Identity and Unity

Yehuda Avner's book, *The Prime Ministers* (Toby Press, 2010), is the most informative, well-written and heart-touching memoir I've read in years.

Avner left Britain at the age of nineteen for British Palestine right before Israel's independence. He joined the Foreign Office and later got a job as an English speechwriter for the Prime Minister –a position he kept under Levi Eshkol, Golda Meir, Yitzhak Rabin, and Menachem Begin. He was a personal witness to those leaders' intimacy, dilemmas, and decisions.

Levi Eshkol comes out as a character that was borrowed from an Isaac Bashevis Singer novel to lead the Jewish state, almost by accident, at its most fateful hour (*"Vus rett der goy?"* [What's the goy talking about?]

he asked his aid, in Yiddish, unable to make sense of President Johnson's Texan babble as the latter was driving high-speed around his ranch).

Golda Meir emerges as down-to-earth and burnt-out grandma who successfully deployed her iron will after the terrifying setbacks of October 1973, but who would rather have been spared the hardships that life had in store for her ("I like nothing better than to sit in an armchair doing nothing" she candidly confessed to Oriana Fallaci).

Yitzhak Rabin reveals himself as a man of impeccable integrity with a strong analytical mind. Jews around the world came to admire him after the Entebbe rescue operation, though some had an awkward way of expressing their admiration (One entry in the Prime Minister's official guestbook after a party hosted for American Jews reads thus: "I congratulate you on your extraordinary rescue feat. But as a clinical psychologist I detect in you a bashful timid reserve. Diagnostically, I would say you have a depressive personality. Its root cause is an inability to elicit love. You're in search of a hero. Henry Kissinger wrestles with the same problem").

As for Menachem Begin, he is the book's hero. And indeed, he was a Jewish hero, as well as a true gentleman who, while constantly haunted by a dreadful past, was always ready to crack a good joke ("Marriage is not a word, it's a sentence" he concluded after unsuccessfully trying to help his wife put on her shoes before landing).

The book also has an anti-hero, albeit a discreet one mentioned *en passant* at the beginning and at the end. He caught my attention for a reason that is relevant to us today.

Yossel Kolowitz was an Auschwitz survivor who had lost his family in the Holocaust, and an Orthodox Jew who was on the ship that brought Yehuda Avner to British Palestine in 1947. In the inner pocket of his long black coat were two letters –both from relatives of his who lived in Palestine and were offering him a home.

The first letter was from his ultra-Orthodox uncle from Meah Shearim[11] who was asking him, as the sole survivor of his family, to perpetuate the Jewish people's tradition and establish a God-fearing family in Jerusalem. The second letter was from another uncle, a member of the secular Mishmar HaEmek kibbutz. He was imploring him to join the kibbutz, to "get rid of that yeshiva garb" and become "a new Jew." Yossel was agonizing about what to do, and the reader is left wondering what happened to him.

But Yossel Kolowitz surprisingly reappears at the end of the book. As Yehuda Avner addresses a crowd of Los Angeles Jews in November 1982, talking about his first sight of Haifa in 1947 from the deck of a ship called the *Aegan Star*, a man with tinted blond hair known by the audience as Jay Cole interrupts Avner claiming that he too had been on the *Aegan Star*. He had. It was Yossel Kolowitz.

Yossel, at the end, had opted for the socialist uncle and the kibbutz life. He married and had two sons. He served in the IDF, was wounded during the Six Day War, and decided he needed a break. He chose California, where he made a living as a plumber. Soon, his two sons joined him and made his plumbing business prosper. They too got married, but to non-Jews.

"Don't think I'm not heartbroken. Of course I'm heartbroken" admitted Yossel to Yehuda Avner. "I'm forever a survivor. So just keep your opinions to yourself, hotshot, and don't start telling me what's right and what's wrong."

We are not allowed to judge people whose travails we haven't experienced, the *Ethics of the Fathers* ("Pirkei Avot") teaches us. Surely, no one is entitled to judge Yossel Kolowitz. But there is a lesson to be learned from his personal tragedy.

---

[11] A Jerusalem ultra-Orthodox neighborhood.

In truth, Yossel had a choice between two unattractive options. Either continue to live and dress as an eighteenth century Polish Jew and stay out of the Jewish national renaissance after nearly two-thousand years of exile. Or abandon an exceptional culture and civilization, while carrying guilt feelings towards his vanished family.

Yossel had a choice between two bad options because too many Jews at the time were torn apart.

Not that the divisions between the secular and religious, Ashkenazi and Sephardic, etc. have disappeared. But it is time to get pass them. In the Bible, the hatred between Joseph and his brothers was due to a lack of respect and humility. Joseph eventually learned humility after spending twelve years in jail. And his brothers recognized the folly of their jealousy after realizing what pain they had caused to their father. Only after Joseph came to fully admit the true source of his powers, and only after his brothers had learned to love their father more than they hated their brother, could the family be re-united.

We Jews need to remember and internalize the meaning of Jewish brotherhood. For the sake of Yossel, let us learn the lesson of Joseph.

Chapter 5:

Trading Truth for Money: How Ben-Gurion University Misleads its Donors

On January 5, 2011, the Knesset decided to establish a parliamentary committee to examine international sources of funding for Israeli organizations that "aid the de-legitimization of Israel through harming IDF soldiers." While the decision enjoyed a wide support (41 in favor, 16 against), it turned into a heated spat between the Right and the Left.

The Knesset's decision was adopted following revelations by organizations such as NGO Monitor and *Im Tirtzu* that many Israeli NGOs (Non-Governmental Organizations) testified against Israel in the Goldstone Report; that they are involved in the issuing of arrest warrants against Israeli politicians and IDF officers in Europe; and that some of those NGOs' funding comes from foreign governments.

Those who oppose the Knesset's decision generally make two points: a. the organizations that stand accused deal with human rights and therefore only deserve praise and protection; b. their sources of funding are already public knowledge, so there is no need to double-check them.

Both claims are half-true.

The same way that the UN "Human Rights Council" is dominated by human rights abusers, many NGOs use the "human rights" fig leaf to harass democracies at war and to whitewash murderous regimes. Why else would the Human Rights Council be dominated by human rights abusers, and why else would Human Rights Watch fundraise in Saudi Arabia (as revealed by the *Wall Street Journal* in July 2009)? Not all human rights organizations in Israel and in the world are a sham, of course. Some actually do care for human rights and dignity. But for many NGOs (including Israeli NGOs that are trying to get IDF officers arrested in London), using the "human rights" agenda has become a clever way of enjoying impunity for political activities that have hardly anything to do with human rights.

Claiming that the sources of funding for Israeli NGOs are already public knowledge is no less misleading. Of course, Israeli NGOs report every penny raised and spent to the Non-Profit Authority. But many funds and foundations that donate money to Israeli NGOs are themselves supported by individuals, organizations and governments whose name and identity do not appear when NGOs report their donations. The public information disclosed by Israeli NGOs on their donations does not reveal the entire money trail –a trail that often includes foreign governments. The same way that many "human rights" organizations have nothing to do with human rights, those organizations call themselves "non-governmental" while being funded by governments.

Many Israeli NGOs have simply gotten used to their sense of impunity. So have Israeli universities. *Ma'ariv* journalist Kalman Liebskind, for example, caught Ben-Gurion University (BGU) red-handed lying to its donors.

Liebskind revealed that BGU's French donors have asked for explanations about reports that the University's Political Science Department has become a uniform hub of radical politics. To which the University replied (via its representative for French-speaking Europe) that many of the Department's professors are "right-wing" and even listed them: David Newman, Dani Filc, and Renée Poznanski. Now, all three proudly define themselves as left-wingers –and for good reasons. They've all signed petitions calling for Israeli soldiers not to serve in the disputed territories. Filc is a Board member of Physicians for Human Rights. David Newman is known for lambasting NGO Monitor and *Im Tirtzu*. One wonders if Newman, Filc and Poznanski will now sue their university for libel...

BGU's reply contains another fantastic claim: that the Israeli Council for Higher Education is dominated by the Right, especially Shas and Israel Beitenu.[12] In truth, however, the Council is a non-political body composed mostly of tenured professors. Claiming that Shas and Israel Beitenu are strongly represented at the Council is pure science fiction.

BGU seems to assume that its donors don't have access to Google. Or rather, it suffers from the same syndrome as the so-called human rights NGOs: the syndrome of abusing your respectability to fool people.

As Abraham Lincoln said: "You can fool some of the people all of the time, and all of the people some of the time, but you cannot fool all of the people all of the time." Thanks to the Internet, most people can't be fooled most of the time, and trading truth for money is no longer a profitable business.

---

[12] "Shas" is a party representing Orthodox Jews of oriental origins. "Israel Beitenu" is a secular and nationalist party whose main constituency is composed of immigrants from the former Soviet Union.

Chapter 6:

Twilight of the Idols: On Israel's Discredited Intellectuals

Israel's intellectuals are worried. The Israeli Holy Trinity (Amos Oz, A.B. Yehoshua, and David Grossman) is getting old. The Hebrew University's Pantheon (Martin Buber, Yehuda Magnes, and Yeshayahu Leibowitz) belongs to history. Avraham Burg tries to mimic Leibowitz, but it is hard to inherit the role of a learned Professor when you didn't finish college. As for Shlomo Sand, Moshe Zuckermann and Ilan Pappé, only European neo-Marxists are willing to attend their lectures and to publish their books.

"It used to be that ... they would call me from Army Radio" complains Moshe Zuckermann to Ofer Aderet from *Haaretz* ("The Shrinking of the Israeli Mind," June 7, 2011). So what happened? "The people have been silenced. They tried to strangle them –and they've succeeded" he says. Zuckermann doesn't specify whom he means by "they" but Daniel

Gutwein blames "market forces." You see, explains Gutwein, "The market … ensures there is no intellectual discussion." As for Shlomo Sand, he blames the Universities themselves: "To become a professor" he says "you have to be cautious."

One only has to look at the political makeup of Israel's social science faculties to wonder (or, rather, to understand) what Sand means by "cautious." As for "market forces" being the enemy of intellectual discussion, I bet Bernard Henri-Lévy would beg to differ: he flies a private jet and yet has quite an audience both at home and abroad (including in Israel). He is mostly excused for his buffoonery because, at the end of the day, he is knowledgeable and knows how to write.

Most Israeli intellectuals, by contrast, are provincial and fossilized. Nowhere but in Israel have I seen academics and journalists who still think that mentioning Foucault and Derrida is in fashion. Those people have been living off the same tired mantras for decades: the occupation is the source of all evil; religion is primitive; the advent of peace depends on Israel alone. It is not that Israelis have become "anti-intellectual" or that they have been "strangled." It is just that they are tired of hearing the nonsense of hypocritical conformists.

One noticeable exception is Yehuda Shenhav. A sociology professor at Tel-Aviv University, Shenhav expresses unorthodox views and has no qualms about being a dissident. His last book, *Bounded by the Green Line* (Am Oved, 2010), exposes the intellectual hypocrisy of Israel's Ashkenazi establishment. By blaming "the occupation" for Israel's problems, Shenhav argues, the Zionist left is lying to itself. Shenhav goes further: the Zionist left's obsession with "the occupation" has less to do with liberalism than with nostalgia for the secular and Ashkenazi pre-1967 Israel. But for the Palestinians (and indeed, for Shenhav himself) the "original sin" is not 1967. It is 1948.

Shenhav is no right-winger trying to demonstrate the absurdity of the Oslo paradigm. He rejects this paradigm precisely because he claims that Israel was violent and racist before 1967. While tenants of the "pre-1967 cosmology" would have us believe that the Six Day War transformed Israel from "Little House on the Prairie" to "The Terminator," Shenhav argues that "The model created in 1948 transformed Israel, for all intents and purposes, into a racial state." Thus does he call for a return to "pre-1948" Israel, to an acceptation of the Palestinian "right of return," and to the establishment of a Jewish-Arab federation.

I found Shenhav's diagnosis and prognosis appalling. Pre-1967 Israel was not a "racial" state. It was (and still is) a nation-state that grants cultural preference to the dominant nation while guarantying equal civil rights to minorities, just like other democratic nation-states such as France, Japan or Sweden. And calling for a pastoral brotherhood between a Jewish minority and an Arab majority in a loose federation simply ignores history. Jews were persecuted and mistreated second-class citizens in Arab lands. Most pre-WWII Arab national movements were fascist. The first Palestinian leader, Hadj-Amin al-Husseini, was a Nazi collaborator who was personally responsible for the Jewish pogroms in Palestine in 1929 and 1936 (as well as in Iraq in 1941). The establishment of Israel in 1948 was more the result than the cause of Arab animosity and violence. The fact that *The Protocols of the Elders of Zion* and *Mein Kampf* are best sellers in Arab capitals and that Palestinian media and preachers describe Jews as "sons of pigs and monkeys" does not bode well for stateless Jews in *Dahr el-Islam*.

But Shenhav has the merit of recognizing that "the occupation" is a delusional excuse for the absence of peace, and that it is Zionism itself that the Arabs reject.

So the choice is not between occupation and peace but between Zionism and peace. Many former believers in the "pre-1967 cosmology" realize this. Some are so attached to peace that they have become post-Zionistic. Others are so attached to Zionism that they have opted for steadfastness.

Avi Shlaim and Benny Morris are the perfect examples. Both self-proclaimed "new historians" separately published a history of the Arab-Israeli conflict shortly before the implosion of the Oslo process (*The Iron Wall* and *Righteous Victims*, respectively). Both authors welcomed the election of Ehud Barak in 1999, predicting he would soon prove their theory to be correct. The very opposite happened. Shlaim reacted by rejecting Zionism, Morris by rejecting the Oslo paradigm. While Shlaim now says that "Zionism today is the real enemy of the Jews," Morris declares that "we are doomed to live by the sword."

Morris even compares himself to Albert Camus. "He was considered a left-winger and a person of high morals, but when he referred to the Algerian problem he placed his mother ahead of morality" Morris declared to Ari Shavit in his famous 2004 interview. And so, Morris declares: "Preserving my people is more important than universal moral concepts." Boaz Neumann, a history professor at Tel-Aviv University, has used the same metaphor and has made the same point.

"Twilight of the Idols" is not only a famous book by Friedrich Nietzsche. It is also a central tenet of Judaism. Idolatry is an abomination because the worshiper knows he is lying to himself. That some Israeli intellectuals are sobering is a sign of hope. Who knows: even the Israeli Holy Trinity might eventually recognize the Holy One.

Chapter 7:

The Faith-Keepers: On Israel's Delusional Academics

Attending the Herzliya Conference's panel on the Israeli-Palestinian conflict is like following Woody Allen's therapy through his movies: you know that the patient is hopeless and that the new movie is going to be a mere repetition of the previous one, and yet you maintain the annual ritual out of snobbism. The 2013 Herzliya Conference, however, was more like a flashback. I felt like I was watching the ending scene of Woody Allen's *Mighty Aphrodite*, when the Greek tragedy turns into a Broadway comedy.

The panel included seven speakers: Tzipi Livni (chairperson of the "Hatnuah" party), Shlomo Avineri (a Hebrew University emeritus professor), Robert Danin (from the US Council on Foreign Relations), Michael Herzog (from the Washington Institute for Near East Policies), Yoaz Hendel (chairman of the Institute for Zionist Strategy), Nati Sharoni (chairman of the Council for Peace and Security), and Dani Dayan (former chairman of the Judea and Samaria Council). The moderator was Barak Ravid, the diplomatic correspondent of *Haaretz*.

Supposedly, the purpose of a panel is to present different opinions and to have a debate. In this panel, however, all but one member expressed support for the "two-state solution" (the only minor differences between the speakers were about technicalities). Even the moderator clearly stated his opinion and sided with the six panelists who expressed their support for the "two-state solution." The only dissident was Dani Dayan, who was added at the last minute (his name was not on the original program, and an extra seat was squeezed-in for him right before the session started). In the end, seven speakers (including the "moderator") said that a Palestinian state must be established in Judea and Samaria, and one speaker begged to differ. It was a 7-1 ratio, or an 86% majority –an impressive display of pluralism and balance.

Tzipi Livni (whose party represents 5% of the Knesset) opened her remarks by claiming that she speaks for the majority. Then she explained why the establishment of a Palestinian state is so urgent: soon Hamas will be in charge and when that happens signing a deal with the Palestinians will no longer be an option. Is Tzipi Livni aware of her argument's silliness? If, as she herself admits, Hamas will eventually take over, what is the point of signing with the PLO today a deal that Hamas will trash tomorrow? But what is telling about Tzipi Livni (and about the "majority" she supposedly represents) is not her comical twisted logic but the way she perceives Israel's rights. She said that a peace agreement is the Archimedes' point of Israel's existence, and that peace grants legitimacy to Israel. In other words, Israel's rights and existence are not *sui generis* but are only valid if the world (especially Israel's enemies) approves them.

Even Ehud Barak said during the Camp David negotiations in July 2000 that the Archimedes' point of Israel's existence (he used the very same expression) is the Temple Mount. For Tzipi Livni, this Archimedes' point is neither divine nor historical (I suspect Ehud Barak was referring to the second option). Rather, Israel only has a right to exist if its enemies agree to it. Tzipi Livni has the same "externality" problem on a personal level, which is why she has metamorphosed over the years into the spokesperson of *Haaretz*. Precisely because Israel's self-proclaimed intellectuals will agree to grant you a certificate of intelligence only if you pledge allegiance to the two-state solution, and precisely because Livni is an intellectual lightweight who suffers from an inferiority complex vis-à-vis the *branja*, she became more royalist than the king. Tellingly, Shlomo Avineri publicly congratulated her during the "debate" for joining the exclusive club of the enlightened ones after years of darkness in the Likud grotto.

"Exclusive club" was the expression used by Barak Ravid to describe those who support the two-state solution. This is typically how the Israeli Left tries to intimidate those who don't toe party line: we are the "star-belly sneetches."[13] Then Ravid harangued the audience about what he called "Israel's Apartheid against the Palestinians" and claimed that, for this "apartheid" to end, a Palestinian state must be established as soon as possible in all of Judea and Samaria.

Robert Danin castigated the Israeli government for claiming that there is no partner for peace. When you keep telling people there is no partner, he said, they end up believing it. Danin didn't discuss whether or not the PLO is a reliable partner for peace. His argument was not about history but about psychology: if you can convince people that there is no partner for peace, then you can also convince them that there is a partner for peace. The truth or falsehood of the argument itself is irrelevant. What's important is to believe. It's not about facts. It's about faith.

---

[13] "The Sneetches" is a satire by Dr. Seuss against discrimination. "Sneetches" are imaginary creatures divided between those who have a star on their bellies, and those who don't.

Michel Herzog made a point which I also find fantastic: we have to negotiate with the Palestinians so that we can say to ourselves and to the world that we tried. Well, what about Camp David in July 2000, what about Taba in December 2000, and what about the Olmert proposal to Abbas in 2008? Didn't we try then? Hasn't Herzog been around for the past twelve years?

Yoaz Hendel publicly confirmed that he agrees with Tzipi Livni (he had briefly considered running on her list for the 2013 Knesset elections). He also claimed that "the Israeli people accepts the two-state solution" (actually, over 50 MKs oppose it: 12 MKs from the Jewish Home, 28 MKs from Likud-Beitenu [if you exclude Netanyahu, Tzahi Hanegbi, and maybe Yuval Steinitz], and at least 2/3 of the 18 MKs from the two ultra-orthodox parties).

Nati Sharoni pledged to "get rid of the occupied territories" and played a short movie by Dror Moreh, the author of *The Gatekeepers*. The movie explains (with a soft background music) how to ethnically cleanse Judea and Samaria of its Jews.

Danny Dayan claimed that a two-state solution is unreachable because the gap is too wide between the maximum that Israel is willing to offer and the minimum that the Palestinians are willing to accept (as proven by Abbas' rejection of Olmert's proposal). He suggested improving the status quo by granting the Palestinians full civil rights under the rule of the Palestinian Authority, while maintaining Israel's exclusive security prerogatives.

To which Shlomo Avineri replied that Dayan's proposal meant denying the Palestinians full national rights, and that this constitutes an injustice. Finally there was a debate (this was the only interesting part of the panel). The difference between Shlomo Avineri and Dani Dayan on this issue is not that wide: Avineri doesn't really believe that a solution is possible, but he wants to keep trying nevertheless. Dayan really doesn't believe that there is a solution, and thinks it isn't worth anyone's time to keep banging your head against the wall.

But the debate between the two raised an important question: is it legitimate to grant the Palestinians full civil rights but to deny them national rights?

My answer to this question is positive, for four reasons.

First, because the "Palestinians" do not constitute a genuine people. They are part of the Arab nation, a nation that has 22 states.

Second, because the Palestinian narrative is a fraud and because the Archimedes' point (to use that expression again) of "Palestinism" is the destruction of Israel.

Third, because the Palestinians openly admit that they won't tolerate any Jewish minority in the "Palestinian state" (by contrast, there is a significant Arab minority in the Jewish state).

Fourth, because such a state would inevitably be militarized, it would incite its population (as the PA currently does) against Israel and the Jews, it would eventually be run by Hamas, and it would be an ally of Israel's worst enemies (especially Iran).

So, yes, there are very good reasons to grant the Palestinian Arabs full civil rights but to deny them national rights.

As the panel was coming to an end, Barak Ravid tried very hard to find out if Netanyahu might actually take concrete steps toward the establishment of a Palestinian state (the dream of the Israeli Left). Shlomo Avineri said he didn't think so because of Netanyahu's "revisionist" upbringing.

Referring to Netanyahu, Avineri said the following: "Beware of people who are true believers, because true believers never admit that they are wrong."

Well said, professor. You obviously didn't realize that you were unintentionally ridiculing the "two-state" believers such as yourself. But I had a good laugh: thank you for turning the Greek tragedy into a Broadway comedy.

Chapter 8:

Israel's "Chienlit" Revolution: Why the Social Protest Fell Flat

As French students and intellectuals were playing Robespierre and Mao on the streets of Paris in the spring of 1968, Charles de Gaulle came-up with a formula that was typical of his linguistic creativity: "La réforme oui, la chienlit non" (Yes to reform, no to anarchy). Journalists and commentators had to look up "chienlit" in the dictionary since nobody had ever heard of that word. Chienlit was used in old French and it means "carnival mask." What could the General possibly mean? A pun of course: divide-up the word with hyphens ("chie-en-lit") and you get "shit-in-bed." Ahem.

Israel was completely disconnected from "Mai 68." France was at the height of its power and de Gaulle's rule was unchallenged. Jean-Paul Sartre's existentialist philosophy offered the perfect antidote to a bored youth. Israel's young generation, by contrast, had just emerged victorious from the Six Day War. Fighting for their survival, and being involved in building a new country, young Israelis had no time for planning revolutions from the terrace of a café.

Aside from the "Black Panthers" in the 1970s, Israel never had a social revolt organized by the youth. Being raised in a conformist society with a uniform public discourse, and being taught to respect authority in the army, Israelis were never known for their revolutionary zeal. Add to this the challenge of making a living in a socialist economy and the stress of being in a permanent state of war, and you understand why Israel never had the equivalent of Mai 68.

So the fact that Israelis are finally taking to the streets is actually good news: It shows that Israel has become so wealthy and secure that people actually have the time and luxury to talk about changing the world with hookahs and guitars. Like the French who had never had it so good in the late 1960s, we too are having our "chienlit revolution" ("chiant," by the way, means "boring" in French).

This is not to say, of course, that there is no economic hardship in Israel. There is poverty and there is hardship. But it is Israel's pervasive oligopolies and unfair tax system that make it impossible for middle class families to make ends meet, let alone save money. Real estate is unaffordable because there is no offer; and there is no offer because Israel's Land Administration abuses its monopoly.

Like the Mai 68 strikes, Israel's current social protest is not led by the union movement. During Mai 68, France's main workers' union, CGT, tried to contain the spontaneous militancy by channeling it into a struggle for higher wages and other economic benefits. Even the Communist Party got cold feet, and Jean-Paul Sartre accused the Communists of "fearing revolution." What rioters really wanted was the ousting of de Gaulle. Although the trade union leadership negotiated a 35% increase in the minimum wage, a 7% wage increase for other workers, and half normal pay for the time on strike, the workers occupying their factories refused to return to work. They demanded new elections.

Likewise, the main organizers of today's protest in Israel are more interested in ousting Netanyahu than in improving the lot of struggling families. This is why the *Im Tirtzu* movement pulled out of the protest: it realized that protesters were looking for a fight, not for solutions.

At the end, Mai 68 was a flop. De Gaulle called for early elections and his party won the greatest victory in French parliamentary history. After the carnival, it was time to go to bed –in clean sheets.

Chapter 9:

Is Elvis Presley Dead? On Israeli Post-Mortem Socialism

August 16 marks the anniversary of Elvis Presley's death. Yet some of the King's fans claim he never died and just went into hiding. The average person rightly scoffs at this science-fiction theory. But how can you ridicule those who believe that Elvis is still alive and, at the same time, continue to believe in socialism or in the Middle East "peace process?" Those Israeli academics and journalists who claim that both socialism and the Oslo accords can be salvaged may consider themselves to be the paramount of sophistication and rationality. In truth, however, they are no less irrational than Elvis Presley's most wacky fans.

When Israel's 2011 social protest movement was in its fourth week, the Government appointed a team of experts (the "Trachtenberg Commission") to suggest ways of making life more affordable for the middle-class. High-rank academics have volunteered to help the protesters formulate their demands. Among those self-appointed consultants is Yossi Yonah, a philosophy professor at Ben-Gurion University. How exactly is Yonah qualified to argue about macroeconomics with the Trachtenberg Commission? True, the same question can be asked about Yuval Steinitz, himself a philosophy professor turned Minister of Finance. But the question is not whether philosophers can understand economics (Karl Marx had a Ph.D. in philosophy, so the answer is "no"). The question is what the presence of Yossi Yonah tells us about the true agenda of some of the movement's leaders.

Yossi Yonah publishes mostly on "multiculturalism" and he summarized his views in an interview published in *Haaretz* in 2005 ("Brave New Multicultural World," *Haaretz*, 14 October 2005). What is Yonah's vision for the future of Israel? "Well" he says, "besides the naturalization of the migrant workers, it will include the annulment of the Law of Return; the cancellation of the arrangement of automatic naturalization for Jewish immigrants; and provision of a worthy solution for the Palestinian refugee problem, based on the Geneva Convention." So, you see, it's not only about economics.

There are economic experts on the team, though, such as Prof. Avia Spivak from Ben-Gurion University. He recommends raising taxes, especially corporate taxes, which would supposedly fill public coffers –as if Israeli companies couldn't pick-up and leave, and as if both economic theory and practice hadn't showed that governments' revenues decrease when taxes are too high.

Then there is *Shas'* brilliant idea on how to lower the price of real-estate. Rent control, of course: the Government should tell landlords what to charge. Such policies have been tried in the past, and they've always had the effect of increasing the price of real estate. The reason is simple: when real-estate investors cannot charge the rent that would make their investment profitable, they stop investing in real-estate. When investments in real-estate decline, so does housing supply. And when supply goes down, prices go up.

The official narrative in Israel's media these days is that the high cost of living and the hardships of the middle-class are the result of "ultra-liberalism" and that Israel must become a "welfare state." The very opposite is true. Israel is not a liberal economy: it is dominated by oligopolies that strangle consumers, and by monopolies (such as the National Land Authority) that control supply. If the Israeli economy is strong and productive, it is partly thanks to the economic liberalization undertaken by Shimon Peres in 1985 and by Benjamin Netanyahu in 2003. What Israel's economy needs is more, not less, freedom and competition.

As for adopting the welfare state model, it is ironical that our know-it-all pundits are suggesting the idea precisely when the welfare state is causing European economies to crumble. If Greece, Spain and Italy are broke, it is partly because their welfare state model was built at a time when the population was young and the economy was hardly exposed to foreign competition. With an aging population and the constraints of a globalized economy, the European welfare system has become unafford-able. Hence the pilling debts of European governments, and hence the nervousness of financial markets.

Israel's provincial public discourse does not end here. The violence in Britain, we are told, is to be blamed on Thatcherism. The fact that Labor was in power between 1997 and 2010 is irrelevant (and anyways, a journalist once told me while interviewing me live on the "Reshet Bet" radio, Tony Blair allied himself to George Bush, so he doesn't count). The truth, of course, is that Margaret Thatcher saved the British economy and that if it weren't for her reforms, Britain's fate today would be similar to Greece's.

If the social protest movement in Israel finally provides the opportunity to lower the cost of living by breaking-up monopolies and cartels and by lowering taxes, it will be remembered as one of the best things that ever happened to the country. But if the movement is hijacked by armchair ideologues to implement policies that have been proven to be counter-productive, then Israel is in trouble.

Those who believe that socialism might actually work at the end and that Israel is just the right place to check the theory again are about as rational as Elvis Presley's fans who "know" he's alive. The Israeli hard Left should be given a chance to implement its economic theories –but only after it finds out where Elvis is hiding.

Chapter 10:

Protecting Israeli Democracy from the New Israel Fund

Israel's 2011 social protest died out with the opening of the school year. In October 2011, the Israeli Government approved the recommendations of the Trachtenberg Committee, which include far-reaching measures aimed at easing the burden of the middle class and at making life in Israel more affordable. Yet it would be misleading to believe that the social unrest is behind us. In fact, the self-appointed leaders of the summer's tent protest announced that they will renew their struggle after the High Holidays.

For a start, they rejected *in toto* the recommendations of the Trachtenberg Committee. Daphni Leef, who emerged as one of the movement's iconic leaders, threatened the government with a popular general strike to shut down Israel's economic activity. Eldad Yaniv, from the "National Left" movement, warned in *Haaretz* (October 11, 2011) that the struggle will continue "until the 120 loafers [i.e. MKs] go home."

The leaders of Israel's social protest talk and behave as if Israel were not a democracy, and as if Israel's government had not been elected by a majority. They claim that most Israelis support their demand. Let them prove that in the next elections. For better or worse, democracy grants power to the people. In representative democracy, the majority runs the government for a set period of time. By trying to impose their demands on an elected government, the unelected representatives of the social protest are breaking the rules of democracy.

Israelis rightly complain about the cost of life, but in the previous elections they did not choose a government whose platform was to over-spend and to turn Israel into Greece.

Yet this is precisely what the unelected leaders of the social protest want to impose on our elected government. They have plenty of time (about a year-and-a-half) to convince Israelis to vote for them and their economic platform in the next elections. In the meantime, the choice of Israeli voters, as it was expressed in the previous elections, must be respected.

Not only are the leaders of the social protest breaking one of the basic rules of representative democracy, but many of them are funded by organizations (such as the New Israel Fund) whose agenda is to pro-mote policies and values that are rejected by a majority of Israeli society. The New Israel Fund (NIF) deceives its donors by presenting itself as an organization bent on promoting the rights of minorities and on helping the poor, but its true agenda is to turn Israel into a multi-ethnic (rather than Jewish) country. The NIF supports the Israeli organizations that constantly petition the High Court of Justice to repeal laws that define and preserve Israel as a Jewish state. In Court, the Government is rep-resented by the State Attorney's Office which has been staffed over the years by former NIF fellows who defend the petitioners rather than the Government.

The NIF's subversive tactics consist of progressively imposing upon Israelis what they reject at the polls. It should come as no surprise that George Soros is a major NIF donor. Or that Stanley Greenberg, whose firm has done work for George Soros' "Open Society Institute," consulted to Ehud Barak in 1999 on how to unseat Netanyahu and is now advising Eldad Yaniv with the same purpose. It should come as no surprise that Daniel Abraham, who helped George Soros set-up "J-Street," gave money to Israel's "tent protest" this past summer. And it should come as no surprise that Daphni Leef works for the New Israel Fund.

Promoting ideas and policies that provide an alternative to the Government is a fundamental right (and even a duty) in a democracy, and this fundamental right obviously applies to Daphni Leef and to the NIF. But there is a difference between promoting a political agenda in an open society, and trying to impose such an agenda against the will of the majority via foreign funding, orchestrated strikes, and legal antics. For the sake of Israeli democracy, everything must be done so that Daphni Leef can express and promote her ideas freely, but everything must also be done to prevent her financial backers from trying to impose upon Israeli society policies and ideas that are rejected by the majority.

Chapter 11:

Israel's Purloined Letter: On the Power-Grabbing of Israel's Judiciary

Edgar Allan Poe's short story "The Purloined Letter" provides the perfect allegory to understand why so many people get so fooled for so long. A letter said to contain compromising information has been stolen by a brilliant thief. The police meticulously search the thief's home, using even microscopes, but to no avail. How did the thief fool the police? By displaying the letter instead of hiding it. It is precisely because the police expected the letter to be hidden that they couldn't see it.

For decades, many people in Israel have been wondering why right-wing governments are generally unable to implement their policies and often end-up adopting the rhetoric of the Left. Witness the fact, for example, that Netanyahu has officially endorsed the establishment of a Palestinian state against his own party's platform, that his government might be toppled if it complies with the High Court of

Justice's injunction to dismantle outposts, and that some Likud ministers and MKs are speaking in unison with the Left on the need to preserve the cooptation system that guaranties the Supreme Court's ideological uniformity.

The answer to this riddle was provided by Tel-Aviv Law Professor Menachem Mautner in his book *Law and Culture in Israel at the Threshold of the Twenty-First Century* (Tel-Aviv University Press, 2008): The Israeli Left lost its monopoly on power with the electoral victory of the Right in 1977, and it has successfully tried to keep its influence via the judicial system, academia, and the media. At the Supreme Court, Judges are selected and appointed by Judges, and they have granted to themselves the right to repeal laws deemed "unconstitutional" (regardless of the fact that Israel has no constitution). Hence the "judicial activism" epitomized by Justice Aharon Barak: if the majority does not legislate according to the will and worldview of the "enlightened ones" (to use Barak's own words), then laws must be repealed by self-appointed judges who know better.

In academia, it is virtually impossible for conservative-minded academics to get tenure in the social sciences and in the humanities outside of Bar-Ilan University. As for "dissident" journalists, there is hardly a payroll to be found outside the *Makor Rishon* and *Israel Hayom* newspapers. The recent legislation advanced by the Right and condemned by the Left (e.g. on boycott, on the funding of NGOs, on the appointment of Supreme Court Justices, or on defamation) suggests that the Israeli Right has finally noticed where the "purloined letter" was displayed, and is taking action to rule according to the will of its voters. But this is only half-true.

For a start, some of the legislation recently initiated by the Right is counter-productive. The fact that boycotters can now be sued for financial damage was meant to deter the Left from taking part in the BDS (Boycott, Divestment, Sanctions) campaign and from boycotting settlements. But according to the same law, Ben-Gurion University (BGU) can now sue the student movement *Im Tirtzu* for asking BGU's donors to keep their money away from this university until its Political Science Department respects pluralism. Likewise, the new legislation meant to increase six fold fines for defamation is more of a threat to a small and conservative newspaper like *Makor Rishon* than to a powerful and liberal newspaper like *Yediot Aharonot*. As for the law limiting foreign government funding for Israeli NGOs, it will certainly hurt the likes of *Shalom Archav* and *Adalah* in their pockets, but it will hardly make fund-raising easier for *Im Tirtzu* or for *My Israel*.[14]

Besides shooting itself in the foot with counterproductive legislation, the Israeli Right is hopelessly absent from the intellectual arena. The Shalem Center was supposed to produce conservative thinkers but it has virtually withdrawn from Israel's intellectual scene because of its focus on starting a new liberal arts college. Shalem is even ending the publication of *Azure*, Israel's only high-quality conservative journal. The Shalem College might be successful in producing another type of intellectual leaders, but it will take a couple of decades to tell. Another Israeli conservative journal, *Nativ*, closed two years ago. The only conservative journal around is *Hauma*. Published by the Jabotinsky Institute (itself located at the Likud headquarter), *Hauma* has a small circulation and preaches to the convert. As for the Institute for Zionist Strategies, its research and papers are mostly kept away from the public's attention by the media.

The Israeli Left is up in arms, but in truth it has little to worry about. Aside from doing a pretty good job at holding on in the judicial system, in academia and in the media, the Israeli Left has one asset that is both

---

[14] "Shalom Archav" and "Adallah" are two left-wing Israeli NGOs that get funding from European governments. "Im Tirtzu" and "My Israel" are two right-wing Israeli NGOs that do not get such funding.

as obvious and as unnoticeable as the "purloined letter": it intimidates the Right. Likud's former "princes" have grown-up with an inferiority complex vis-à-vis the Left. They are petrified by *Haaretz* and by the accusation of not respecting "the rule of law." They are imbued with the idea that people who read *Haaretz* and who live in Tel-Aviv are smarter, and that you need their seal of approval in order for your IQ to be declared above average. *Haaretz* has recently canonized Menachem Begin as Israel's most impeccable democrat, but three decades ago it decried him as a warmonger, as a bigot and as a fascist. Why? To make sure that his son gets the message: continue to be a good boy and to keep your hands off the Supreme Court.

What the Israeli Right needs to do is to produce intellectuals. This is what institutions and movements such as the Jewish Statesmanship Center, *Im Tirtzu*, the Tikva Fund and the future Shalem College are trying to achieve. But those important initiatives are emerging nearly forty years after the electoral victory of the Right. For all its kicking and screaming, the Israeli Left can relax: surely if it took forty years for the Right to find the purloined letter, there is no reason to be hypochondriac.

Chapter 12:

An Israeli Tribute to Margaret Thatcher

I was a ten-year-old child growing-up in France when I first heard the name Margaret Thatcher. Maggie, as she came to be known, had just liberated the Falklands (which French journalists insisted on calling "Les Malouines"). Mitterrand gave full support to Britain in that war (including vital information on French missiles sold to Argentina), and his feelings toward "La dame de fer" oscillated between admiration and envy ("Je l'admire. Ou je l'envie?" he confessed to his advisor Jacques Attali). When it came to economics, however, the socialist President thought he knew better. He privately derided Thatcher as "a shopkeeper," echoing Napoléon's dismissive description of the British as "a nation of shopkeepers." As a child, I thought Mitterrand was right. As an adult, I know he was wrong.

In a way, Britain gave liberalism and conservatism to the world. John Locke, Adam Smith and David Ricardo were liberals (in the original and British sense of the word) because they believed that there could be no political freedom without economic freedom. Edmund Burke was a conservative because he doubted the feasibility of Rousseau's grand social designs and because he firmly believed that no society could function without cherished traditions and shared beliefs.

Both liberalism and conservatism took a blow in the 20th century, though. The economic crisis of the 1930s made people wonder where Adam Smith's "invisible hand" was hiding. European fascism discredited nationalism. In post World War Two Europe, economic thought and policy were dominated by Keynesianism, and the political discourse was mostly monopolized by Marxism ("The opium of the intellectuals" as Raymond Aron pointedly quipped).

The 1970s changed the fortunes of the Keynesian and Marxist duopoly. The enduring "stagflation" put Keynesians on the defensive, and the lowering of trade barriers within the EEC and the GATT turned demand side economics into a "help-thy-neighbor" policy. In addition, Alexander Solzhenitsyn's revelations about the Soviet Gulag embarrassed the European Left. The time was ripe for liberalism and conservatism to make their case again.

The task was daunting. The fact that Keynesianism was no longer delivering and that Marxism's true colors had been revealed did not produce an overnight upheaval. Indeed, Germany's Willy Brandt was busy appeasing the Soviets with his *Ostpolitik*, and in France Mitterrand added Communists to his Socialist government. Liberalism was in need of leadership. Margaret Thatcher provided it.

When Margaret Thatcher was elected in 1979, the British economy was in decline and the West was in retreat. In 1979 alone, the West suffered three international humiliations (mostly thanks to Jimmy Carter):

the Soviet invasion of Afghanistan; the Islamic revolution in Iran; and the Sandinista coup in Nicaragua.

Thatcher faced those challenges by battling for freedom both in economics and in foreign affairs. Her outlook on economics had been influenced by Friedrich von Hayek and by Milton Friedman. Her conduct of foreign policy was based on Churchill's warning that whoever chooses dishonor to avoid war ends up with both dishonor and war.

Hence did she pass an unpopular budget in 1981 despite calls from within her own party to operate a U-turn ("You turn if you want. The lady is not for turning"). And hence did she deal with the miners' 1984-1985 strike with unflinching determination. Thatcher lowered Britain's punishing income tax, privatized government-owned behemoths, took away from the unions the power of shutting down the country, and stopped throwing taxpayer money into industrial black holes. While her reforms put many people out of work in the short run, they lowered unemployment in the long run. As a result of her policy, Britain has less unemployment and more economic growth than France. Indeed, London has become a refuge for French entrepreneurs who flee punishing taxes and unaffordable labor laws.

Her reforms have served as a model of economic liberalization in India, in South America, and in Eastern Europe. Even Israel's 1985 economic stabilization program was pure Thatcherism —except for the ironical fact that in Israel Thatcherism was introduced by Shimon Peres while he served as Labor Prime Minister.

Thatcher was also right not to join the Euro. The European monetary union has become a trap for growth-prone and disciplined countries (Germany, basically) who end-up supporting profligate and irresponsible ones. Indeed, the Euro is like a dysfunctional couple that wants to separate but is deterred by the cost of divorce.

Thatcher's foreign policy was also a change for the better. In lieu of the moral relativism and diplomatic appeasement of the European Left, she proudly proclaimed the moral superiority of democracy and made it clear to tyrants that she was out to get them. She ordered military action against the Argentinean junta and brushed aside calls for caution and conciliation. As a result of Britain's victory, the junta fell and democracy returned to Argentina. Argentineans may revile Thatcher, but they owe her their freedom.

She rightly believed that there could be no peace with Russia without a victory over the Soviet regime. She allowed US nuclear missiles to be stationed in the UK in order to boost the West's deterrence vis-à-vis Moscow. She made it clear to Gorbachev that he had to free his country before expecting the West's largesse. The Soviet Union may have been doomed to implode, but Thatcher and Reagan decisively accelerated the process that brought the Evil Empire to its knees.

Thatcher had no patience either for the clownish reincarnations of Saladin. She supported the bombing of Tripoli in 1986, severed diplomatic ties with Iran in 1989, and convinced George Bush senior to use military force against Saddam Hussein after the invasion of Kuwait. She stepped down shortly before the Gulf War, but that war might never have been fought if she hadn't been on board from day one.

Like everyone else, of course, Thatcher had a less savory side. Her tolerance for Chile's Pinochet and for South Africa's Apartheid government were unforgivable.

But, on balance, she gave back to liberalism and conservatism their *lettres de noblesse*. The struggle is far from being over but, thanks to Maggie, it is no longer hopeless.

Chapter 13:

Hilarious Hillary: Reading *Haaretz* does not Make you Smart

Hillary Clinton expressed concern about the future of Israeli democracy because the Knesset is considering curtailing foreign governments' funding for Israeli NGOs, and because some rabbis in Israel say they want men and women to seat separately on buses. Does Hillary realize how disingenuous she is? In the United States, NGOs that receive money from foreign governments are considered foreign agents. And why is separate sitting between men and women on "haredi" (ultra-orthodox) buses a threat to democracy in Israel but not in New York (a common practice in Clinton's home state)?

In July 2011, the FBI arrested Syed Ghulam Nabi Fai, a US citizen accused by the US Department of Justice of not informing the US government that he was on the payroll of the Pakistani government while lobbying for the Kashmir cause and donating funds to Congressmen.

Fai, who is director of the Washington-based NGO Kashmiri American Council (KAC), allegedly received millions of dollars for the KAC over the last two decades. Fai is accused of a decades-long scheme with one purpose – to hide Pakistan's involvement behind his efforts to influence the US government's position on Kashmir. His handlers in Pakistan allegedly funneled millions through the Kashmir Center to contribute to US elected officials, fund high-profile conferences, and pay for other efforts that promoted the Kashmiri cause to decision-makers in Washington. If found guilty, Fai could face up to five years in prison.

US law states that any American citizen or organization that receives money from foreign governments must register as a foreign agent. The foreign agent must report all its income and spending, and the Attorney General can demand, at any time, the list of the agent's donors. Many Israeli NGOs receive money from foreign governments in order to influence the policy of Israel's government. In the United States, such NGOs would have to register as foreign agents, and their books would be scrutinized by the Government. Why is the United States, a superpower no longer threatened by communism, entitled to take self-protecting measures from political NGOs funded by foreign governments, but not Israel, a tiny country that faces existential threats?

Clinton is making a fool of herself because she is buying into the nonsense of the English version of *Haaretz*. This radical newspaper read by less than 1% of the Israeli population (it prints 70,000 copies a day for a population of 8 million) is the Bible of foreign journalists and diplomats –the very people who write about Israel and who report to their capitals. Clinton is not the only victim of the "*Haaretz* effect." Recently, President Sarkozy said that a state cannot be Jewish just like a table cannot be Catholic. He was repeating almost word by word what Amos Oz regularly writes in *Haaretz*.

Haaretz has been writing that it is undemocratic to curtail foreign governments' funding for Israeli NGOs bent on influencing the policies of Israel's government; that only in autocracies and in third world countries do the executive and legislative branches have a say on the appointment of Supreme Court Justices; and that fining journalists for lying intentionally is contrary to the freedom of speech. *Haaretz* knows that it is writing nonsense, but its ideological agenda comes before the truth. Hillary Clinton obviously knows that in her country Supreme Court Judges are appointed by the President and that organizations that receive funding from foreign governments have to register as foreign agents. Is Clinton simply being hypocritical, or is she orchestrating a campaign against the Netanyahu Government, just like her husband did when he was President?

The second possibility does make sense, since Tzipi Livni was quick to come to Hillary Clinton's defense. Livni justified Clinton's statements despite the fact that Clinton went as far as to compare Israel to Iran —or maybe because of it: after all, Livni is about to lose her job as Kadima's Chair to the Iranian-born Shaul Mofaz. The problem with reciting the content of *Haaretz* and of *The New York Times* is that it makes you look smart in front of *Haaretz* and *New York Times* readers (the kind of people who attend the Saban Forum), but it also makes you look like a fool in front of the rest of the world.

The fact that Livni expressed support for Clinton's comments goes to show that Clinton and Livni deserve each other. But it also goes to show that both Israel and America deserve better.

Chapter 14:

Sarkozy, c'est fini

French songwriter Hervé Vilard became famous overnight in 1965 with his love song "Capri, c'est fini" (Capri, it's over). The song literally sounds like a broken record, but Vilard made a fortune out of it (he sold 2.5 million records). Could it be that disappointment is so universal a feeling that it speaks to our hearts even with the dullest melody? And would I get 2.5 million downloads on I-tunes if I were to write a song called "Sarkozy, c'est fini?" After all, there are more than 2.5 million people who are disappointed in Sarkozy. I'm no musician, though, so I shall settle for the following words.

Since "making aliyah" (immigrating, ascendency-wise) to Israel eighteen years ago, I forwent my right to vote in French elections. I no longer share the destiny of France, a country I voluntarily left. In 2007, however, I made an exception. Nicolas Sarkozy impressed me, and I made a special trip (twice) to the French consulate to give the guy my vote. Sarkozy was an outsider. The son of a Hungarian immigrant, he was raised by a Jewish grandfather and grew-up as the ugly duckling in Paris' posh Neuilly suburb. As opposed to the rest of France's political leadership, he was not intellectually cloned by ENA, the French elite school for government. But, mostly, he sounded sincere when he said that he intended to replace French economic dirigisme with pro-market policies, and when he spoke fondly of Israel and of America. Indeed, it seemed too good to be true –and it was.

Sarkozy turned out to be a temperamental control-freak whose economic reforms are meager and whose foreign policy record is disastrous. His "Mediterranean Union" project was a flop. Besides angering his European partners (especially Germany) for not consulting with them on his half-cooked ideas (yet expecting them to share the cost of their implementation), Sarkozy made a fool of himself. In July 2008, he threw a grand party in Paris to launch his now defunct "Mediterranean Union" with embarrassing guests such as Hosni Mubarak and Bashar Assad. Sarkozy thought that his "Mediterranean Union" would convince Turkey to give-up its EU bid, while Erdogan had already made the choice of a pan-Islamic foreign policy.

Worse, Sarkozy went out of his way to rehabilitate Muammar Kaddafi in order to sell French nuclear plants and military aircrafts to Libya. Shortly after his election, Sarkozy hosted Kaddafi in Paris and then went to Tripoli to celebrate "a strategic partnership" between France and Libya. While candidate Sarkozy gave fine speeches on France's international role to promote human rights, President Sarkozy did business with Kaddafi ("I'm about to sign multi-billion contracts with Libya," Sarkozy proudly declared to the French media). Except that Sarkozy underestimated the risks of doing business with an airplane blower. Kaddafi pocketed Sarkozy's "rehabilitation certificate" but failed to deliver. Aside from being furious at Kaddafi, Sarkozy was embarrassed by the Arab revolts which revealed his government's cozy relations with Arab dictators. He subsequently and opportunistically decided to rebrand himself as Zorro, now bombarding Kaddafi with the planes he wanted to sell him.

Sarkozy unsuccessfully tried to play the tough peace-maker vis-à-vis Russian President Medvedev when the latter bombarded South Ossetia in the summer of 2008. It is not done to try and preserve your bygone empire by using military force against independence-minded leaders, Sarkozy explained to Medvedev. Yet Sarkozy himself did just that in the former French colony of Côte d'Ivoire, where the French army toppled Laurent Gbagbo, the outvoted President who had been instrumental in undoing France's neo-colonialism in his country.

Sarkozy's hot-headedness and duplicity are by now music to Israel's ears. Sarkozy has Jewish origins, and he started his political career as Mayor of Neuilly –an affluent Paris suburb with a powerful Jewish community. As Interior Minister under President Chirac, he acted firmly against anti-Semitism. His speeches were full of praise for Israel. He became friendly with Benjamin Netanyahu. His address to the Knesset in June 2007 was as good as it could get (except, that is, for the line on dividing Jerusalem).

Today, Sarkozy's attitude toward Israel is undistinguishable from that of his predecessors: he is obnoxious and confrontational, and France's "Arab policy" is back in full gear. In 2009, Sarkozy granted the Légion d'Honneur (France's equivalent of the Presidential Medal of Freedom) to Charles Enderlin, the French journalist who falsely accused Israel of killing Muhamad Al-Dura, thus igniting the second Intifada as well as "revengeful" acts such as the beheading of Daniel Pearl. Sarkozy blamed Netanyahu and absolves Abbas for the Israeli-Palestinian stalemate, despite Netanyahu's gestures and despite Abbas' refusal to negotiate. He encouraged Abbas' statehood bid at the UN and recently voted in favor of UNESCO's admission of "Palestine" as a full member state. He has reportedly declared that Israel's demand to be recognized as a Jewish state by the Palestinians is "ridiculous." In a private conversation with

President Obama, Sarkozy badmouthed Israel's Prime Minister calling him a "liar" and saying he couldn't stand him.

Sarkozy's speech at the UN General Assembly in September 2011 was no less than idiotic. He blamed the Israeli-Palestinian stalemate on a "method problem" and yet he suggested to try again that very method in order to solve the conflict: negotiate the final status of Jerusalem, borders and settlement within a pre-set timetable. This is precisely what the Oslo process, the Road Map and the Annapolis conference unsuccessfully tried to achieve.

Most French Jews and most dual French-Israeli citizens voted for Sarkozy in 2007. Sarkozy mistakenly calculates that he can still count on their votes despite his antics, because the alternative is allegedly worse. He is mistaken. In the Socialist Party's primaries, the rabid anti-Israel Martine Aubry was defeated by the moderate and conciliatory François Hollande. On the far-right, Marine Le Pen is at pains to prove her pro-Israel credentials and to distance herself from her anti-everything (including anti-Semitic) father.

Sarkozy has lost the Jewish vote and his defeat in the 2012 French elections will be well deserved. Sarkozy, c'est fini.

Chapter 15:

For me, not for thee: On Freedom of Speech in Israel

In July 2001, the new Republic of South Soudan became a member state of the United Nations. After being oppressed, massacred and plundered for decades by Khartoum, the people of South Sudan finally obtained the independent state they fought for. Theoretically, the Palestinians should rejoice and ask the UN why they are denied what the South Sudanese were granted. Instead, Mahmoud Abbas delivered a letter to Sudanese President Omar Hassan Al-Bashir (a man accused of genocide and of crimes against humanity by the International Criminal Court) to express his opposition to South Sudan's independence.

It's called self-determination for me, not for thee.

Just as Abbas was about to reap the gold medal for hypocrisy, Catherine Ashton broke a new record. After the Knesset passed a law that enables Israeli citizens to bring civil suits against people or organizations instigating anti-Israel boycotts, Ashton expressed public concern for freedom of speech in Israel. Which makes Ashton eligible for the gold medal of hypocrisy too, because in Europe anti-Israel boycott is a criminal offence. In France, for example, you can go to jail for three years and pay a €45,000 fine for trying to impede economic activity out of political, ethnic, or religious prejudice (Articles 225-1 and 225-2 of the "Code pénal").

The French law is more stringent than the one recently passed by the Knesset. The new Israeli law does not criminalize boycott. It only allows "citizens to bring civil suits against persons and organizations that call for economic, cultural or academic boycotts against Israel, Israeli institutions or regions under Israeli control." So the New Israel's Fund's statement that the new law "criminalizes freedom of speech" is false and misleading. The new Israeli law does not criminalize boycott, let alone freedom of speech. French law, by contrast, does criminalize boycott.

US law also prohibits anti-Israel boycott. The Anti-boycott laws under the US Export Administration Act of 1979 (as amended in August 1999) prohibit American companies from furthering or supporting the boycott of Israel. The penalties imposed for each violation can be a fine of up to $50,000 or five times the value of the exports involved (whichever is greater), and imprisonment of up to five years.

It is ironical that the same people in Israel who claim that freedom of speech can suffer no infringement said the very opposite two weeks ago when the police arrested Rabbi Dov Lior. We were told, at the time, that freedom of speech can and should be curtailed when it borders incitement. True, there is a difference between incitement and boycott (though boycott often turns into incitement). But either freedom of speech suffers no limitation, or it does. And democracies such as the United States and France do limit freedom of speech in order to prevent incitement as well as boycott. So you are allowed to limit freedom of speech in order to prevent discrimination in America and in France, but not in Israel.

It's called freedom of speech for me, not for thee.

No less ironical is the fact that the very same people in Israel who said after the arrest of Rabbi Lior that the law is sacrosanct are now making a point of publicly defying the law by boycotting Israeli goods produced beyond the "green line" (in France, as explained above, they could be jailed for doing that). Two weeks ago, the law was sacrosanct. Now, it is a moral duty to break it.

It's called rule of law for thee, not for me.

So who gets the gold medal for hypocrisy? Mahmud Abbas, Catherine Ashton, or Zehava Gal-On?[15] The contest being so tight, here is a compromise. Let's grant French citizenship to Zehava Gal-On to deter her from discriminating between Israeli products for political reasons. Let's have Catherine Ashton write an essay on "why civil lawsuits are more dangerous to freedom of speech than criminal prosecutions." And let's appoint Mahmoud Abbas as "UN Special Envoy for the Universal Implementation of the two-state solution including, inter alia, in Sudan, Libya, Lebanon, Morocco, Cyprus, Belgium, Canada, and China."

It's called making of fool of thee, not of me.

---

[15] Zehava Gal-On is the Chairperson of Israel's left-wing "Meretz" party.

Chapter 16:

Putting an End to Outrageousness: On the Toulouse Tragedy

There are no words to express the horror of the Toulouse shooting (March 2012), but EU Foreign Affairs Representative Catherine Ashton did manage to find the words that add insult to injury. "When we think about what happened today in Toulouse," she said, "we remember what happened in Norway last year, we know what is happening in Syria, and we see what is happening in Gaza and other places - we remember young people and children who lose their lives."

Three Jewish children lost their lives in Toulouse on Monday because a murderer intentionally shot them in their school. There are sometimes civilian casualties, including among children, when Israel targets missile launching sites in Gaza. Israel's military operations in Gaza are always a reaction to the shooting of missiles launched from Gaza and aimed at Israeli civilians. The former is a lawful act of self-defense while the latter is a war crime. The civil casualties of Israel's military operations in Gaza are both unintentional and unavoidable, and Hamas is ultimately responsible for those casualties.

Even though Ashton reacted to the uproar caused by her remarks by declaring that she "drew no parallel whatsoever between the circumstances of the Toulouse attack and the situation in Gaza," the comparison she made is outrageous.

Unfortunately, however, Ashton's comparison is not an isolated act of clumsiness or malignity. Many world leaders and international organizations have gotten used to being outrageous when talking about Israel. Even worse, those leaders and organizations simply get away with their outrageousness. This tendency must, and can, stop.

The same Bashar Assad who murders thousands of his own citizens has condemned Israel for retaliating to the shooting of missiles from Gaza. The same Recep Erdogan who uses military force against Turkey's Kurds (a violence that caused the death of 34 innocent Kurds, mostly teenagers, in December 2011) has accused Israel of "massacring" the Palestinians. The same Vladimir Putin who strongly condemned Israel's raid on the Gaza flotilla in 2010 has sent military reinforcement to Assad's murderous regime.

Then there is the UN and the Arab-funded NGOs.

The "Israel Apartheid Week" recently ended on US and European campuses. While Israel is the only country in the Middle East where Arab citizens enjoy civil rights, and while Arab states are notorious for their apartheid policies against minorities, Israel is singled out for the crimes of its accusers.

In March 2012, The UN Human Rights Council (HRC) endorsed a report in which the human rights record of the Gaddafi regime in Libya was enthusiastically praised by some of the world's most repressive governments. The HRC singles out Israel as the world's only country whose human rights record must be examined at every session. While the HRC is silent on Assad's mass murder, it discussed a resolution this week condemning Israel's human rights record in the "occupied Syrian Golan."

Also in March 2012, the United Nations Office for the Coordination of Humanitarian Affairs (OCHA), released a report that accused Israel of "stealing" water from the Palestinians. In truth, however, the "Water Agreement" signed by Israel and the PA in Washington in September 1995 is respected by Israel and systematically violated by the Palestinians.

This outrageousness will continue as long as Israel adopts a defensive position instead of going on the offensive.

Rather than reacting to Erdogan's outbursts with appeasing statements, Israel should condemn Turkey's opposition to Kurdish statehood and Turkey's occupation of Cyprus. Israel should also remind the world that Syria normalized its relations with Turkey despite Turkey's refusal to relinquish the Alexandretta province.

Rather than echoing the absurd accusation of "Israeli Apartheid," Israel should organize an "Arab apartheid week" on US and European campuses.

Rather than imploring the Palestinians to return to the negotiations table (as Israel's ambassador to the UN in Geneva Aharon Leshno Yaar did this week after hearing his Palestinian counterpart Ibrahim Khraishi declare that Israel's retaliation to Hamas' rocket fire was "unjustified"), Israel should ask the world why it accepts Mahmoud Abbas' position that there will be no room for a single Jew in the Palestinian state envisioned by the PA.

The Toulouse tragedy is a reminder of a simple truth: acts of violence are preceded by words, and there are consequences to portraying Jews as segregationists, as human rights abusers, and as water stealers.

Jews will be vulnerable as long as they are defamed, and this defamation will only end when we go on the offensive and when we have the confidence to stand for the truth.

Chapter 17:

J'Accuse! On the Israeli Establishment and the al-Dura Affair

Emile Zola's open letter published on the front page of *L'Aurore* on 13 January 1898 has become the epitomic expression for denouncing State lies. This expression fits perfectly to denounce the French Republic for sacrificing truth in the name of *raison d'État* in the Al-Dura Affair. In February 2004, French President Jacques Chirac sent a letter to Charles Enderlin, the author of the Al-Dura report, praising his faithfulness to truth. In 2008, French journalists published an open letter to express their support for Charles Enderlin. In 2009, President Sarkozy granted Enderlin the *légion d'honneur*, France's highest decoration. The French State has behaved in the Al-Dura Affair the way it behaved in the Dreyfus Affair —except for the fact that in the Dreyfus Affair, the State eventually admitted that it had orchestrated a lie. And during the Dreyfus Affair, many French "intellectuels" (the word was coined at the time) took personal risks in the name of truth. In the Al-Dura Affair, by contrast, most French journalists and public figures have circled the wagons around Enderlin.

The behavior of the French establishment in the Al-Dura affair is shameful, but not surprising. What is surprising is the fact that the *Israeli* establishment also circled wagons around Enderlin.

The "Affair" started on September 30, 2000, when French state television France 2 broadcast images showing a boy and his father (Mohammad and Jamal Al-Dura) supposedly caught in gunfire between the IDF and PA forces at Gaza's Netzarim junction. France 2's Israel correspondent Charles Enderlin did not personally witness the incident but he claimed, while commenting on the images filmed by his Palestinian cameraman Talal Abu-Rahmah, that the boy had been killed by Israeli bullets. Enderlin's words were that the boy and his father were the *target* ("la cible" in French) of the IDF. The message was clear: the IDF had intentionally killed a helpless Palestinian child (Enderlin later claimed that he hadn't meant that Israel *intentionally* killed the child, but that is nevertheless what could unmistakably be understood from his words).

In 2004, France 2 sued French politician and media analyst Philippe Karsenty for claiming that Enderlin's report was a forgery. In 2008, the Paris Appellate Court acquitted Karsenty of defamation, concluding that the defendant had grounds for questioning the authenticity of Enderlin's report.

The images broadcast by France 2 and Enderlin's claim had a devastating effect. They inflamed the "Second Intifada" as well as anti-Israel demonstrations around the world. Horrendous crimes such as the lynching of Israeli soldiers in Ramallah in October 2000 or the beheading of Daniel Pearl in February 2002 were justified by their perpetuators as a revenge for Mohammad Al-Dura's death.

And yet, Mohammad Al-Dura could not possibly have been killed by Israeli bullets. Worse, there is strong evidence that the whole scene might have been staged in the first place. Which means that Charles Enderlin and France 2 are responsible for a blood libel that caused the death of hundreds of Jews and that had devastating consequences on Israel's international image.

On 19 May 2013, the Israeli Government published a report that demonstrates the inconsistencies and falsehoods of Enderlin's claim. Why it took nearly thirteen years for the Israeli Government to react to Enderlin's accusation is an intriguing question that will be addressed at the end of this chapter.

The Israeli Government's report is based on previous studies and inquiries, including those of Philippe Karsenty, of German journalist Esther Schapira, of American History Professor Richard Landes, of Israel ballistic expert Nahum Shahaf, of French ballistic expert Jean-Claude Shlinger, and of French-born Israeli surgeon Yehuda David. The commission established by the Israeli government concludes that Enderlin's accusation is baseless. There is nothing to support the claim that Muhammad and Jamal Al-Dura were "targets of gunfire from the Israeli position." Indeed, nothing in the video supports the claim that they were hit by any gunfire.

Enderlin committed a grave professional mistake at best and an act of felony at worst by relying entirely on Abu Rahmah's unsubstantiated claim that the boy had been killed by Israeli bullets. Indeed, CNN refused to air Enderlin's report (which France 2, for some reason, gave out for free) precisely because its central claim was not confirmed by the images and were only based on the sayings of Abu Rahmah, himself a Palestinian militant who has declared that he became a journalist "to promote the Palestinian cause."

The Israeli government and the IDF have asked many times to receive the full and unedited footage filmed by Abu-Rahmah. France 2, Charles Enderlin and their lawyers have consistently refused to hand the entire raw footage to Israel (only part of it was submitted to Court in France because the Judges demanded it). Right after the broadcast of Enderlin's report, the IDF Spokesman asked for the full raw footage (27 minutes according to Abu-Rahmah), but was only given a tape which contained basically the same footage that had already been aired. France 2 has also turned down similar requests by the Commander of the Southern Command and by the Prime Minister's Office. Between September and November 2007 the IDF Spokesperson and Deputy Spokesperson repeatedly requested the unedited footage from France 2's lawyers, but to no avail. France 2 wouldn't refuse to produce the entire raw footage if it didn't have anything to hide.

CRIF, the representative council of French Jewry, has been asking for years for a professional inquiry into the Al-Dura Affair. In 2008, France 2 accepted to set-up an independent and international commission, but then it backed down.

But the most troubling part of the Al-Dura affair is that it took over twelve years for Israel to officially deny Enderlin's claims.

Charles Enderlin is a Franco-Israeli journalist who moved to Israel in the late 1960s and started working for French TV channel Antenne 2 (today's France 2) in the early 1980s. He defines himself as "a Zionist up to the green line" (apparently unaware that Mount Zion is beyond the green line) and openly identifies with the Israeli Left. He has many friends in Israel's political and media establishments. When the Al-Dura affair erupted, Enderlin could –and did- count on those friends.

After the failure of the Camp David Summit in July 2000, Enderlin became personally involved in further attempts to reach an agreement between Israel and the PA. He offered his help to his friend Gilead Sher, who was Israel's co-chief peace negotiator in 1999-2001. Today, Sher is Enderlin's lawyer.

Since 2000, Enderlin's line of defense has been that the Israeli government never officially contested his report and never accused him of forgery. He had a point, but then there was a reason why the Israeli government never accused Enderlin of forgery. Enderlin has many friends at the Israeli Ministry of Foreign Affairs (MFA), in the IDF, and in the Israeli media. Prominent among them are former Israeli ambassadors to France Nissim Zvili and Danny Shiek, Israeli politicians Tzipi Livni and Israel Hasson, and Israeli journalists Gideon Levy and Daniel Bensimon.

Since 2000, the official position of the MFA and of the IDF was that it was preferable not to talk about Al-Dura (Gideon Meir was, and still is, a fierce defender of this theory on behalf of the MFA). The MFA's spokesman Yigal Palmor declared that "The [Israeli] government does not have an official stand as to what exactly happened on September 30, 2000 at Netzarim and sees the issue as an internal French affair, not Israeli" and that "Karsenty's work is counterproductive."

Enderlin could use his contacts at the MFA, at the IDF, and in the Israeli media to keep Israel quiet, but he had no such leverage on Moshe Ya'alon, who was appointed Minister of Strategic Affairs in 2009.

It is the Ministry of Strategic Affairs that issued Israel's official rebuttal of Enderlin in May 2013. So now Enderlin can no longer claim that Israel does not dispute his accusation of murdering Mohammad Al-Dura. What was Enderlin's reaction to Israel's official rebuttal? To threaten to sue Moshe Ya'alon. And who sent this threatening letter to Ya'alon on May 28, 2013? Gilead Sher's law firm.

On the one hand, Enderlin has been explaining the lack of official rebuttal of his theory by the Israeli government's silence (a silence which he was instrumental in preserving). On the other hand, now that the Israeli government finally rebutted his theory, Enderlin is threatening to sue. This bullying and intimidation are reminiscent of the way France 2 and Charles Enderlin "convinced" the ARTE TV channel not to air Esther Schapira's documentary on the Al-Dura affair.

I accuse senior MFA and IDF officials as well as major Israeli journalists, because their cover-up of Enderlin was cowardly and criminal.

The official MFA/IDF/*Haaretz* et al. claim that ignoring the whole story and letting it fade away was preferable to fighting for Israel's reputation was, and still is, moronic, hypocritical, and wrong. Why should we let ourselves be accused of intentionally murdering a helpless child? Why? As for the "let it fade away" theory, it has been constantly contradicted by facts: the Al-Dura myth is pervasive in the Arab world. Jamal Al-Dura tours the world as a hero, monuments keep being dedicated to the memory of Muhammad Al-Dura, children are taught in school about "the hero Muhammad Al-Dura," and in March 2012 the perpetuator of the Toulouse massacre justified his murder as a revenge for the killing of Palestinian children in Gaza. So how, exactly, did Al-Dura fade away?

Prof. Shmuel Trigano wrote recently that the Al-Dura affair is the Dreyfus Affair of anti-Zionism. I beg to differ: the Al-Dura affair is rather remindful of "The *Saison*" (i.e. the collaboration between the Jewish Agency and the British Mandate against *Irgun* fighters) and the *Altalena* (i.e. putting the monopoly of power before Jewish lives).

Enderlin's Israeli defenders should be ashamed of themselves. They are a disgrace.

Chapter 18:

Government-funded NGOs and the Challenge to Israeli Democracy

A bill sponsored by MK Ayelet Shaked on NGO funding has raised the ire of many, especially on Israel's political left. The bill aims to impose a 45-percent tax on donations from foreign governments to NGOs that support armed struggle by an enemy state or terror organization against Israel; that try to indict Israeli soldiers for war crimes; and that promote the BDS (Boycott, Divestment and Sanctions) campaign against Israel. Both proponents and opponents of the bill claim that their motivation is the preservation of Israeli democracy. Who is to be believed? Neither.

Many NGOs that operate in Israel are funded by European governments and by the European Union with the explicit purpose of influencing public discourse and of infringing on government policies. The scale of European interference in Israeli politics via NGOs is unprecedented and unparalleled in relations between democratic countries. European governments would never get away with funding American NGOs that oppose drone killings in Afghanistan or promote the teaching of Darwinism in conservative private schools. Indeed, NGOs that operate in the United States and receive funding from foreign governments are required by the Foreign Agents Registration Act to register as foreign agents, and the Attorney General can demand to see their donor list at any time.

I wonder if the US administration (or the Israeli government for that matter) would be allowed to fund European NGOs that promote independence for Scotland, New Caledonia, Corsica, Catalonia or the Basque region. And how about NGOs that advocate the annexation of Northern Ireland by the Irish Republic? Or NGOs that campaign against the French government's ban on the Islamic veil and against the expulsion of illegal Roma immigrants? The British, Spanish, and French governments would obviously not put up with such foreign interference. Indeed, France would likely evoke article 411-5 of its "Code pénal" which states that contact with foreign governments or organizations which are likely "to undermine the fundamental interests of the nation" is punishable by a 10-year jail sentence and a €150,000 fine.

Saying that some of the NGOs which operate in Israel "undermine the fundamental interests of the nation" is an understatement.

Because there is no standing for petitioners in Israeli law (i.e. the requirement that a petitioner should have a proven stake in the dispute for which he is petitioning the court), Israel's High Court of Justice is constantly petitioned by NGOs that try to prevent, by judicial means, the implementation of government policies. Some of these NGOs are funded by foreign governments, and this funding undermines the sovereignty and authority of the Israeli government.

The 2009 Goldstone Report, which accused Israel of war crimes and of intentionally targeting civilians in the Cast Lead operation in Gaza (a claim that Judge Richard Goldstone himself retracted in April 2011), was based on the testimonies of Israeli NGOs such as *B'Tselem, Breaking the*

Silence, Adalah, The Palestinian Center for Human Rights, Al-Haq, and *Human Rights Watch*. These organizations, which were out to defame Israel, receive significant funding from European governments and from the EU.

Other NGOs funded by the EU and by European governments implement policies that clearly undermine Israel's sovereignty and interests. These include *Ittijah*, which actively promotes the BDS campaign against Israel, the indictment of IDF officers in European Courts, and the repealing of the tax-deductible status for donations to Zionist NGOs and institutions in the US and in Europe; *Ir Amim*, which challenges Israel's sovereignty in Jerusalem; *Adalah*, which advocates the Palestinian "right of return" (which would turn pre-1967 Israel into a bi-national state); the *Alternative Information Center*, which campaigns for repealing Israel's definition and identity as a Jewish state; *Coalition of Women for Peace*, which was involved in attempts to indict Justice Minister Tzipi Livni for war crimes; and *Bimkom*, which challenges Israel's sovereignty in the Negev.

The list goes on. The phenomenon of foreign government funding for organizations that challenge Israeli democracy and sovereignty violates accepted norms among democratic nations. But this serious issue was already addressed by the "NGO Funding Transparency Law" passed by the Knesset in February 2011, which requires NGOs to fully disclose the identity of their donors and enables Israel to hold European governments accountable for their interference in Israeli politics and for their support of agendas (such as the "right of return") that clearly contradict the two-state solution.

The ill-named "human rights NGOs" are looking for every excuse to avoid the full enforcement of the 2011 law. The new bill provides them with the perfect diversion because it enables the wrongdoers to depict themselves as victims. Yet, no matter how repulsive and disingenuous those NGOs are, penalizing political agendas is clearly illiberal and undemocratic. One should stand by Voltaire's motto that no matter how much I hate your ideas, I shall fight to the death for your right to express them.

Chapter 19:

If Israel is an Apartheid State, Why do so many Africans Flock Here?

Here is a question for those who accuse Israel of apartheid: Why would an apartheid country attract massive illegal immigration from Africa, and why would Africans put up a huge fight to stay in an apartheid regime? As opposed to Eyad El Sarraj, a Palestinian BDS activist who boycotted Israel and yet was treated in Israeli hospitals for his leukemia, those illegal African immigrants did not trespass Israel's southern border for medical treatment. They came to Israel because they know exactly where in the Middle East there is freedom. They know what their fate would be in Arab countries whose language uses the same word ("Abed") for "slave" and "African" – a reminder of the Arab slave trade in Africa.

The phenomenon of mass illegal immigration from Africa to Israel started reaching large-scale proportions in 2007. Most illegal immigrants came from Eritrea, Sudan, Ethiopia, and Somalia. By 2012, there were an estimated 60,000 illegal African migrants in Israel (nearly one percent of its total population). Israel managed to put an end to this flood by building a physical barrier on the Egyptian border, but it still has to find a solution for those already here, most of whom live in southern Tel Aviv and in the Red Sea port city of Eilat. The level of crime in those cities has increased exponentially, with residents complaining that their daily life has become an ordeal.

Like every sovereign state, Israel has the right to accept or decline immigration applications, and it has the right to deport illegal migrants. So why doesn't it do just that?

According to its "Anti-Infiltration Law," since Sudan is an enemy country, Israel is entitled to expel Sudanese migrants. But in 2007, Israel's Attorney General ruled that the government cannot enforce this law indiscriminately and must instead grant temporary refugee status to illegal migrants from Sudan. There have also been many petitions submitted by NGOs to the Israeli High Court of Justice to stop the government from expelling illegal immigrants. These NGOs include ASSAF (the Organization for Psychological Aid to Refugees and Asylum Seekers), the Association for Civil Rights in Israel (ACRI), the Hotline for Migrant Workers, Kav LaOved, Physicians for Human Rights Israel, and the African Refugees Development Center.

As a signatory of the United Nations Convention Relating to the Status of Refugees, Israel cannot expel asylum seekers if they face danger in their home country. According to the UN High Commissioners for Refugees (UNHCR), as well as NGOs, Israel cannot expel those migrants because they are political refugees. But are they? While their home countries are definitely no paragons of democracy, most illegal immigrants are actually migrant workers. Recently, Eritrea's ambassador to Israel was violently attacked by illegal Eritrean immigrants because he claimed that they fake their refugee status and are not persecuted in Eritrea.

All illegal migrants claim that they are political refugees, whether they migrate to Western Europe, to North America or to Israel. But why is Israel expected to be more lenient than Europe toward these illegals?

French politician Michel Rocard declared when he was prime minister back in 1988 that "France cannot absorb all of the world's misery." Neither can Israel.

In October 2013, France deported to Kosovo a 15-year-old illegal immigrant. In 2006 alone Greece deported 54,700 immigrants, Spain 33,000, and France 21,000. In 2008, the Council of the European Union published a "European Pact on Immigration and Asylum" which stated that "The European Union ... does not have the resources to decently receive all the immigrants hoping to find a better life here." The document included a decision to "take rigorous action through dissuasive and proportionate penalties against those exploiting immigrants without legal authorization to reside in an EU country." In 2009, France deported 10,000 Romani immigrants back to Romania and Bulgaria. In 2010, it deported 9,530 Romani immigrants and demolished 51 Romani camps. In 2011, France deported 32,912 illegal immigrants of all origins.

In 2009, the Italian parliament passed a law that punishes illegal immigration with a €10,000 fine and enables the state to deport illegal immigrants without the need for legal procedure. A shocking video that recently went viral online revealed how Italian authorities treat their illegal immigrants.

The same European governments that are tough on their own illegal immigrants fund the Israeli NGOs (such as ACRI and Physicians for Human Rights) which demand from the Israeli government a more lenient policy toward illegal immigrants.

So not only do I challenge Israel bashers to explain why an allegedly apartheid state attracts African immigrants. I also challenge European governments and their local minions to explain why Israel should treat migrant workers as political refugees while Europe should not.

Chapter 20:

Will Avigdor Lieberman be Crowned as the Left's Next National Hero?

Foreign Minister Avigdor Lieberman surprised many in January 2014 by declaring that John Kerry's proposal is the best peace deal Israel could get, provided that the land swaps with the purported Palestinian state be over populated areas instead of empty ones. His statement was immediately condemned by the Israeli left, which endorses the idea of Jewish population transfer (from Gaza in the past, from Judea and Samaria in the future) but abhors that idea when applied to Arabs (even though, in Lieberman's plan, there would be no population transfers but only a redrawing of borders). And yet, the very same Left will very likely end-up canonizing Lieberman as a national hero. After all, it did just that with Ariel Sharon eight years ago, transforming him overnight from demon to angel.

Why will this happen? Because Lieberman wants to be prime minister, because he knows exactly what political down-payment he will have to pay to achieve that goal, and because he is as pragmatic as he is cynical.

The very fact that Lieberman has been labelled a "radical right-winger" goes to show how disingenuous his critics are and how cynical he his. Both he and his critics know that he is no "radical right-winger" but this label served him politically (to attract Russian speaking voters) and his opponents as well (to avoid addressing Lieberman's actual platform).

For what, exactly, is "radical right-wing" about Lieberman's platform? On state and religion and on military service his positions are hardly different than those of the centrist "Yesh Atid" party or of the leftist "Meretz." On the issue of the Arab-Israeli conflict, his positions are similar to those of the Zionist left: he supports the creation of a Palestinian state and the partition of Jerusalem (in stark contrast to Likud's platform), as well as land swaps (Likud rejects land swaps because they implicitly endorse the mistaken idea that any Israeli presence over the 1949 is illegal and must therefore be "compensated").

Lieberman has been decried as a radical because of his tough talk on Arab citizens. But his talk is just that: talk. It has not been followed by any meaningful legislation.

The legislative record of Lieberman's party ("Israel Beitenu") on the "no citizenship without loyalty" issue is nearly nonexistent and the little that passed is mostly counterproductive. A case in point is the Admission Committee Law promoted by "Israel Beitenu" and passed in 2011. In 2000, the High Court of Justice ruled in the "Kaadan" case that Arab citizens are entitled to purchase land in villages built and funded by the Jewish Agency for the Jewish population. In 1989, however, the same High Court had ruled (in the "Avitan" case) that a Jew is not entitled to buy land in a village built for Bedouins. As a result, "Israel Beitenu" initiated a law ostensibly intended to protect the Jewishness of Jewish villages. In the end, the law passed in 2011 upon the initiative of "Israel

Beitenu" did the very opposite and effectively turned the "Kaadan" ruling into law.

If Lieberman were serious about his nationalistic agenda, he would never have allowed the passing of such a law. But what Lieberman really cares about is being labelled a fascist in order to attract nationalist voters.

Such, at least, was his interest until recently. Since being acquitted in court, Lieberman's objective is to become prime minister. And for him to reach that goal, his strategy must change.

The relationship between Lieberman and Netanyahu is reminiscent of the one between Ariel Sharon and Menachem Begin. Begin would not have signed the Camp David Agreement without Sharon's seal of approval, the same way that Netanyahu will seek and need Lieberman's backing for any deal with the Palestinians. Like Sharon under Begin's premiership, Lieberman wants to replace his boss.

Sharon's lifelong friend and aide-de-camp Uri Dan said after Sharon's dismissal following the Sabra and Shatila massacres that those who did not want Sharon as minister of defense will have to deal with him as prime minister. It took twenty years for his prophecy to materialize, but as soon as it did Israel's legal establishment was out to get Sharon. An old cynic and brilliant tactician, Sharon knew just how to defeat his enemies. In 1973, he bypassed and surprised the Egyptian army from its rear. In 2003, he announced that he would deliver 8,600 settlers to the Israeli Left on a silver platter. Suddenly and miraculously, the State Attorney got off his case. And the same media who had been depicting him as the incarnation of evil for two decades turned him overnight into a national hero.

Lieberman knows that. Like Sharon, he is ambitious, ruthless, and cynical. Those on the Right who see him as their best hope would be well-advised to remember the precedent Sharon set and to connect the dots. As for the Israeli Left, I am hereby publicly betting that if Lieberman does follow Sharon's steps as I suspect he will, the very people who demonize him today will praise him tomorrow.

Chapter 21:

Ariel Sharon's Leadership was about the Economy, Stupid

There is something maddening about the Israeli left's eulogy of Ariel Sharon. He was the left's *bête noire* until the 2005 retreat from Gaza. The anti-Sharon bashing culminated in the first Lebanon War but did not start with it. The hero of the 1973 Yom Kippur War was also one of the founders of the Likud party, a union of nationalists and liberals that Sharon had engineered to defeat the left.

After the massacre of Palestinians in Sabra and Shatilla, Sharon was commonly slammed as a "murderer" by his political foes. In 2001, Israelis massively voted for Sharon to end the daily massacre of civilians by Arab terrorists, but the Israeli left obsessively claimed that there was no military solution to terrorism (a demagogic formula factually contradicted by Operation Defensive Shield). Then came the "disengagement plan" and the overnight re-labeling of Sharon from Pinochet to de Gaulle.

When the Israeli left today praises Sharon for his "leadership" and "courage," it does so only in reference to the uprooting of 8,600 settlers from the Gaza Strip. For the Israeli left, "leadership" is measured by territorial retreat, and "courage" is tested by the resolve to uproot settlers. But, in fact, the disengagement was not a courageous decision. It was motivated by cowardice. After his reelection in 2003, Sharon was under criminal investigation. He would have been indicted and compelled to resign. As documented by Israeli journalists Raviv Drucker and Ofer Shelah in their book *Boomerang*, Sharon conceived the disengagement plan, together with his close advisor Dov Weisglass, in order to get the state prosecutor off his case. It worked. But this was neither courage nor leadership.

Sharon, however, did display courage and leadership on many occasions: when he heroically saved the honor of the IDF in October 1973; when he kicked Arafat and his gang out of Lebanon in 1982; when he masterminded and oversaw the airlifting of Ethiopian Jews to Israel in 1984-85 and in 1991; when he built homes for hundreds of thousands of Soviet Jews in the 1990s; and when he defeated Arafat's war in 2004.

Sharon also displayed courage and leadership in 2003, when he fully backed the unpopular policy of his finance minister Benjamin Netanyahu, a policy that restored growth to the Israeli economy. When the Israeli left praises Sharon's "courage" and "leadership" it does not mention Sharon's key role in Israel's Thatcherite revolution. Yet Sharon showed courage and leadership by embracing economic liberalism.

Netanyahu's 2003 supply-sides economics undid the last and choking vestiges of Israeli socialism by breaking-up inefficient monopolies, by cutting taxes and government expenditures, and by lowering welfare entitlements. By the time Netanyahu unveiled his plan, the Israeli economy had suffered from two years of negative growth, which had cut 7% from its GDP. Unemployment was at 11%, the budget deficit was 6%, and the debt/GDP ratio was 103%. Government spending was capped for three years, personal tax rates were cut from 64% to 44%, and corporate tax rates were slashed from 36% to 18%. Pension ages were increased from 60 to 64 for women and from 65 to 67 for men.

There were also major reforms in the welfare system. In the twelve years that preceded Netanyahu's 2003 reform, the number of welfare recipients had grown by 600% while the population had grown by 30%. The combination of high taxes and generous welfare had created a disincentive to work. Capping the support at $40 per child addressed the underemployment of Arab women and of Orthodox men. A Wisconsin-like program was introduced to encourage people to go back to work instead of living off the dole. Those reforms brought back economic growth and eventually lowered Israel's unemployment from 11% to 6%.

Similar reforms were actually undertaken around the same time in Germany by Socialist Chancellor Gerhard Schröder. Also in 2003, the Schröder government launched "Agenda 2010," which included tax cuts as well as drastic cuts in pension and unemployment benefits. This program, which was the boldest reform of the German social security system since World War II, was initiated by a Socialist government.

French President François Hollande is also abandoning his socialist dogma for economic realism. Elected in 2012 to end austerity and to tax the rich, Hollande declared in his 2014 New Year address that France's high taxes are deterring job creation and that its generous welfare system is being abused.

Schröder and Hollande's ideological "apostasy" is, simply, about facts: population aging and trade globalization have spelled the demise of the post WW2 European welfare state. Thanks to the foresight and courage of Sharon and Netanyahu, Israel undertook the necessary reforms ten years ago that spared Israel a Greece-like bankruptcy.

Sharon should indeed be thanked for the leadership and courage that he displayed by embracing economic liberalism.

Chapter 22:

Israel's anti-boycott law is tame compared to other countries'

Israel's High Court of Justice was petitioned in February 2014 to determine whether or not the "anti-boycott law" is constitutional. This law, passed by the Knesset in July 2011, enables Israeli companies, institutions or individuals to sue those who publicly call for their boycott, and to seek financial reparations for any proven monetary loss. The law also entitles the finance minister to deny tax benefits and tenders to organizations that publicly call for the boycott of Israel.

Branded "anti-democratic" by its critics, this law is actually much tamer than what French and American legislation has in store for boycotters.

In France, boycott is a criminal offense. A person trying to prevent the sale of a product or of a service because of the identity of the seller can be fined up to €45,000 and jailed for a year (Articles 225-1 and 225-2 of the Code pénal and Article 24-8 of the 30 December 2004 Law). In September 2009, France's court of final appeal, "Cour de Cassation," confirmed the condemnation of a French mayor who had called for the boycott of Israeli products in his town. The decision was upheld by the European Court of Human Rights in July 2009. In December 2007, the "Cour de Cassation" ruled that boycotting Israeli companies in France is illegal and criminal. In January 2014, the "Cour de Cassation" confirmed the condemnation of a pro-Palestinian French NGO that had called for the boycott of Israel's SodaStream™ in France.

In the United States, the 1976 and 1977 amendments to the Export Administration Act (EAA) and to the Tax Reform Act (TRA) prohibit US companies from furthering or supporting the boycott of Israel. Taking part in the boycott of Israel is punishable by a $50,000 fine and by up to 10 years imprisonment. Penalties for violation of the Anti-boycott Regulations are governed by the International Emergency Economic Powers Act (IEEPA), which provides for up to $1 million in fines and 20 years of imprisonment per violation for criminal anti-boycott violations.

Freedom of speech, like other rights, is limited by the principle that "Your right to swing your fist ends where my nose begins." That's why calls for boycotts are illegal (and even criminal) in democracies like the US and France. Why should Israel be the only democracy where limits to freedom of speech are "undemocratic" when tougher limitations are common in the West?

To that question, opponents of the Israeli anti-boycott law answer that the law penalizes their right to boycott Israeli settlements because it applies to the State of Israel and to "areas under its control" (i.e. the West Bank and the Golan Heights). There is a difference, however, between expressing opposition to settlements (a right that the law neither denies nor affects) and causing economic damage to companies or individuals that operate in those settlements. Britain's Supreme Court recently ruled that the constitutional right to express opposition to Israel's control of the West Bank does not justify attempts to cause economic damage to Israeli companies that operate there.

Moreover, the Israeli organizations that petitioned the High Court of Justice against the "anti-boycott law" admitted in court that their chief concern is not that the law is applicable to territories conquered by Israel during the Six Day War. When asked by the Court if the petitioners would still oppose the law were it not to apply to the West Bank and to the Golan Heights, but only to pre-1967 Israel, their lawyer Hassan Jabareen answered a clear "yes." In doing so, the petitioners contradicted their previous claim that all they want is to preserve their "right" to boycott settlements. What they actually want, is to be able to promote the international boycott of Israel without having to bear the economic consequences of the damage they cause to others.

One can understand their concern: the boycott of Israel, after all, is "made in Israel." It is a tool used by a certain brand of academics and politicians who fail to convince Israelis at the polls, and therefore try to impose their rejected policies by attempting to hurt Israelis in their pockets. This manipulative strategy is as immoral as it is efficient. In 1991, senior members of Israel's Labor Party were dispatched to Washington to convince the Bush Administration not to sign a $10 billion loan guarantee to Israel (for the integration of Jewish immigrants from the Soviet Union) unless then-Prime Minister Yitzhak Shamir would commit not to invest the money beyond the Green Line. Since Shamir refused, the Labor Party ran (and won) the 1992 elections, "warning" Israelis of imminent economic disaster.

The same strategy is used today by people who warn us of the very fire they lit themselves. The "anti-boycott law" ensures that these people don't have their cake and eat it too.

Chapter 23:

Does Israeli Negotiator Tzipi Livni truly want a Jewish State?

The recognition of Israel as the nation-state of the Jewish people has been demanded by Israeli Prime Minister Benjamin Netanyahu and rejected by Palestinian Authority Chairman Mahmoud Abbas because of both leaders' understanding that such recognition would bury the co-called "right of return" and put a final end to Palestinian claims. When Abbas says that it is for Israel to decide how it wants to define itself, he fails to explain why he cannot accept Israel's self-definition. Inadvertently, however, Abbas brings to our doorstep the intriguing fact that Israel's chief negotiator, Tzipi Livni, is the one preventing the official and legal definition of Israel as a Jewish state.

Israel did define itself as a Jewish state in its Declaration of Independence ("We ... hereby declare the establishment of a Jewish state in the land of Israel, to be known as the State of Israel"). But the legal status of the Declaration of Independence is that of a declaratory document with no constitutional value since the High Court of Justice's 1948 "Ziv vs. Governik" ruling. And because Israel does not have a constitution, its declaratory self-definition as a "Jewish state" is not legally binding.

Instead of a constitution, Israel passed "basic laws" defining the powers of the three branches of Government (such as the "Knesset Law") and protecting human rights (such as the "Human Dignity and Freedom Law"). No basic law, however, defines the state's Jewish identity. The constitutions of nation-states, by contrast, generally cover the three issues of national identity, of separation of powers and of human rights (the French Constitution, for example, was proclaimed in the name of the "French People" and it defines the Republic as "secular, democratic, and social").

There are, potentially, far-reaching consequences to the fact that Israel is a Jewish state de facto, but not de jure. De facto, Israel's symbols and national anthem express the historical legacy and culture of the Jewish people; the Law of Return accords an automatic immigration right to Jews; Hebrew is the official language and national holidays are based on the Jewish calendar; the IDF protects all Jews and not only Israelis (such as the 1976 rescue of hostages in Entebbe); taxpayer money was used in the past to airlift Jews in distress and it is used today to fund Jewish education in the Diaspora.

Those de facto expressions of Israel's self-declared identity as a Jewish state are legally challenged by Israel's Arab minority and by Jewish post-Zionists. This legal challenge calls for a legal answer.

Nation-states (and Israel among them) express and protect the right of nations to self-determination. This national and collective right does not affect (at least in democratic nation-states) the civic and human rights of minorities. As Israeli writer A.B. Yehoshua points out, nobody expects Denmark to add a Muslim symbol to its flag in order to make its

Muslim minority feel good: Denmark is the nation-state of the Danish people, and yet all Danish citizens (including naturalized Muslim immigrants) are equal before the law. The same applies to Israel.

While justifiable and justified, however, Israel's right to be a nation-state is challenged both conceptually and legally. The legal challenge could theoretically undo the Law of Return and state funding for Jewish educational programs overseas, for example. In light of the recurrent (and often successful) petitioning of the High Court of Justice in the past two decades, to repeal laws and government decisions, such a prospect is not far-fetched.

This is why former MK Avi Dichter (from the centrist Kadima party) submitted a bill in 2011 to legally define Israel as the nation-state of the Jewish people. The bill was bipartisan, having been co-signed by Kadima, Labor and Likud MKs. While most Kadima MKs co-signed the proposed bill, then Kadima Chairperson Tzipi Livni ordered them to withdraw their signatures when the bill was brought to her attention.

In an academic event organized in February 2014 by the Kohelet Policy Forum (an Israeli think-tank dedicated to national sovereignty and to personal freedom) on the stalled "Jewish state" bill, Tzipi Livni reiterated her opposition to the bill. She explained that it does not define Israel as a democratic state and claimed it could turn halakhah (Jewish rabbinical law) into a source of legislation (both claims are factually wrong: Article 3 of the proposed bill does define Israel as a democratic state, and nowhere does the bill refer to halakhah as a source of legislation).

In a way, Mahmoud Abbas is right: Israel should decide how it wants to define itself. How absurd, then, that Israel's chief negotiator, Tzipi Livni, is the one blocking the official and legal definition of Israel as the nation-state of the Jewish people. Why should Abbas be more royalist than the king?

Chapter 24:

The realistic Right Turn of Israeli Defense Minister Ya'alon

Some Israeli politicians have a selective and instructive way of reacting to the latest public declarations on the tortuous negotiations between Israel and the Palestinian Authority (PA).

On March 6, 2014, PA Chairman Mahmoud Abbas declared that any deal with Israel would be submitted to a referendum among all Palestinians around the world, explaining that he would not waive the "right" of 5 million Palestinians to become citizens of Israel. Abbas made it clear that he only has a right to waive his own "right of return," (to Israel) but certainly not that of his children and grandchildren, and that Palestinian "refugees" (i.e. the descendants of the actual refugees of 1948) will be entitled to financial reparation on top of their "right" to become Israeli citizens.

As for the referendum among the Palestinians "from Canada to Japan," Abbas did not get into the details of the logistics that such an unprecedented worldwide consultation would entail. Besides logistics, however, Abbas' suggested referendum begs disbelief. He does not have any say on the Gaza Strip, which is controlled by Hamas. Since being elected PA Chairman in 2005, Abbas has refused to hold new elections. One may wonder why a man who has systematically ignored the will of his constituents for the past nine years is suddenly eager to hear their opinion. And since Abbas just "promised" 5 million Palestinians that they will be entitled both to become Israeli citizens and to receive financial compensation, why should they approve, in a hypothetical referendum, a deal that will obviously not include such fantasies?

If Abbas actually believes what he says, then he is obviously not a man with whom Israel can make peace. If he is just being provocative and obnoxious, then he is not trustworthy. So Israel's Defense Minister Moshe Ya'alon expressed a perfectly reasonable opinion when he declared on March 15 that Abbas is no partner for a genuine peace deal.

Yet chief negotiator Tzipi Livni and Member of Knesset Zehava Gal-on (who chairs the left-wing "Meretz" party) expressed outrage at Ya'alon for drawing conclusions from Abbas' statements, but not at Abbas for making those statements in the first place. Nor did Livni and Gal-on have anything to say about the fact that, on March 12, senior PA official Abbas Zaki declared on Palestinian television: "Allah will gather the Israelis so that we can kill them."

Livni and Gal-on's condemnation is not only selective, but also instructive. Gal-on criticized Ya'alon for "not believing in peace," and Livni claimed that "our responsibility is to change reality." Galon and Livni did not address the merit (or lack thereof) of Ya'alon's assessment. They castigated him for lacking "belief" in peace and for facing reality rather than "changing" it.

The reason Ya'alon incurs the ire of the Israeli left is that he is an "apostate." A son of Israel's secular and socialist founding generation, Ya'alon is a kibbutz member who excelled in the army and who eventually became chief of staff. Like other secular and Ashkenazi generals who emerged from the Labor movement, Ya'alon could have become a poster boy of the Labor Party. When the Oslo Agreement was signed in 1993, he truly and sincerely hoped for their success. But as head of the IDF's intelligence unit, he became aware of the extent of Yasser Arafat's doublespeak, incitement, and illegal armament. Realizing that the "peace process" was a sham, Ya'alon broke ranks with the left.

Ya'alon is not the only IDF veteran who refuses to follow the herd. Earlier this week, he attended the funeral of Meir Har-Zion, a war hero once described by Moshe Dayan as "the best soldier ever to emerge from the IDF." Together with Ariel Sharon, Har-Zion founded the "Unit 101" commando and, like Sharon, he became a farmer upon retiring from the army. But when Sharon announced and implemented his 2005 "disengagement plan" from Gaza, Har-Zion publicly spoke out against his former commander. Taking a stance against disengagement cost Har-Zion his friendship with Sharon. It cost Ya'alon his job as army chief of staff.

Ya'alon is a political realist. True, reality can always be said to be in the eye of the beholder, but being pessimistic about human nature and skeptical about man's ability to change reality is precisely what thinkers like Hobbes and Machiavelli meant by "realism." By contrast, Rousseau and Kant's faith in human goodness and in man's ability to subjugate reality is generally what is understood by "idealism."

Gal-on and Livni clearly identify with the latter school of thought. That is perfectly legitimate, but accusing political rivals of lacking faith is reminiscent of the rhetoric of "revolutionary" regimes.

Livni and Gal-on would be well advised to engage in debate rather than in inquisition. It is for them to justify their optimism. After all, no Middle East observer has ever lost money by betting on pessimism.

Chapter 25:

Being less phony than others does not a leader make

Winston Churchill quipped about Stanley Baldwin, the inter-war British PM who infamously denied in 1934 that the Luftwaffe was approaching parity with the Royal Air Force, that "he occasionally stumbled over the truth, but hastily picked himself up and hurried on as if nothing had happened." Derided by his opponents as a warmonger and a political has-been in the 1930s, Churchill was called to the rescue in May 1940 at age 65. After the collapse of France one month later, French Chief of Staff Maxime Weygand predicted that "England will have her neck wrung like a chicken." To which Churchill echoed after the Battle of Britain: "Some chicken! Some neck!"

Great leaders have this ability to grasp reality, to master history and to infer what the future has in store. They are willing to pay whatever personal price it takes to do what is right for the sake of their country.

In time of acute crisis, and at the edge of the abyss, they are begged by their former scoffers to save the motherland.

Thankfully, Israel's current situation is neither comparable to that of Britain in May 1940, nor to that of France in May 1958. Still, with the Israeli-Palestinian chess game having come to a draw, Israel is in dire need of a leader able to envision and implement a way out. Alas, no Churchill or de Gaulle is in sight.

Prime Minister Benjamin ("Bibi") Netanyahu likes to boast that he has no serious contender. He has a point. Yair Lapid (leader of the "Yesh Atid" party) is a former TV anchor who owes his career to his good looks and to his journalist-turned-politician father. Opposition leader Yitzhak Herzog, also a political heir, fails to convince even himself when he promises peace and social justice (not least because Israel's Labor party treats its leaders like the guillotine used to treat aristocrats).

Bibi, however, is a lame duck whose leadership is threatened by an emerging alliance between Foreign Minister Avigdor Lieberman and former Likud Minister Moshe Kahlon.

Netanyahu has been Prime Minister for eight years (a record of political longevity by Israeli standards). His English rhetorical skills are unsurpassed, but few still believe him when he pledges that Iran will never go nuclear. A self-declared free-marketer, he has done precious little to undo Israel's cartels and the state's monopoly over land ownership (two major sources of Israel's high costs of living). He has alienated the right by endorsing the idea of a Palestinian state and by freeing terrorists, and yet he is accused by the left of being insincere about his commitment to a two-state solution. Netanyahu has virtually lost control of his own Likud party, as he himself recently admitted. His claim that Israel has no credible alternative leader sounds more and more desperate and unconvincing.

Yet the alleged alternative of the Lieberman-Kahlon duo is charlatanic, at best. Lieberman is an authoritarian and demagogical cynic, who alternates between hawkishness and pragmatism, depending on the polls of his political consultant, Arthur Finkelstein. Many of Lieberman's voters have taken notice of the fraud, and his Yisrael Beiteinu party is in free fall. Lieberman had hoped that the 2012 joint Knesset list between Likud and Yisrael Beiteinu would eventually put him at the helm of a merged party, but a merger is off the table.

Lieberman's only hope, therefore, is to run in the next elections together with Moshe Kahlon, a former Likud poster boy turned Likud-basher, who recently announced a political comeback. The son of Libyan Jewish immigrants, Kahlon would supposedly bring Lieberman the vote of Sephardic Israelis and of social conservatives (two constituencies that would otherwise shun the Soviet-born and secular Lieberman). The only problem with this scheme is that it is too fraudulent to go unnoticed.

Kahlon attacked his former party for having become "too right-wing" and for having abandoned its social justice agenda. Yet as a Likud MK and Minister, Kahlon always and openly identified with (and was elected thanks to) the most right-wing factions of Likud. Self-proclaimed as one of Likud's most right-wing politicians in the recent past, Kahlon has now re-branded himself as "pragmatic" and "moderate." Kahlon's alleged conversion to social democracy also begs disbelief. As a Minister of Communications, he implemented free-market policies by introducing true competition, lowering the prices of cell phone service. His current economic advisors are all free-marketers.

A political realist and an economic liberal, Kahlon is talking the language of peace and of social justice out of opportunism and demagogy. This is the very opposite of leadership. He and Lieberman deserve each other, but Israel deserves better.

Netanyahu may be correct about a lack of challengers, but being merely the least phony of all falls short of the leadership that Israel needs and lacks.

Chapter 26:

Why Israel Must Legally Define itself as a Jewish State

Prime Minister Benjamin Netanyahu's decision to promote a bill officially defining Israel as the Jewish nation's state may seem bizarre to outsiders. At home, it was immediately criticized by Justice Minister Tzipi Livni, by Israel's opposition, and by the *Haaretz* newspaper.

The standard argument against the proposed bill is that Israel is both Jewish and democratic and that the bill would favor Jewish values over democratic ones. But why is this alleged contradiction between national identity and democracy only considered an issue in Israel's case? Does anyone question the fact that the Czech Republic is both Czech and democratic? All EU members (arguably with the exception of Belgium) are both nation states and democracies. They all belong to a dominant nation, yet all citizens are equal before the law. The fact that Jewish identity combines nationality with religion (to different degrees depending on one's personal beliefs) is not particular to Israel, either. Japan's national identity intertwines with Shinto; Catholicism is intrinsic to the Polish ethos; Evangelical Lutheranism is the state religion of Denmark; the Queen of England is both head of state and head of the Anglican Church.

Haaretz argues that the 1992 Basic Law: Man's Dignity and Freedom already defines Israel as "Jewish and democratic" and, therefore, the proposed bill is unnecessary. In fact, *Haaretz* wishes Israel would stick to the "Jewish and democratic" definition spelled out back in 1993 by then Chief Justice Aharon Barak: "The concept of 'Jewish State' should be interpreted in the most abstract manner, and in no way based on Jewish law. Israel's values as a Jewish state are the universal values of a democratic society."

During his 28 years as a Supreme Court Justice (from 1978 to 2006), and his 11 years as President of the Supreme Court (from 1995), Barak confirmed many times that his understanding of "Jewish and democratic" is "democratic." But he also promoted and implemented what he called a "constitutional revolution" whose intention and outcome was to replace the separation of powers with a hierarchy of powers dominated by the judiciary.

Barak implemented his "revolution" (the only revolution in history which took place without the people's awareness, as former MK Michael Eitan quipped) by annulling the principle of standing and thus by opening the floodgates of politically-motivated petitions; by deciding that the High Court of Justice is entitled to invalidate Knesset laws; by empowering the Court to cancel government decisions not only based on their illegality but also on their "unreasonableness" (an arcane concept whose interpretation belongs to the Court); and by declaring that everything (including political decisions) is "justiciable."

The effects of Barak's unilateral extension of the Court's authority became palpable in the 1993 "Pinhassi" ruling. Deputy Interior Minister

Rafael Pinhassi had been indicted by the Attorney General on corruption charges. By law, he was under no obligation to resign since he had neither been convicted nor stood trial. NGOs petitioned the Court to oblige then Prime Minister Yitzhak Rabin to fire Pinhassi. They did not meet the requirement of standing, but such a requirement no longer existed since a 1986 ruling by Barak. The law did not require Rabin to fire Pinhassi, but Barak decided that keeping Pinhassi in his job would be "unreasonable." Deciding Pinhassi's fate was a purely political question of the executive branch, but Barak ruled the Prime Minister's decision "justiciable." And so the Court ordered the Prime Minister (whose opinion the Court deemed irrelevant in its ruling) to fire his Deputy Interior Minister.

For the past two decades, Barak's "constitutional revolution" has enabled individuals and NGOs to petition the Court to cancel Knesset laws and government decisions that express and preserve Israel's Jewishness. Thus, the Court forbade the Jewish Agency in 2000 ("Kaadan" ruling) to allocate land purchases only to Jews; thus was the Court petitioned in 2006 to repeal a law meant to prevent the implementation of the Palestinian "right of return" through the back door by way of "family reunification" (the Court eventually rejected the petition against Barak's minority opinion).

As explained by law professor Menachem Mautner, Barak's "constitutional revolution" was meant to enable Israel's liberal elite to preserve its power despite the left's electoral defeat of 1977. And as confirmed by former Justice Minister Daniel Friedmann: "The struggle is not for the rule of law, but for the rule itself."

One of the side effects of the "constitutional revolution" was to enable post and anti-Zionists to challenge Israel's Jewishness via the High Court of Justice. This side effect may not have been intended by Barak, but today the Court lacks the law it needs to defend Israel's Jewishness when petitioned. Hence the necessity of the proposed bill. The opposition of post-Zionists is understandable; that of liberal Zionists less so.

Chapter 27:

Why Israel Needs a President

"Power," quipped former Italian Premier Giulio Andreotti, "only wears out those who don't have it." This was the typical Andreotti way of rebuffing the claim that he had been in power for too long: sharp, witty, cynical. But power does wear out politicians who stay too long at the helm: it gives them a feeling of entitlement and impunity. Andreotti was not immune. Neither, it seems, is Benjamin Netanyahu.

The Prime Minister's attempt to postpone the presidential election and to dismantle the presidency altogether seems like a real-life version of Alfred Jarry's play *Ubu roi*. Netanyahu does not want Reuben ("Rubi") Rivlin, the front runner, to succeed President Shimon Peres for three reasons: a. The President has discretionary power to designate the party leader of his choice to form a government after general elections, and Netanyahu fears that Rivlin will not pick him after the next elections; b. Rivlin has been vocally critical of Netanyahu, especially of his decision to free terrorists; c. Rivlin has infuriated Netanyahu by saying that he doesn't let his wife boss him around – a mischievous allusion to Sarah Netanyahu's alleged influence over her husband.

The fact that Netanyahu feels entitled to play around with political institutions and to change the rules in the middle of the game is alarming. The idea of dismantling the presidency is plainly wrong.

In presidential regimes, the President is both head of state and head of government. In parliamentary regimes, the Prime Minister heads the government while the King or President is head of state. This bi-cephalous structure is the outcome of a historical process that progressively transferred powers from Kings to the elected governments. Republican parliamentary democracies replicated this model, but replaced the inherited monarchy with an elected, yet no less ceremonial, head of state. Such is the case of Germany today. Such was the case of the third and fourth French republics.

Israel adopted that model. David Ben-Gurion, Israel's first Prime Minister, was not willing to share his executive powers with the President, and so the office became mostly ceremonial (the first President, Haim Weizmann, complained that all he was empowered to do was to stick his nose into his handkerchief). Weizmann was a renowned scientist and a respected statesman who had been instrumental in obtaining the Balfour Declaration from Britain in 1917 and the UN's recommendation to establish a Jewish state three decades later.

While Ben-Gurion was unwilling to share his executive powers with the head of state, he realized that the President had to be a prestigious and unifying figure. After Weizmann passed away in 1952, Ben-Gurion asked Albert Einstein to replace him. Einstein declined, but Weizmann's predecessors were (with rare exceptions) respected and prestigious statesmen.

Yitzhak Ben-Zvi was a renowned historian; Zalman Shazar a man of letters; Efraim Katzir a biophysics professor; Yitzhak Navon an author; Haim Herzog a diplomat and historian. All were recognized for their life achievements and personal integrity. The election of Ezer Weizmann in 1993 was a break with tradition. Weizmann, a former commander of the Israeli air force, was the first "sabra" elected to the job. His claim to fame was his family (he was Haim Weizmann's nephew) and his military career. His political allegiances switched as unexpectedly as his mood. Once elected President he entered the fray of partisan politics and brazenly criticized the government – breaching the code of conduct of an apolitical office. He resigned amid accusations of financial wrongdoing.

Ezer Weizmann undoubtedly caused damage to the prestige of the President's office and to its unifying role. His successor, Moshe Katzav, was also his antithesis: the son of Iranian Jewish immigrants, he grew up poor and represented the "other Israel." His modest origins and composed demeanor earned him the respect he subsequently lost upon revelations of sexual misconduct and subsequent conviction and imprisonment. Shimon Peres restored the prestige of the office.

When Charles de Gaulle spelled out his vision of the French constitution in 1946, he said that the head of state in a parliamentary democracy should be "a national arbiter above political tides, an anchor of stability among endless intrigues." Israel, with its proportional voting system for the Knesset, its unstable coalition politics, and its social schisms, cannot afford to abandon an institution that symbolizes and embodies stability and unity.

Netanyahu's initiative is wrong and he is promoting it for the wrong reasons. I wish I could grant him the benefit of the doubt, but then I am reminded of another Andreotti punch line: "If you think ill of others, you commit a sin - but you often get it right."

Chapter 28:

Jewish Freedom of Worship and Israeli Sovereignty must Apply to the Temple Mount

A bi-partisan bill drafted by MKs Miri Regev (Likud) and Hilik Bar (Labor) was submitted in May 2014 to the Knesset to allow Jews to pray on the Temple Mount, including with ritual objects such as a tallit (prayer shawl) and tefilin (phylacteries). The Temple Mount is holy to Jews because the first and second Jerusalem Temples once stood there. However, Rabbis disagree about the permissibility of Jewish access to the Temple Mount: some rabbis (generally the ultra-orthodox) forbid the Jews' access altogether, fearing that it might desecrate the Holy of Holies; others (generally the Zionist rabbis) allow Jewish access in designated areas. However, Jews who follow the second stance are not allowed by the Islamic Wakf and by the Israeli police to pray on the Temple Mount for fear of Muslim violence.

The proposed bill only refers to the Temple Mount plaza, not to the Al-Aqsa mosque. And yet, Mohammad al-Madani, chairman of the Palestinian Committee for Interaction of Israeli Society, has said that allowing Jews to pray on Judaism' holiest site would constitute a violation of "the sanctity of Islamic and Christian holy places." Palestinian political analyst Abdel Raouf Arnaout falsely claimed in the Saudi daily *Al-Watan* that the bill is meant to allow Jews to pray inside the Al-Aqsa mosque. PA Chairman Mahmoud Abbas himself had warned in an interview with the same *Al-Watan* newspaper (on June 3, 2013) of an Israeli "plot" to destroy the Al-Aqsa mosque and to build the Third Temple in its stead.

The Temple Mount is one of the "core issues" of the Arab-Israeli conflict.

At the Camp David Conference in July 2000, Yasser Arafat shocked the American and Israeli delegations by claiming that the Jerusalem Temple was a myth (Arafat first said that the Temple had been built in the Biblical town of Shechem (today's Nablus), but he later denied the Temple's existence altogether). And yet, when Arafat launched his terror war against Israel in September 2000, he aptly named it the "Al-Aqsa intifada" calling upon Muslims to protect the Al-Aqsa mosque from a Jewish plan to destroy it and rebuild the Jerusalem Temple in its stead. There is no lack of irony in the self-contradictory Palestinian position on the Temple Mount: on the one hand, it denies the past existence of the two Jerusalem Temples; on the other hand, it claims that Israel plans to "re-build" the Temple.

Neither is this contradiction new. Haj Amin al-Husseini, the Jerusalem Mufti in the 1920s and 1930s, triggered the 1929 violence and the Jewish pogrom of Hebron after claiming that the Jews were planning on destroying the Al-Aqsa mosque and on rebuilding the Jerusalem Temple. In 1931, al-Husseini hoped to repeat the bloodbath on a larger scale when he convened a pan-Islamic conference in Jerusalem at which he disseminated photomontages of Jews with machine guns attacking the Dome of the Rock.

Since September 1996, when Arafat launched a wave of riots against Israeli civilians, the Islamic Waqf has ceased to cooperate with Israel on its activities on the Temple Mount, carrying out instead illegal construction projects. As a result, the Waqf built two new mosques on the Temple Mount: the Solomon's Stables mosque in 1996 and the Al Aqsa Al-Qadim mosque in 1999. In the process, the Waqf removed tons of archeological rubble containing artifacts dating back to the First Temple period. Decorations and inscriptions were polished away from ancient stones, and stones with Hebrew writings and Hasmonean stars were thrown into Jerusalem's municipal garbage dump. Thus do the Palestinians publicly deny the Temple's existence even as they actively erase proof to the contrary.

Nevertheless, at Camp David, the Israeli delegation agreed to share Israel's sovereignty over Jerusalem with a future Palestinian state. The United States suggested Palestinian custodianship over the Temple Mount and full Palestinian sovereignty in the Muslim and Christian quarters of the Old City. The deal faltered only when the Palestinians rejected the American proposal. Even after the failed Camp David summit, Israel suggested a division of sovereignty over the Temple Mount whereby a future Palestinian state would control the upper level, and Israel the lower one. In December 2000, then Israeli Foreign Minister Shlomo Ben-Ami offered the Palestinians full and exclusive sovereignty over the Temple Mount (including the lower level), provided merely that they recognize the sites' holiness to the Jewish people and prevent the destruction of Jewish remnants on the Mount. Yet even that proposal was rejected by the Palestinians.

Preventing Jews from praying on the Temple Mount is a capitulation not only to threats and violence but also to Palestinian mythology and denial of historical facts. The proposed bi-partisan bill is a partial yet overdue step to enforce the Jews' freedom of worship and Israel's sovereignty in the heart of its capital and on Judaism's holiest site.

Chapter 29:

Yes to the Death Penalty in Israel, in Extreme Cases

When the bodies of the three kidnapped youths - Eyal, Gilad and Naftali were found - I was touring the D-Day beaches in France with two of my children. I wanted to commemorate the 70th anniversary of Operation Overlord by explaining to my children that the world had sunk into madness not that long ago, and that we owe our freedom to the foresight of a few leaders and to the sacrifice of many soldiers.

Shortly after leaving the Normandy American cemetery, the terrible news from Israel reached us. As my children and I were coping with the grief, I couldn't help wondering if I hadn't misled them with my lectures on freedom: how free can you claim to be when you can still be murdered for who you are in your own country?

The next day I watched the heartbreaking scene of the three fathers saying the Kaddish prayer for their murdered sons, and of the devastated faces of the bereaved mothers. In the darkness of this inconsolable pain, the unity and dignity of our nation was an almost comforting ray of light. There was a feeling, if not certainty, that we Jews would never go down the road of our enemies thanks to our values and principles. But with the appalling murder of the Palestinian teen Mohamed Abu Khdeir, even that certainty was shattered. Sherri Mandell, whose son Kobi was murdered by Arab terrorists in 2001, asked the murderers of Mohamed a question that is hard to answer: "What can we believe about our own society now that you have weakened our integrity?"

True, our thugs and killers are a minority reviled by the mainstream. True, our government (unlike the Palestinian Authority) will not pay a monthly income to their parents and will not name streets and summer camps after them. There still is, thankfully, a moral gap between our enemies and us. But that is no consolation and no excuse. The murder should be a wake-up call for our society.

In addition to soul-searching, we must ask ourselves if we punish murderers adequately. Less than three months ago, on April 14, Baruch Mizrahi was murdered in front of his wife and five children by Ziad Awed, who was among the 1,027 terrorists freed by Israel in exchange for the liberation of soldier Gilad Shalit from Hamas captivity. The freed terrorists also included Ali al-Nasser Yataima, convicted of planning the 2002 Passover massacre, in which 30 civilians were killed and 140 were wounded; Walid Abd al-Aziz, who took part in the execution of the 2002 bombings at Café Moment (11 killed), at the Hebrew University (9 killed), and in the town of Rishon-LeZion (16 killed); Maedh Waal Taleb Abu Sharakh, Majdi Muhammad Ahmed Amr and Fadi Muhammad Ibrahim al-Jaaba, who were responsible for the attack on bus No. 37 in Haifa in 2002 (17 killed). This macabre list is much longer. These people are now walking around free. They spent less than a decade in jail and they now get a nice salary from the Palestinian Authority.

The death penalty is often said to be immoral. But I fail to understand, for the life of me, what is moral about these people walking around free. Precisely because Israel has freed such terrorists in the past and will likely and unfortunately do so again in the future, the time has come to discuss the implementation of the death penalty in Israel.

In 1954 Israel passed a law restricting the death penalty to convicted perpetrators of genocide, crimes against humanity, war crimes, crimes against the Jewish people, and high treason in time of war. The penalty was administered to the architect of Hitler's Final Solution, Adolph Eichmann, in 1962. Military tribunals in Israel can administer the death penalty, but military death sentences have always been commuted to imprisonment. In 2003, the prosecution sought death for the Palestinian "policeman" responsible for the lynch of two Israeli soldiers in Ramallah in October 2000. Only two of the three judges agreed, short of the unanimous verdict required by law. The author of the lynch was sent to jail, and since then the Israeli military prosecution has never asked for the death penalty - not even for the murderers of the Fogel family (a father, mother, and three young children, including a baby, murdered in their sleep on the 11th of March 2011). The murderer, Amjad Awad, is in jail. Like other murderers before him, he might be freed in a future swap of prisoners.

Because of the unfathomable cruelty of the murders, and because of Israel's immoral release of murderers, administering the death penalty in extreme cases such as the ones we just witnessed is actually the moral thing to do —whether the murderer is Arab or Jewish.

Chapter 30:

The Israeli Left is Barking up the Wrong Tree

Former French Prime Minister Edith Cresson once claimed that most Britons are gay. Her "diagnosis" was based on the observation that men across the Channel did not seem to be attracted to her. Most British males could easily think of another explanation, but desperation tends to produce delusion. The way the Israeli left "explains" why less and less Israelis endorse its ideas is a case in point. Since those ideas cannot possibly be nonsensical, the explanation must lie elsewhere. The explanation, you see, is that the left is being silenced.

The claim that the left is being silenced keeps being repeated these days. Earlier this month (on August 13), Prof. Zeev Sternhell wrote in *Haaretz* that his fellow Israeli intellectuals are guilty of "absolute conformism" and of "intellectual bankruptcy." A few days later (on Aug. 17), Israeli author David Grossman warned during a political rally in

Tel Aviv that Israel is in danger of turning into a "radical and isolated cult." Even former French Prime Minister Dominique de Villepin wrote in *Le Figaro* (on Aug. 1st) that Israel's "peace camp" is "being silenced." This claim was echoed on *124news* by Amalia Rosenblum, who wrote that there is "censorship and pressure on citizens to 'get in line' with the right wing nationalist views."

As a lone conservative surrounded by ultra-liberal colleagues at Tel Aviv University, I am always amused when I hear the left complaining about being silenced. Indeed, this is a case of the pot calling the kettle black.

After Zeev (Vladimir) Jabotinsky (the founder of "Revisionist" Zionism) was barred by the British from re-entering Mandatory Palestine in 1929, the monopoly of Ben Gurion's Mapai party over the pre-state political system went unchallenged. In 1934, Ben Gurion and Jabotinsky reached (from the latter's exile in London) a reconciliation agreement, but Mapai rejected it, seeing no reason to share power. Mapai controlled the economy via its Histadrut labor union and made it almost impossible for Jabotinsky's followers to obtain immigration permits to Mandatory Palestine. In the 1940s, Mapai denounced and delivered Jewish fighters from the politically rival Irgun to the British authorities (the so-called "saison"). Menachem Begin, leader of the Irgun, and later of the Herut party, was not invited by Ben Gurion to the 1948 declaration of independence ceremony. Ben Gurion never addressed Begin by his name, and refused to have Jabotinsky re-buried in Israel.

If there was a time when Israeli democracy was in fact a tyranny of the majority, it was under Ben Gurion's rule. Revisionists could not get a job in government offices and agencies, Mapai mostly controlled the media, and the judiciary did not dare to challenge Ben Gurion's arbitrary decisions.

This unchallenged rule lasted for 29 years, until Menachem Begin's electoral victory in 1977. The reactions to Begin's victory were hysterical (journalist Doron Rosenblum, for example, wrote that the Likud victory marked "the beginning of the end of the State of Israel"). And yet, as opposed to Ben Gurion, Menachem Begin was a true gentleman and an impeccable democrat. He did not replace senior civil servants (Israel's ambassador to the US, Simcha Dinitz, couldn't believe his ears when Begin asked him to stay in his job) and he bowed to the decisions of the High Court of Justice that went against his will ("there are judges in Jerusalem," he famously said).

Having lost at the polls, the left kept running the country and setting its agenda via the judiciary, the media and academia. This is no conspiracy theory: Prof. Menachem Mautner explains in his book *Law and Culture in Israel at the Threshold of the Twenty-First Century* (2008) that those whom he calls "the former hegemons" unilaterally expanded the powers of the judiciary to prevent the government from governing. Prof. Daniel Friedman shows in his book *The Purse and the Sword* (2013) how, in Israel, the separation of powers has been replaced by a hierarchy of powers dominated by an ultra-liberal and self-appointed judiciary.

In academia, the intellectual monopoly of the left is mostly unchallenged and unchallengeable in the humanities, in the social sciences and in law. In the media, the left had a monopoly until the establishment of the *Israel Hayom* newspaper in 2007 – a newspaper that the left is trying to close down through legislation (to preserve Israeli democracy, of course).

During the "Oslo years" (1993-2000) Israel's intellectuals definitely displayed the "absolute conformism" and "intellectual bankruptcy" that Zeev Sternhell denounces today (Sternhell only has a problem with conformists who don't agree with him).

If the Israeli left is not being heard, it is not because of some "censorship and pressure," but because of the bankruptcy of its ideas. Instead of barking up the wrong tree, the Israeli left would do our imperfect democracy a favor by producing ideas worthy of being debated and endorsed.

Chapter 31:

Israel's High Court of Justice Undermines Democracy and Sovereignty

Israel's High Court of Justice ruled in September 2014 that the "infiltrators law" (which enables the government to detain illegal immigrants) is unconstitutional. According to the Court, a law in Israel is unconstitutional if it contradicts two basic laws passed in 1992 ("Human dignity and freedom" and "Freedom of occupation"). This "constitutional revolution" was unilaterally proclaimed by then Justice Aharon Barak. The "human dignity and freedom law" was passed by 32 MKs who had not intended to grant this basic law constitutional status, nor to empower the High Court to repeal regular laws. Yet Barak did just that, in effect granting the Court veto power over legislation.

In the absence of a constitution, there is no clear separation of powers in Israel. Barak was able to unilaterally expand the powers of the Court and, in effect, to establish a hierarchy of powers dominated by the judiciary because there was no constitution to stop him from doing so. Barak was harshly criticized for his judicial activism by leading legal scholars, such as Prof. Daniel Friedman and Prof. Ruth Gavizon. Barak was also criticized for the way he handled the dilemma between human rights and national security. Former Justice Michael Cheshin, for example, accused Barak of being willing to sacrifice national security and Israeli lives for the sake of human rights.

The Court's decision to repeal the "infiltrators law" typically belongs to Barak's legacy: it treats the legislative branch as a subordinate and it puts human rights before the national interest. Even the President of the Supreme Court, Justice Asher Grunis, wrote in his minority opinion that "If my colleagues' opinion were to prevail, then the Court would establish norms that leave no freedom of action to the legislator. I cannot subscribe to this constitutional stance because it turns the Court into a legislator, if not in theory then in practice."

Israel adopted the "infiltrators law" in order to deter further illegal immigration. Those who oppose the law claim that it has become unnecessary since illegal immigration has dropped significantly. This is a sophistic argument: illegal immigration has dropped precisely because the law deters potential illegal immigrants (and, of course, because the physical barrier built by Israel along the border with Egypt makes it nearly impossible to enter Israel illegally from Sinai).

Israel took special measures to stop illegal immigration because it is the only Western country that has a common border with Africa (notwithstanding the British jibe that Africa begins at Calais). As opposed to other Western countries, Israel cannot expel illegal Sudanese migrants because it does not have diplomatic relations with Sudan. Israel is a refuge to all Jews in danger, but it cannot afford to be a refuge to all the world's persecuted individuals. In 1977, Israel granted refugee status and Israeli citizenship to 66 Vietnamese boat people who had been ignored by passing ships from East Germany, Norway, Japan, and Panama. What Israel was able to do for 66 Vietnamese refugees, it would not have been able to do for two million boat people.

Despite its special position among developed countries, Israel took measures against illegal immigration that are actually similar to, and often milder than, those adopted by other Western nations, many of which have a policy of immigration detention.

In the United States, about 31,000 non-citizens are held in over 200 detention centers, a practice made mandatory by legislation passed in 1996.

In Canada, immigration detention has no maximum time limit. In 2010, the Canadian government introduced a bill that imposes mandatory 12-month detention without access to independent review for illegal immigrants. In December 2011, a rejected Iranian asylum seeker was released by Canada after being detained for six years.

Australia puts all foreigners who arrive in the country without a visa in indefinite detention. The Australian High Court of Justice ruled in 2004 that the indefinite detention of illegal immigrants is constitutional. In 2014, the Court ruled that detention should be limited in time, so Australia transferred its indefinite detention centers to Papua New Guinea.

In Italy, illegal immigrants are sent to "Identification and Expulsion Centers" (illegal entry to Italy became a criminal offense in 2009). There are 14 detention centers in the UK and three in the Netherlands. In 2003, the Maltese government replaced its indefinite detention policy with an 18-month detention (the maximum under EU law).

By contrast, Israel's "infiltrators law" limited the detention of illegal immigrants to one year. While Israel's detention policy is justified by its small size, by its common border with Africa, and by the absence of diplomatic relations with Sudan, the High Court of Justice has imposed on the government, via self-granted powers, higher standards than those of Canada, Australia and of many EU members. This is an affront to Israeli democracy and sovereignty.

Part Two:

Regional Challenges - Two-State Problem

Chapter 32:

Yitzhak Rabin was no Starry-Eyed Peacenik

How did the man who declared that he would "break the bones" of the Palestinians become the Mahatma Gandhi of the Israeli Left? Like every year, the commemoration of Yitzhak Rabin's murder is an exercise in historical falsification and emotional intimidation. It is time to set the record straight.

Rabin grew up in the nationalistic *Palmah* movement. He was a pure sabra: a Jew from Sparta, not Athens, who was told to fight rather than to think. A talented officer, he followed the ideal career of the Ashkenazi ruling class: IDF Officer, Chief of Staff, Ambassador to the US, Labor MK, Prime Minister —a true WASP (White, Ashkenazi, Sabra Paratrooper).

In his two three-year stints as Prime Minister (1974-1977 and 1992-1995), Rabin was maneuvered into foreign policy decisions he had originally opposed, and in both cases he paved the way for the electoral victory of the Right. In 1975, Rabin was basically coerced by Gerald Ford and Henri Kissinger to withdraw from about 20% of the Sinai Peninsula in order for the U.S. to convince Sadat that abandoning the Egyptian-Soviet alliance made sense. And when Rabin came back to power in 1992, he was not a leader who had "seen the light" as some would have us believe, but rather a man who was manipulated into signing a deal he rightly suspected to be risky.

Rabin wanted to organize elections in the territories to set up a local Palestinian leadership with which Israel would negotiate the interim status of the West Bank and Gaza, as outlined in the 1989 Israeli Peace Initiative. Rabin believed that a moderate, non-PLO Palestinian leadership could emerge in the territories. By contrast, Peres was of the opinion that Israel should establish direct contacts with the PLO and test the seriousness of the Palestinian leadership in Tunis.

Upon the presentation of his government to the Knesset in July 1992, Rabin declared Israel's commitment to the strengthening of "strategic" settlements in the West Bank ("The Government will continue to enhance and strengthen Jewish settlement along the lines of confrontation, due to their importance for security, and in Greater Jerusalem"). Rabin also ruled out any negotiation over Jerusalem ("The Government is firm in its resolve that Jerusalem will not be open to negotiation;" "whoever believes that any Government of Israel can compromise on united Jerusalem fools himself. We, Israel, the Jewish people, will never negotiate the fate of Jerusalem. It is ours and ours forever"). And he warned that Israel would favor its security over its search for peace ("Security takes preference even over peace").

After the June 1992 elections, Rabin reluctantly gave the Foreign Affairs portfolio to his rival Shimon Peres. It was agreed between Rabin and Peres that Rabin would be responsible for Israel's relations with the United States and for the bilateral negotiations with the Palestinian delegation in Washington, and that Elyakim Rubinstein would remain head of the Israeli delegation in Washington. Peres' role with regard to the peace process was to be confined to the "multilateral negotiations." One month after the formation of his government, Rabin reluctantly agreed to nominate Yossi Beilin as Deputy Foreign Minister.

In September 1992, as Beilin was frustrated with his lack of control over the bilateral negotiations, his Norwegian counterpart Jan Egeland paid a visit to Israel and reminded Beilin about the idea of the secret channel on which he had agreed three months earlier with Yair Hirschfeld, Faisal Husseini and Terje Larsen. Beilin and Egeland agreed to start secret talks between Israel and the PLO in Oslo. Since Rabin had forbidden Peres himself to meet with Faisal Husseini, Beilin could not reasonably expect Peres to allow him to meet with PLO representatives in Oslo. Consequently, Beilin asked Hirschfeld to travel to Oslo and to start secret negotiations with the PLO. Rabin himself was unaware of these secret talks.

When Peres reported to Rabin about the Oslo channel, Rabin was not enthusiastic, and he warned Peres not to torpedo the Washington talks. However, Rabin apparently did not believe that the secret discussions in Oslo would bring substantial results, and so he let Peres go ahead.

During his elections campaign in 1992, Rabin had committed to sign an interim agreement with the Palestinians within nine months. In March 1993 (eight months after the elections), there was no prospect of an interim agreement with the Palestinians through the Washington talks. By contrast, Hirschfeld (together with Ron Pundak) had agreed on a declaration of principles with Mahmoud Abbas, and all they needed was Rabin's green light.

In early May 1993, Peres managed to convince Rabin that the Oslo track was the Government's last hope, and Rabin agreed to send the Director General of the Foreign Ministry, Uri Savir, to Oslo. However, a few days later, Rabin sent a letter to Peres, in which he denounced the Oslo process. Rabin claimed in his letter that the secret Oslo talks were actually undermining the peace process and that the PLO in Tunis was manipulating Israel in Oslo in order to torpedo the Washington talks.

Eventually, Rabin gave his green light to Oslo because he had been unable to reach an agreement with the Palestinians in Washington. But he did not initiate this process and he had serious reservations about it.

Rabin was an honest and decent man who cared about the well-being of his soldiers and the safety of his country. He was a talented army officer; as a political leader he was altogether uncharismatic, gauche, and pragmatic. He eventually endorsed and signed an agreement which others had conceived and negotiated without his knowledge and against his electoral platform. The fact that he paid with his life for the controversial Oslo Agreements is a tragedy, and nobody has a monopoly over the pain and shame that fell upon us in November 1995.

Turning Rabin into a born-again peacenik is a factual and historical fraud. The two gigantic doves that ornate the Rabin Center in Tel-Aviv are a mixture of esthetical bad taste and intellectual dishonesty. As we commemorate Rabin's tragic death, let us honor his memory by respecting him for what he was rather for what he was not.

Chapter 33:

Can a state be Arab and Democratic?

When Natan Sharansky published *The Case for Democracy* shortly after the 2003 US-led invasion of Iraq, he ignited a debate about the likeliness of democracy in the Arab world. President Bush loved the book (*The Economist* said he was having an intellectual affair with Sharansky) and he recommended it to his aids. The idea that democracy was not incompatible with Arab culture and that its promotion would generate peace in the Middle-East neatly fitted the attempt to justify invading a country where no weapons of mass destruction could be found. But the question of whether democracy can flourish in an Arab country was both tricky and relevant at the time. With the recent upheavals in the Arab world, the answer to this question is critical.

As Israel's Prime Minister recently observed with a well-deserved dosage of scorn, even *The New York Times'* editorialists do not know what will be the outcome of the Arab revolts. Are we witnessing a repetition of 1989 Eastern Europe or of 1979 Iran? How strong is the Muslim

Brotherhood? Can democracy take hold in societies with no real middle class?

Because the answer to these questions is partly speculative, the debate is mostly ideological. Liberals call upon the Google workers of the world to unite, and they accuse skeptics of being party poopers. Conservatives roll their eyes at a déjà-vu situation and accuse the Obama administration of not having learned from Carter's betrayal of the Shah.

While neither Sharansky, nor *The New York Times* or Middle East scholars can know for sure whether democracy will spread in the Arab world, lessons can be drawn from the past and reasonable guesses can be made about the future.

First, signing peace deals with autocrats is indeed a gamble. Since the 1979 peace treaty with Egypt, Israel's academics and journalists have dismissed with corporatist consistency the idea that true peace can only prevail between democracies. Although the "democratic peace" theory was originally spelled out by the liberal Immanuel Kant, our know-it-all academics would have us believe that it is actually a cheap excuse made up by the Right to prevent the otherwise inevitable advent of peace.

Second, no previous anti-autocratic revolt in Arab societies has so far ended-up in democracy. The Nassers and Gaddafis of the post-colonial era overthrew monarchs only to break records of longevity and ruthlessness. The Lebanese, who in 2005 revolted against their Iranian-backed Syrian masters, are now ruled by Hezbollah.

Third, the rare (and one-time) free elections held in Arab countries and societies have generally been won by Islamists. The Front islamique de salut (FIS) won the 1991 elections in Algeria, and Hamas won the 2006 elections in the Palestinian Authority. The same way that the European Commission considers referenda to be a type of exam with a correct and a wrong answer, the State Department seems to assume that free elections simply must be the prelude to free societies.

Fourth, the United States will not let the Egyptian army cut-and-run with the $50 billion of aid invested over three decades. It will do its utmost to keep the Egyptian army in charge while paying lip service to democratic reform. If America is too vocal in its support for democracy in Egypt, the Muslim Brotherhood will use this to depict liberal parties as pro-Western traitors. If America keeps a low profile while the army pushes off elections, the military regime will be accused of stealing the revolution for the sake of US interests. In both cases, the Islamists will benefit and America will be blamed.

Israel's detractors claim that a country cannot be both Jewish a democratic. But do they think that a country can be Arab and democratic? Theoretically, it could: if national identity and the rights of minorities can be reconciled in democratic nation-states such as Japan, Sweden or Israel, why can't they be reconciled in an Arab nation-state? It is hard to answer this question, since history has yet to produce one example of a truly democratic Arab state. Meanwhile, the Arab contention that a country cannot be both Jewish and democratic looks more like a manifestation of what psychologists call "projection."

Sharansky concludes his book on democracy by saying that all peoples, and not only all people, are created equal. Fair enough. But both his native Russia and his adopted Middle-East strongly suggest that not all cultures have the same attitude toward democracy.

Joseph de Maistre famously dismissed the French concept of the "rights of man" with his typically aristocratic wit: "I have met in my life Frenchmen, Britons, and Russians. I have even heard, thanks to Montesquieu, about Persians. But for Man, I confess that I have never met him, and if he exists it is without my knowledge." All people, and peoples, are and should be equal. But they are also different. The same way that the Arabs are "projecting" when they accuse Israel of not being democratic, the Americans are "projecting" when they expect the Arabs to give the "correct" answer at the ballot box.

Chapter 34:

The Core Fallacies of the Arab-Israeli Conflict

Most diplomats and journalists repeat at will that Israel and the Palestinians need to address the "core issues" such as borders and refugees in order to make peace. Yet on both issues, historical and legal fallacies have become the conventional wisdom.

On borders, the conventional wisdom is that Israel must "return to the 1967 borders." Indeed, the Palestinian Authority (PA) is asking the world to recognize a Palestinian state "within the 1967 borders." But such "borders" never existed. The 1949 Rhodes Agreements established an armistice line between Israel and Jordan, a line that was defined as "temporary" upon Jordan's insistence, and that had no political or legal significance so as not to prejudice future negotiations on final borders. The armistice demarcation line represented nothing more than the lines of deployment of the forces involved in the conflict on the day a ceasefire was declared. The line was demarcated on the map attached to the Rhodes Agreements with a green marker pen and hence received the name "Green Line."

UN Security Council Resolution 62 (November 16, 1948) stressed the temporary nature of the armistice lines that were to be maintained "during the transition to permanent peace in Palestine." This meant, and still means, that future permanent borders would be negotiated in the framework of a peace agreement, and that those borders would be different from the temporary armistice lines. As Judge Steven Schwebel (former President of the International Court of Justice) explained: "The armistice agreements of 1949 expressly preserved the territorial claims of all parties and did not purport to establish definitive boundaries between them." This is why UN Security Council Resolution 242 (November 22, 1967) calls for Israel's withdrawal "from territories" to agreed-upon and defensible boundaries –not to the temporary and indefensible armistice lines of 1949.

On refugees, the conventional wisdom is that the Palestinians' claim is legally and historically justified but that its actual implementation would turn the two-state solution on its head. But the Palestinians' claim on refugees is baseless both legally and historically.

The PLO claims that Palestinian refugees are entitled to "return" to Israel according to UN resolutions. This is untrue. The often-quoted UN General Assembly resolution 194 (December 11, 1948), like all General Assembly resolutions, is not binding in international law. General Assembly resolutions are mere recommendations. Resolution 194 states among other things that "the refugees wishing to return to their houses and live at peace with their neighbors should be permitted to do so." How would such "refugees" possibly live at peace with their neighbors today, more than sixty years after their parents and grandparents left? As Abba Eban said, "hundreds of thousands of people would be introduced into a state whose existence they oppose and whose destruction they are resolved to seek."

The Palestinians' claim on refugees is not only legally baseless. It is also historically absurd. The 1948 Arab aggression against Israel created a double refugee problem. About 900,000 Jews were expelled from Arab and Muslim countries, while about 600,000 Arabs fled the British Mandate. For tragic as they were, these two refugee problems only represented about 3% of the world's refugee population at the time. And while the world's refugees were all treated by the United Nations High Commissioner for Refugees (UNHCR), it is only for the Palestinians that a special UN agency was created (UNWRA). UNHCR defines a refugee as a person outside the country of his or her nationality as a result of expulsion, but UNRWA extends this definition to the refugees' descendants. As a result, the number of refugees worldwide has decreased from about 60 million in 1948 to about 17 million today, while the number of Palestinian "refugees" has increased from about 600,000 in 1948 to about five million today.

If the UN were to abandon this double standard, the "Palestinian refugee problem" would be easily solved. Of the 600,000 refugees from 1948, about 50,000 are still alive, and most of them are old. Israel would have no problem integrating them. Alternatively, if UNRWA's definition of a refugee was to be applied to the 15 million refugees from the partition of India in 1947, to the 14 million German refugees who fled Eastern Europe in 1945, or to the 1.5 million refugees of the 1922 conflict between Turkey and Greece, then dozens of millions of German "refugees" would have to "return" to Poland, and hundreds of millions of "refugees" would have to re-cross the border between India and Pakistan.

The Palestinians want to invade Israel with the descendants (or alleged descendants) of the 1948 Arab refugees, but they won't accept a single Jewish refugee into the Palestinian state that they want to establish. Jews had lived peacefully and uninterruptedly in Hebron for generations. The Arab pogrom of 1929 emptied Hebron of its Jews for the first time in history. But the Arabs deny the rights of the Jews whose parents were murdered in 1929 to return to their homes, while they demand that the descendants of the Arab refugees who fled because of the Arab war of aggression in 1948 return to what is Israel today. This is as absurd as it is immoral.

This also raises the question of minorities in the framework of the "two state solution." Why should there be an Arab minority in the Jewish state and no Jewish minority in the Arab state? There are Hindus in Pakistan and Muslims in India. About 20% of Israel's citizens are Arabs, but the Palestinians will not tolerate a Jewish minority. Indeed, PA Chairman Mahmoud Abbas declared to journalists in Ramallah on December 25, 2010, that there will be no room for Israelis in a Palestinian state.

Western diplomats and journalists must ask themselves why they tolerate this Arab intolerance. They must also be taken to task for laundering Palestinian propaganda. For none of the "core issues" will be solved as long as they are based on historical and legal falsifications.

Chapter 35:

The Price of Madness: On the Murder of the Fogel Family in Itamar

I first heard of the horror in Itamar (the murder of the Fogel family on 11 March 2011) on Saturday night. Sickened and nauseated to the depth of my soul, I tried to keep my mind occupied by finishing the book I had been reading over the Sabbath –Stef Wertheimer's autobiography *A Man near a Machine*. Wertheimer ends his book with an article of faith: by providing work to our Arab neighbors with industrial parks, we shall achieve peace.

Really? Is unemployment what pushes someone to stab with a knife an entire family, including a baby? I very much admire and respect Stef Wertheimer. Fleeing Nazi Germany in 1937, he learned his trade as an apprentice to a refugee who developed an early camera for Zeiss, an optical company. At age 26, he started a cutting-tool factory from his backyard with a borrowed lathe and a loan from a local butcher. Six decades later, the lathe in the backyard is one of the world's largest manufacturers of metal cutting tools, which are used by car makers like General Motors and Ford. The company, ISCAR, employs 6,000 people and has 50 branches around the world. In 2006, Warren Buffet bought 80% of ISCAR for $4 billion.

As an industrialist, Wertheimer is a genius. But if he thinks that creating industrial jobs in the PA will diffuse hatred, he is dangerously mistaken.

Arab barbarism has nothing to do with statelessness or unemployment. On August 23 and 24, 1929, the Jewish community of Hebron was massacred by Arab mobs armed with clubs, knives and axes. 67 Jews were savagely murdered, and hundreds fled to Jerusalem.

Photographs of this massacre display unbearable scenes: a girl struck over the head with a sword and her brain spilling out; a woman with bandaged hands; people with their eyes gouged out.

This was twenty years before Israel declared its independence and 38 years before it took control of the West Bank. Obviously, the Arab perpetuators of the Hebron massacre were not acting out of despair because of "the occupation" or because of economic hardship. When we Jews were occupied by the British, we never stabbed children in the middle of their sleep. The occupied peoples of Tibet, of Northern Cyprus or of Western Sahara have never committed such crimes either.

Nor are the murderers of the Fogel family social outcasts condemned by their people. The murder of the Fogel children and their parents was greeted with jubilation in Gaza. Carnivals were held in the streets as Hamas members handed out sweets. A society that celebrates when babies have their throat cut is sick and sickening. No less sick and sickening are those journalists who describe the victims as "settlers" and the killed baby as a "settler baby." This language justifies the murder and blames the victims.

As for Abbas, he is a hypocrite. Just two months ago, he awarded $2,000 to the family of a terrorist who attacked IDF soldiers. In March 2012, the PA's official daily Al-Hayat Al-Jadida announced a football tournament named after Wafa Idris, the first female Palestinian suicide bomber. Three weeks ago, Abbas' PA TV broadcast videos glorifying the terrorist Habash Hanani, who in May 2002 entered Itamar and murdered three Israeli students. Twice (in 2008 and again this past summer), the PA named summer camps after the terrorist Dalal Mughrabi, who in 1978 led the most deadly attack in Israel's history in which 37 civilians were killed in a bus hijacking.

While European media have been mostly ignoring the Itamar massacre only to mention, en passant, some "settlers" killed by "militants" in a typical "cycle of violence," French Foreign Minister Alain Juppé couldn't think of a better reaction than to declare that his country is considering recognizing a "Palestinian state." All this while the Israeli navy just caught a freighter of Iranian weapons heading toward Gaza. So what do the Palestinians get for glorifying throat-cutters and for creating an Iranian basis on Israel's southern shore? A European declaration that the Palestinians urgently need a state. As for the Libyan victims of Gaddafi's madness, they might get their "no-flight" zone after they're all dead.

Which brings me back to Wertheimer. Stef's father, Eugen, was a German soldier during World War I and he lost a leg in combat. When Hitler stripped the Jews of their German citizenship, Eugen realized that Germany was going mad. He decided to pick up and leave with his family for Palestine. In a way, his amputation saved his life: it is because he had become an invalid for Germany that he could not stand the idea of being stripped of his German citizenship. Pain can make you lucid.

Will the overwhelming pain of the Itamar massacre make us lucid too? It is about time. As we approach the Purim festival we have, like every year, the opportunity to internalize the clear-cut message of the Book of Esther: that when the hatred of Jews reaches a point of no-return, the only way for us to save our lives is to make our enemies pay the price of their madness.

Chapter 36:

My Kingdom for a Hoax: On Palestinian Diplomatic Threats

A specter is haunting Israel. As the Palestinian Authority is threatening to declare statehood in September 2011 with UN recognition, many Israelis seem to believe that the Apocalypse is near. What is approaching, however, is not a Big Bang but a Big Flop.

The creation of a Palestinian state has already been proclaimed, and the admission of this "state" to the UN has already been recommended by the General Assembly. On November 15, 1988, Yasser Arafat proclaimed in Algiers the establishment of "The State of Palestine" with Jerusalem as its capital and Arafat as its President. One month later, the UN General Assembly adopted a resolution that acknowledged "the proclamation of the State of Palestine" and that replaced the PLO with "Palestine" at the UN. One hundred and four states voted in favor of the resolution, forty-four abstained, and two (the US and Israel) voted against. Since then, the UN General Assembly has passed many resolutions supporting Palestinian statehood.

UN General Assembly resolutions, however, are not binding (as opposed to Security Council resolutions). They are mere recommendations. The General Assembly does not and cannot establish states. Contrary to a widespread misconception, the UN did not establish the State of Israel. On November 29, 1947, the General Assembly only approved the recommendation of UNSCOP (the United Nations Special Committee on Palestine) to divide the British Mandate between a Jewish state and an Arab state. This approval was a non-binding opinion. What established the State of Israel were seven decades of labor and a war of Independence in which the Jews fought by themselves without any help from the UN (though with the military backing of a Soviet satellite –Czechoslovakia).

Nor can the General Assembly admit new members at the UN without the approval of the Security Council. If one of the five permanent members of the Security Council uses its veto, the "State of Palestine" will not be accepted to UN (Kosovo is not a UN member because of Russia's veto). Hence the diplomatic efforts deployed by Israel and by the PA to lobby the Security Council's two wavering veto-holders (Britain and France).

The difference between 1988 and 2011, of course, is that the PLO and Hamas partially control the West Bank and Gaza. Back then, the PLO was operating from Tunis and Hamas was in its infancy. Territorial control, even a partial one, makes the Palestinian "declaration of independence" more potent. The 1933 Montevideo Convention on Rights and Duties of States lays down the most widely accepted formulation of the criteria of statehood in international law: 1. A permanent population; 2. A defined territory; 3. A government; 4. A capacity to enter into relations with other states. The PA fits the bill, but with two caveats that will nurture the upcoming diplomatic struggle between Israel and the Palestinians.

The Palestinians don't have one government but two: a Fatah government in the West Bank and a Hamas government in Gaza. An attempt, in 2011, to form a Hamas-Fatah government was short-lived. The Palestinians try to obtain the "moral laundering" of Hamas (they can count on the support of countries such as Russia, Turkey, Norway, and Switzerland), while Israel tries to convince the EU not to remove Hamas from its list of terrorist organizations.

The second caveat has to do with territory. The "Palestinian territory" is not defined. It is disputed. Hamas openly claims all of Palestine, while Fatah will officially do with the entirety of the West Bank, of Gaza, and of East Jerusalem (a review of PA schoolbooks, TV programs, and public speeches in Arabic suggests otherwise). Mahmud Abbas' claim that the entire West Bank "belongs" to the Palestinians lacks both historical and legal basis. The 1949 "Green Line" was a temporary armistice line between Israel and its Arab aggressors. UN Security Council Resolution 242 does not require an Israeli withdrawal to those lines. The West Bank was ruled (and annexed) by Jordan between 1949 and 1967; there never was a Palestinian state there in the past. The Palestinians are trying to obliterate these facts by arguing that their territorial claims are backed by international law. They are not. Most countries, however, endorse the Palestinians' territorial claims. As for the Obama administration, it has neither endorsed nor repudiated President Bush's letter to Ariel Sharon (from April 14, 2004), which stated inter alia that "it is unrealistic to expect that the outcome of final status negotiations will be a full and complete return to the armistice lines of 1949."

The true purpose of the September 2011 vote is not to declare and recognize a state that has already been declared and recognized in the past. Its true purpose is to obtain three things from the international community: 1. To abandon the demand that the Palestinians renounce their claim about the "right of return" as a condition for statehood; 2.

To grant legitimacy to Hamas; 3. To de-legitimize any Jewish presence beyond the "green line" (including in Jerusalem's Old City).

While the September vote at the UN General Assembly will be legally meaningless, it will implicitly recognize the "right of return" and whitewash Hamas' hideous ideology and crimes. As we Israelis are about to celebrate 63 years of independence, our struggle for it is far from being over.

Chapter 37:

Yair Lapid and the Oslo Syndrome

Psychoanalyzing the Israeli left requires a vocabulary that is to be found in the Fenno-Scandinavian capitals. The Stockholm syndrome refers to a victim's empathy for his aggressor. The Helsinki syndrome is a case of group think and intellectual blindness. As for the Oslo syndrome, I would suggest that the definition of Prof. Kenneth Levin from Harvard University (i.e. identifying with your enemy's narrative) does not grasp the whole phenomenon. Victims of the Oslo syndrome have seen their "solution" blow up in their faces (and ours) for two decades and yet they dismiss their critics, with breathtaking chutzpah, as dangerous extremists and hopeless morons.

Finance Minister Yair Lapid has officially joined the club. In his address to the 2014 Herzliya Conference, Lapid provided the "branja" (code word for Israel's self-proclaimed elite) with its favorite sound bites on the two-state solution (a different outcome will eventually come of the same experiment) and on public funds (there is no money for education because of the settlers).

Lapid said that Israel should submit a map to PA Chairman Mahmoud Abbas showing the future border between Israel and Palestine. Is Lapid ignorant, disingenuous, or both? Because former Prime Minister Ehud Olmert did submit such a map to Abbas in September 2008. Olmert offered Abbas 99.5% of the West Bank, with land swaps (Israel was to annex 6.3% of the West Bank, and the Palestinian state was to annex 5.8% of pre-1967 Israel). Olmert also accepted the partition of Jerusalem, with Israel relinquishing its sovereignty over the Temple Mount and the "holy basin" to an international trusteeship composed of the United States, Saudi Arabia, Jordan, Israel and the proposed Palestinian state. Olmert also agreed to absorb thousands of Palestinian refugees and to create a safe passage (which did not exist before 1967) between the West Bank and the Gaza Strip.

Olmert's original proposal was actually submitted to Abbas via US Secretary of State Condoleezza Rice back in May 2008, way before Olmert was considered a political lame duck. When Abbas justified his rejection of the proposal, first to Rice and then to American journalist Jackson Diehl, he did not mention Olmert's legal troubles, nor did he complain about being offered 99.5% of the West Bank instead of 100%. Abbas clearly stated that he could not relinquish the "right of return" of "millions" of Palestinian refugees.

Does Lapid believe that Abbas will accept the Olmert proposal and give up the right of return, now that he has formed a coalition government with Hamas? Or is Lapid suggesting that resubmitting the rejected Olmert map would convince the Palestinians not to vote for Hamas? If so, I have news for Lapid. On 24 January 2006, literally the day before the elections for the Palestinian legislative council, then interim Prime Minister Ehud Olmert addressed the Palestinians in his closing remarks at the Herzliya Conference. In essence, Olmert told the Palestinians that their choice of a "moderate leadership" (i.e. not Hamas) shall be reciprocated by Israeli "painful concessions for peace." Hamas won a majority the next day.

As for Lapid's claim that settlements are wasting the state's money, it is demonstratively false. Israeli towns and cities in Judea and Samaria are populated by hard-working, tax-paying citizens and businesses. Those Israeli citizens and businesses contribute to Israel's GDP and state income no less than their brethren on the other side of the Green Line, and therefore the government is not throwing money down the drain by building and maintaining those flourishing communities.

But if Lapid is trying to find an answer to his 2013 election slogan ("where is the money?") he should look into the cost of the Oslo Accords. Israel spent $1.4 billion on a security fence meant to stop human bombs that started appearing after the Oslo Accords. Since Oslo, Israel has had to add $11 billion to the budget of the Shin Bet (Israel's security services) to handle the wave of terrorism that emerged after 1993. Hiring security guards all over Israel to stop potential human bombs is estimated to have cost $64 billion. As for the loss of tourism revenues to post-Oslo terrorism, this is estimated at $44 billion.

In truth, however, there is no need for psychoanalysis to understand the "Oslo syndrome." One of the architects of the Oslo Accords, the late Ron Pundak, candidly admitted what Oslo was all about: "Peace is not an end in itself. It is a means to move Israel from one place to another: Israelization of society rather than its Judaisation." So it is not that Oslo believers suffer from a syndrome. They are, simply, hypocrites who use peace as an excuse to advance an otherwise unpopular agenda.

Chapter 38:

What to do with Thomas Friedman

Thomas Friedman has a way of getting attention with provocative statements and inaccurate facts. His new recipe for solving the Arab-Israeli conflict ("What to do with Lemons," *NY Times*, 18 June 2011) is a case in point.

When Friedman claimed that *The World is Flat* in his 2005 book on globalization, all he meant, obviously, was to get a catchy title. The book begins with the story of Christopher Columbus, who set out to find India only to reach the Americas. Friedman claims that this proved Columbus's thesis that the world is round. Actually, proof that the world is round came later, in 1522, when the sole surviving ship from Ferdinand Magellan's fleet returned to Spain.

When it comes to the Middle East, however, Friedman's belief that the world is flat seems to be sincere. No amount of evidence will make him budge from the dogma that the establishment of a Palestinian state along the 1949 armistice lines will bring the conflict with Israel to an end. This is why he twists facts in order for the theory to look correct.

For a start, UN General Assembly Resolution 181 (from November 29, 1947) did not partition the British Mandate between a Jewish state and an Arab state. It only endorsed the recommendation of the United Nations Special Committee on Palestine (UNSCOP). General Assembly resolutions are not binding upon UN members. Resolution 181 became moot anyway after the Arab states rejected it and attacked Israel.

Turning Resolution 181 into a Security Council Resolution, as Friedman suggests, will accomplish nothing. Such a resolution would not be adopted under Chapter 7 of the UN Charter. It would be adopted under Chapter 6, which deals with finding a peaceful solution to international disputes via negotiations. So the Security Council would officially ask Israel and the Palestinians to negotiate. What an achievement: they have been doing just that, to no avail, for the past two decades.

Besides, there is already a Security Council resolution on the Arab-Israel conflict: it is Resolution 242. This Resolution does not require from Israel a withdrawal to the temporary 1949 armistice line. The future border between Israel and its eastern neighbor is to be negotiated. When Friedman claims that "The dividing line should be based on the 1967 borders," he not only invents a border that never existed. He also turns Resolution 242 on its head.

Aware of the fact that reverting to the 1949 armistice line is technically impossible, Friedman calls for "land swaps" that would enable "5 percent of the West Bank where 80 percent of the settlers live" to "be traded for parts of pre-1967 Israel."

Why should there be "land swaps" when Israel is entitled, according to Resolution 242, to retain parts of the West Bank in the framework of a peace agreement? In his recent address to AIPAC on May 22, President Obama claimed that the 1967 lines with land swaps "has long been the basis for discussions among the parties, including previous

U.S. administrations." This is untrue. The only US Administration that mentioned land swaps was the Clinton Administration during the Camp David negotiations in July 2000.

Friedman concludes his op-ed by quoting Gidi Grinstein's gloomy prediction that "September can be a confrontational zero-sum moment with potentially disastrous consequences." Actually, Abbas is bluffing. "Palestine" was already recognized by the UN as a state in 1988. In addition, one of the conditions for state recognition in international law is to have a government. This is why Abbas tried to work out a deal with Hamas in order to put an end to the Gaza/West Bank dichotomy. With this deal falling apart, there are still two, not one, Palestinian governments.

The world is not flat, but Thomas Friedman is flat-wrong about the Middle East. "You know what they say to do with lemons?" he asks in his piece. "Make lemonade." Well, do you know what I say to do with prima donnas whose judgment is blurred by an inflated ego? Ignore them.

Chapter 39:

The True Meaning of September: On Palestinian Statehood at the UN

The mounting diplomatic tension over the upcoming UN vote on Palestinian statehood is somewhat puzzling since this vote already took place twice. On December 15, 1988, the UN General Assembly passed a resolution with an overwhelming majority (104 in favor, 2 against, and 36 abstentions) calling for the establishment of a Palestinian state on the entire West Bank and Gaza Strip. The General Assembly passed a similar resolution on December 18, 2008. The new resolution expected to pass in the General Assembly will thus be redundant.

It will also be irrelevant since General Assembly resolutions are not binding in international law. They are mere recommendations. The UN Charter does not grant the General Assembly the power to establish states, and the idea that Israel owes its existence to a UN vote is a misconception. On November 29, 1947, the General Assembly endorsed the recommendation of UNSCOP (United Nations Special Committee on Palestine) to divide the British Mandate between a Jewish state and an Arab state. This was a mere recommendation that became moot as soon as it was passed since the Arab League rejected it flatly and since the Arab armies attacked the nascent Jewish state.

Nor can the General Assembly accept a new member state without the Security Council's recommendation. Kosovo (which is recognized by 75 countries) is not a UN member because Russia is blocking its membership at the Security Council. The US Government has already announced that it will veto the admission of "Palestine" at the UN without a prior peace agreement with Israel. France and Britain, for their part, are wavering. Yet, even without a US veto, how can the Security Council accept a state that has not been declared and therefore doesn't exist?

States need to be declared by their leaders. Were Abbas to do so, he would blatantly violate Article 31 of the Oslo Agreement ("Neither side shall initiate or take any step that will change the status of the West Bank and the Gaza Strip pending the outcome of the Permanent Status negotiations"). Once the Oslo Agreement is officially cancelled by the Palestinian Authority (PA), Israel will be free to act unilaterally as well (it probably will).

The PA does not meet all the legal criteria to become a state (i.e. a permanent population; a defined territory; a government; the ability to interact diplomatically with other governments). The PA's territory is not defined; it is disputed. There never was a Palestinian state before; there never was a border between Israel and Jordan between 1949 and 1967 but a "temporary armistice line" defined as such in the Rhodes Agreements; and UN Security Council Resolution 242 does not require from Israel a withdrawal to those arbitrary and indefensible lines. Moreover, there isn't one Palestinian government but two: a PLO government in Ramallah and a Hamas government in Gaza. This is why Abbas tried to reach a deal with Hamas, but this deal fell through.

A Palestinian statehood declaration at this point would thus be illegal, and a General Assembly resolution will be both redundant and meaningless.

And yet, the expected UN vote will have far-reaching political and moral consequence, especially if European countries decide to endorse it.

The PA Chairman complains about the absence of negotiations with Israel while he is the one who has refused to talk to Israel for the past two years. His behavior is remindful of the famous anecdote in which a man murders his parents and then asks the Judge for mercy on the ground that he is an orphan.

The true reason why Abbas has opted for unilateralism is that he has come to realize that Israel will not sign a peace agreement that includes the so-called Palestinian "right of return." Abbas also knows that Western governments stand with Israel on that issue, because the Palestinian definition of the so-called "right of return" would turn Israel into a bi-national state with an Arab majority, while the Palestinian state will not tolerate a single Jew (Abbas explicitly said so recently). The "two-state solution" and the "right of return" are mutually exclusive.

Unilateralism will enable the Palestinians to obtain statehood (even virtually and illegally) without having to pay the price demanded by Israel and the West, i.e. making peace with Israel and abandoning the so-called "right of return." Unilateralism, then, will perpetuate the conflict and will legitimize the idea that accepting and recognizing Israel as the nation-state of the Jewish people is no longer a condition and a requirement for the establishment of a Palestinian state.

UN members who will vote in favor of the Palestinian move at the General Assembly will in effect be accomplice to the perpetuation of the conflict and to the de facto denial of the Jewish people's right to self-determination.

Chapter 40:

Cousins in Arms: French State Television and the "Palestinian Cause"

Until Mahmoud Abbas delivered his speech at the UN General Assembly on September 23, 2011, there was some mystery about the Palestinian state applying for UN membership. Abbas did not proclaim statehood before his UN bid, so how could a state that was not proclaimed apply for membership? Abbas provided the answer to that question: the Palestinian state applying for membership was the one proclaimed by Arafat in Algiers on November 15, 1988.

The proclamation of the "State of Palestine" in Algiers did not specify its borders; it did not designate the former armistice lines between Israel and Jordan (often and wrongly called today "1967 borders") as the borders of the proclaimed state. Rather, the proclamation spoke of a "State of Palestine on our Palestinian territory with its capital Jerusalem." The proclamation's reference to the 1947 Partition Plan might have been interpreted as a de facto acceptation of the Plan's suggested (and moot) separation lines as the borders of the Palestinian state. Aware of this ambiguity, Arafat's deputy, Salah Khalaf, declared in his keynote closed-session speech on November 14, 1988 that "at first [the Palestinian state] will be small ... God willing, it will expand eastward, westward, north-ward and southward ... I am interested in the liberation of Palestine, but step by step."

On the very day Abbas delivered his speech at the UN on September 23, one of his deputies, Fatah Central Committee member Abbas Zaki, declared on Al-Jazeera that "the greater goal cannot be accomplished in one go ... If Israel withdraws from Jerusalem, evacuates the 650,000 settlers and dismantles the wall, what will become of Israel? It will come to an end. If we say that we want to wipe Israel out, it's not accept-able to say so. Don't say these things to the world. Keep it to yourself." Unfortunately for Abbas Zaki, it is hard to keep things to yourself in the age of the Internet, especially after you've admitted your true intentions on TV.

In his speech to the General Assembly, Mahmoud Abbas declared that "The goal of the

Palestinian people is the realization of their inalienable national rights in their independent State of Palestine, with East Jerusalem as its capital, on all the land of the West Bank, including East Jerusalem, and the Gaza Strip." On the face of it, the borders of the Palestinian state claimed by Abbas, "only" encompass the West Bank, Jerusalem, and Gaza. But the Palestinian state envisioned by Abbas will emerge next to a Jewish state that will cease to be Jewish through the implementation of the "right of return."

For, as Abbas said in his speech, there must be a "just and agreed upon solution to the Palestine refugee issue in accordance with resolu-tion 194" and "the time has come to end the suffering and the plight of millions of Palestine refugees in the homeland and the Diaspora, to end their displacement and to realize their rights." The refugees "in the homeland" are the ones in the West Bank and Gaza, and what Abbas means by putting an end to their "suffering and plight" is having their descendants becoming citizens of pre-1967 Israel. The Palestinians mistakenly interpret UN General Assembly Resolution 194 as granting them a "right of return" to Israel, and Abbas explicitly referred to that resolution. So the "two-state solution" means two Arab states: a Palestinian state without a single Jew, and a State of Israel with an Arab majority. "Step by step" as Khalaf said. And "keep it to yourself" as Zaki advised.

On the week of the UN speeches, I spoke almost daily on radio and TV. One of my radio debates was on France Culture, France's highbrow radio. During that debate, I made the obvious point that the Palestinian definition of the "right of return" is incompatible with the two-state solution. While the panelists couldn't argue with that, one of them came out with a "solution." Huda Al Iman, who teaches International Relations at Al-Quds University, reassured me: don't worry, she said, the "right of return" will be implemented in phases and not in one shot.

When I mentioned the plight of the 900,000 Jewish refugees expelled from Arab and Muslim countries after Israel's independence, another panelist, Al-Quds University law professor Anwar Abu Eisheh, came up with an interesting answer. In 1974, he said, the PLO "decided" that Jewish refugees from Arab and Muslim lands should be allowed to come back to their countries of origin –which, means that Oriental Israelis (and their offspring) should settle in Iran, Iraq, Egypt, Syria, and Libya. Abu Eisheh is at least soft-spoken –unlike PLO spokesman Mahmoud Labadi who yelled at me during a debate on Voice of America: "Go back to Morocco!"

To their credit, my co-panelists were being honest: they admitted that their goal is to progressively undo Israel via demography (Jewish "return" to Arab lands, and Arab "return" to Israel). Mahmoud Abbas, by contrast, cannot be so candid about his true intentions without being dismissed by Western leaders (Remember: "Don't say these things to the world"). In order for his ultimate goal to gain legitimacy in the free world, Abbas sells a narrative that presents the Palestinians as helpless victims, and whose only aspiration is to achieve justice by peaceful means. And, indeed, Abbas' UN speech was a paragon of hypocrisy.

The hypocrisy started right at the beginning of the speech when Abbas congratulated South Sudan for its newly acquired independence. Two month before his speech, Abbas delivered a letter to Sudanese President Omar Hassan Al-Bashir (a man accused of genocide and of crimes against humanity by the International Criminal Court) to express his opposition to South Sudan's independence. Abbas' state media described South Sudan's independence as an Israeli plot to weaken the Arab world.

Abbas said that negotiations with Israel "broke down" without mentioning the fact that he had refused to negotiate with Israel despite the 10 month settlement freeze which he demanded as a precondition for negotiations. Abbas claimed that "the occupying Power also continues to undertake excavations that threaten our holy places," but the truth is that Israel is the only country in the Middle East that preserves the integrity of other religions' holy places, while the PA has vandalized Jewish antiquities on the Temple Mount since 1996 and has desecrated two Jewish religious sites that fell under its control (Joseph's tomb in Nablus and the antique Jericho synagogue).

Abbas mentioned Arafat's speech at the UN in 1974, claiming that this speech had been about the "pursuit of peace." Really? This is what Arafat said in his speech: "Zionism is an ideology that is imperialist, colonialist, racist; it is profoundly reactionary and discriminatory ... The General Assembly partitioned what it had no right to divide — an indivisible homeland." He called upon the establishment of a state of Palestine, not next to Israel but instead of it.

Abbas called the PLO "the sole legitimate representative of the Palestinian people," yet Hamas won the 2006 elections in the Palestinian Authority and is in full control of Gaza. Abbas said that the Palestinians will continue their "peaceful resistance" –a "peaceful resistance" of terrorist attacks that have claimed the life of thousands of Israelis. He said that the Palestinians are "armed only with their dreams" without mentioning the thousands of missiles pointed at Israel from Gaza, as well as the heavy weapons that have been illegally introduced to the West Bank since 1995. Abbas claimed, with a straight face, that his decision to unilaterally achieve statehood at the UN without a peace agreement with Israel "is a confirmation that we do not undertake unilateral steps." He asserted that Israel's partial presence in the West Bank "is the only occupation in the world" while, in truth, there are dozens of occupations in the world, including the occupation of Tibet by China, the occupation of Cyprus by Turkey, or the occupation of Western Sahara by Morocco.

If Abbas' case were strong, he would not rely on so long a list of distortions. His ability to convince will be determined by the number of people who buy into his falsifications. And like his predecessor, Yasser Arafat, Mahmoud Abbas can count on a faithful ally: France's state television France 2.

On September 30, 2000, France 2 broadcast a tragic scene that was almost certainly staged and faked: the "murder" of Muhammad al Dura by "the Jews." The images, shot by Palestinian cameraman Talal Abu Rahmah and irresponsibly broadcast without due diligence by France 2's Israel correspondent Charles Enderlin, became a major trigger of the "second Intifada." Violence in Gaza and the West Bank erupted accompanied by the cries "revenge for the blood of Mohamed al Durah!" Daniel Pearl was beheaded with a picture of Mohamed al Dura behind him and with pictures of the scene spliced into the slitting of his throat.

Eleven years later, France 2 is once again signing up for the Palestinian cause –this time by actively taking part in Abbas' propaganda. On

October 3, 2011, France 2 broadcast a special report on "Palestine." In a nutshell, it goes like this. The 1947 UN Partition Plan didn't work out and both parties are to be blamed for it; the PA government in the West Bank is the Switzerland of the Middle East; as for Gaza, all Hamas wants is peace and whenever rockets are shot at Israel, it is only and always in retaliation to Israeli unprovoked attacks and aggressions; Israel steals the Palestinians' water and in the Jordan Valley it turned a green land into a desert; Jewish "settlers" first came to Hebron in 1968 and since then they terrorize helpless Palestinians; the Palestinians' "resistance" is always peaceful and harmless; the only reason why Israel still enjoys US support is because of AIPAC's money, threats and control of US politicians and media; the 7 millions descendants of Palestinian refugees from 1948 cannot and should not be integrated in their host countries (such as Lebanon) and they have the right to return to Israel.

The scenario of France 2's special report could have been written by Mahmoud Abbas himself. Its effects will probably not be as dramatic as those of the al Dura hoax. But the third Intifada –an Intifada of lies and propaganda- has been launched, and France 2 is once again giving it a hand.

Chapter 41:

Tom, Gideon, Yossi and Amira: On Tom Friedman and his Israeli Pals

Tom Friedman's column "Newt, Mitt, Bibi and Vladimir" (*New York Times*, 13 December 2011) makes two points: a. Alleged friends of Israel such as Newt Gingrich and Mitt Romney are blind to the fact that Israel is sinking into the Dark Ages because of the mad-cap policies of Netanyahu and Lieberman; b. The critical voices of Tom Friedman and Gideon Levy are unfairly rebuked as "anti-Israel" when, in truth, those voices are the only ones today that are trying to save Israel from itself, out of foresight and true love. There is also a subliminal message in the title of Friedman's article: The world's Axis of Evil is composed of the two Republican frontrunners, of Israel's Prime Minister, and of Russia's President-for-Life.

What ignited Friedman's op-ed was Newt Gingrich's claim that the Palestinians are an "invented" people. Friedman calls Gingrich's claim "a new low." So for Friedman stating the truth constitutes a "low" (for

Hillary Clinton it's simply "unhelpful"). What, exactly, did Gingrich say? That there never was a sovereign country called "Palestine," and that the Arabs who lived in the South-East of the Ottoman Empire were known as Arabs and not as "Palestinians." These two facts are undisputable. Now, were the Palestinians "invented"? Yes, they were.

During the Ottoman rule in the Middle East (from 1516 to 1918), there was no "Palestine" but "sanjaks" (i.e. administrative divisions): The Sanjak of Acre, the Sanjak of Nablus, and the Sanjak of Jerusalem. Arabs who lived in those "sanjaks" were a disconnected bunch of tribes who had little in common. There was not "Palestinian" culture, language, religion or national identity separate from that of the wider Arab nation.

The name "Palestine" appeared in the 20th century when Britain established its rule on the ruins of the Ottoman Empire (the British revived the Latin word "Palestina" coined by the Romans to replace the name "Judea" with one remindful of the Philistines –the Jews' histori-cal foes). All people living in the British Mandate were "Palestinians," including the Jews. *The Jerusalem Post* used to be called *The Palestine Post*, and it is only after Israel's independence that the Palestine Philharmonic Orchestra became the Israel Philharmonic Orchestra.

In February 1919, the first Congress of Muslim-Christian Associations met to consider the future of the territories formerly ruled by the Ottoman Empire. The Congress declared: "We consider Palestine as part of Arab Syria as it has never been separated from it at any time." Arab leader Auni Bey Abdul-Hadi told the British Peel Commission in 1937: "There is no such country as Palestine. 'Palestine' is a term the Zionists invented. There is no Palestine in the Bible. Our country was for centuries part of Syria. 'Palestine' is alien to us. It is the Zionists who introduced it." The respected Arab scholar Philip Hitti testified before the Anglo-American Committee in 1946 that there never was such a thing as "Palestine" in history.

The United Nations Special Committee on Palestine (UNSCOP) wrote in its September 1947 report that Palestinian nationalism was a new phenomenon. Indeed, UNSCOP recommended the partition of the British Mandate between a Jewish state and an Arab state (not a "Palestinian state"). Arab Spokesman Ahmad Shuqeiri told the UN Security Council in 1956 that Palestine was nothing more than southern Syria. The head of the Military Operations Department of the PLO, Zuheir Muhsein, declared on March 31, 1977: "There are no differences between Jordanians, Palestinians, Syrians and Lebanese. We are all part of one nation. It is only for political reasons that we carefully underline our Palestinian identity... Yes, the existence of a separate Palestinian identity serves only tactical purposes. The founding of a Palestinian state is a new tool in the continuing battle against Israel."

"Palestinism" is a reaction to Zionism. If the Zionist movement had not existed, no one would ever have heard of a Palestinian people. In 1925, for example, the new British High Commissioner for Palestine, Sir Herbert Plumer, attended a sporting event at the end of which the "God Save the Queen" and "Hatikvah" anthems were played. Arab representatives protested to Plumer about the playing of the Jewish national anthem. Since Plumer was in favor of a strict status quo between Jews and Arabs, he apologized for his faux pas and promised that next time the Arab anthem would be played as well. At that point, the Arab leaders had to admit it: they didn't have a "Palestinian Arab anthem." Well, you'd better start working on one, Plumer said.

So Gingrich is right. The fact that stating the truth about the Middle East has become an act of pyromania goes to show that intellectual terrorism does indeed work. But it also goes to show that the "Guardians of Middle East Truth" (such as Tom Friedman, Gideon Levy, Yossi Beilin, and Amira Hass) have double standards.

Thomas Friedman did not express any outrage when Shlomo Sand published his book *The Invention of the Jewish People* (nor did Hillary

Clinton protest that it is "unhelpful" to claim that the Jewish people was invented). Claiming that the Palestinian people was invented is a "low" and is "unhelpful" but claiming the same about the Jews is an act of academic courage.

Friedman wrote that the standing ovations Netanyahu got at the US Congress in May 2011 "were bought and paid for by the Israel lobby" (an accusation for which New Jersey Representative Steve Rothman demanded an apology). Why, then, didn't Friedman write that the likely boycott Netanyahu would face at the University of Wisconsin is bought by the Saudi lobby? Why does this logic only apply to Israel? If the Jewish lobby is so strong and so wealthy, how come it has not yet bought the support of University campuses in America? Like Stephen Walt and John Mearsheimer (co-authors of *The Israel Lobby and U.S. Foreign Policy*), Friedman cannot think of a reason for the pro-Israel stance of the US Congress other than "Jewish money." But, like them, he would not venture to say that the pro-Arab discourse on American campuses has anything to do with the millions of dollars donated by Saudi Arabia. Only Jewish money is capable of perverting the American mind.

Finally, Friedman's description of Israel's alleged descent into fascism is either hypocritical or ignorant (or both). In his article, Friedman only quotes the New Israel Fund, *Haaretz*, and the *Financial Times* as his sources of information. With such pluralistic sources, Friedman surely knows what's happening in Israel: Gideon Levy quotes Thomas Friedman, and Thomas Friedman quotes Gideon Levy. It's the vicious circle of circular logics.

Friedman quotes the *Financial Times* to grant credit to his claims, but the *Times'* article is full of inaccurate facts and of slanderous accusations. First, there is no law in Israel that allows Israeli communities to exclude Arab families. Second, the "boycott law" does not impose penalties on Israelis advocating a boycott of products from West Bank Jewish settlements. The law merely enables victims of boycotts to file a civil suit for their economic loss. The law has nothing to do with settlements: a non-kosher butcher from Tel-Aviv, for example, is now able to sue a rabbi calling for the boycott of his store. Third, the purpose of recent proposals to reform the nomination process of Justices is to put an end to the Supreme Court's cooptation system, which generates ideological uniformity and bars non-liberal Judges from the Court. In Israel, Supreme Court Judges are nominated by a committee in which the Judiciary has a veto. One of the proposals is to let the Knesset approve the nomination of Judges for the Supreme Court ("Political oversight!" cries Friedman). In America, Supreme Court Justices are appointed by the President and approved by Congress –but that's not "political oversight."

Friedman ends his article by claiming that more than a few Israelis are asking "who are we?" (he knows, because Gideon, Yossi and Amira told him). I wonder if Tom Friedman ever asks himself who he is. But I have the answer for him: a hypocrite.

Chapter 42:

The Myth of "Israel's Internationally Recognized Borders"

South Africa's Trade and Industry Minister Rob Davies declared in June 2012 that he intended to issue an official notice "to require traders in South Africa not to incorrectly label products that originate from the Occupied Palestinian Territory (OPT) as products of Israel." Davies added that Pretoria recognizes the State of Israel "only within the borders demarcated by the United Nations (UN) in 1948."

The UN did not demarcate Israel's borders in 1948. On November 29, 1947, the United Nations General Assembly approved the recommendation of the United Nations Special Committee on Palestine (UNSCOP) to divide the British Mandate on Palestine between an Arab state and a Jewish state (Resolution 181). This vote constituted a mere recommendation since General Assembly resolutions are not binding in international law. Thus, the idea that the UN "created" the state of

Israel with Resolution 181 is mistaken (the General Assembly can approve the admission of new states to the UN, but it cannot create states). This resolution became moot as soon as it was passed since the Arab states flatly rejected it.

Resolution 181 suggested borders that never came into being. When Israel declared its independence on May 14, 1948, it did not specify its borders (Israel's Declaration of Independence does refer to Resolution 181, but not to the borders suggested by the resolution). The war launched by six Arab countries (Egypt, Transjordan, Iraq, Syria, Lebanon, and Saudi Arabia) against the newly declared State of Israel ended with the armistice agreements signed in Rhodes in 1949. Those agreements did not establish borders but armistice lines, which were different from the borders suggested by UNSCOP. The armistice line between Israel and Transjordan was specifically defined as "temporary" upon the latter's insistence.

This "temporary" line lasted for 18 years, until Jordan attacked Israel on June 5, 1967. When Israel conquered the West Bank in self-defense, it did not occupy a sovereign country or part of a sovereign country. Transjordan annexed the territories it had conquered west of the Jordan River during Israel's War of Independence, but this annexation was never recognized by the international community (only Britain and Pakistan recognized Jordan's conquest and annexation). As for Israel, it regained in June 1967 a territory that had been granted to the Jewish People for self-determination by the Treaty of Sèvres in 1920 and by the League of Nations Mandate in 1922 –a territory that, incidentally, was given to the Jews according to the Book on which US Presidents are administered the Oath of Office.

UN Security Council Resolution 242 (adopted on 22 November 1967) does not demand an Israeli withdrawal to the 1949 armistice lines. The resolution calls for "secured and recognized" boundaries (the 1949 armistice lines were neither) and for an Israeli withdrawal "from territories" ("the" was intentionally dropped to leave room for negotiations). Negotiations between Israel and Jordan (between 1967 and 1988) and between Israel and the PLO (between 1993 and 2008) have failed to establish "secured and recognized" boundaries. Blaming Israel alone for that failure flies in the face of the historical record.

So when South Africa recognized Israel on 24 May 1948 (for Rob Davis' information), it did not recognize Israel "within the borders demarcated by the United Nations (UN) in 1948." The UN suggested borders in 1947, not in 1948, and those borders never came into being. When South Africa recognized Israel, Israel did not have borders. It was in the middle of a war that ended-up in armistice lines which disappeared eighteen years later as a result of Arab aggression.

"Two things are infinite: the universe and human stupidity; and I'm not sure about the universe" Albert Einstein is said to have quipped. In the Middle-East, two things are hopeless: the Arab-Israeli conflict and human ignorance; and I'm not sure about the Arab-Israeli conflict.

Chapter 43:

The Myth of "Israeli Occupation"

In July 2012, a panel of three Israeli legal experts (former Supreme Court Judge Edmond Levy, former District Judge Tchia Shapira, and the former legal advisor of Israel's Foreign Ministry Alan Baker) submitted to the Prime Minister and to the Minister of Justice a "Report on the Status of Building Activities in Judea and Samaria" (the "Levy Report"). The report was immediately condemned by the US State Department whose spokesman, Patrick Ventrell, declared: "We do not accept the legitimacy of continued Israeli settlement activity and we oppose any effort to legalize settlement outposts."

Less expected was the condemnation coming from mainstream North American Jewish leaders. In a letter to Prime Minister Netanyahu, those leaders expressed concern "about the recent findings of government commission led by Supreme Court Justice (Ret.) Edmond Levy." They went as far as to claim that the endorsement of the Levy Report by the Israeli government would place the "prestige of Israel as a democratic member of the international community in peril."

I found it hard to believe that a report whose purpose was to analyze the legal status of Israeli constructions beyond the armistice lines of 1949 would, if officially endorsed, imperil the "prestige of Israel as a democratic member of the international community." So I read it.

The three authors clarify (on Page 2) that their report does not constitute an opinion on the wisdom (or lack thereof) of Israel's settlement activity. Indeed, the report quotes testimonies from experts and organizations from all sides of the political spectrum (including "Peace Now," "Betslem," "Yesh Din" and "Addalah").

The Levy Report only repeats a legal opinion that has been known for decades and expressed many times in the past (including by Israel's Foreign Ministry) regarding the legal status of Judea and Samaria. This opinion states that Judea and Samaria cannot be defined as "occupied" in international law, since a territory is occupied only if it has been conquered from a recognized sovereign country. Judea and Samaria were not a sovereign country or part of a sovereign country when Israel conquered that territory in June 1967.

Judea and Samaria were part of the British Mandate until May 1948. During Israel's War of Independence, those areas were conquered by Jordan in a war of aggression. Jordan annexed (in April 1950) the territories it had conquered west of the Jordan River, but this annexation was never recognized by the international community (with the exception of Britain and Pakistan). Jordan itself waived its sovereignty claims over Judea and Samaria in 1988. So the 1949 Fourth Geneva Convention does not apply to Judea and Samaria, even though Israel has been respecting the Convention *de facto* since 1967.

When Israel conquered Judea and Samaria in June 1967, it lawfully recovered (in an act of self-defense) a territory that had been granted exclusively to the Jewish People for self-determination by the Balfour

Declaration (1917), by the San Remo Conference and by the Treaty of Sèvres (1920), by the League of Nations Mandate for Palestine (1922) –a mandate that was confirmed by the UN Charter (1945).

Claiming that Israel's civilian presence in Judea and Samaria is "illegitimate" (as President Obama said in his Cairo Speech in June 2009) is historically absurd. Claiming that it is illegal is factually wrong.

Many Israelis, however, claim that their fellow-citizens' presence in Judea and Samaria is both illegitimate and illegal. In 2005, a report was submitted to then-Prime Minister Ariel Sharon by Attorney Talia Sasson. Sasson is hardy an apolitical figure: she ran for Knesset in 2008 as a Meretz candidate, is a board member of the New Israel Fund and of "Yesh Din," and was among the initiators of the "Geneva Initiative." She has called Israeli settlements in Judea and Samaria a "cancer."

Talia Sasson's report listed what she defined as "unauthorized outposts" in Judea and Samaria, but her claim that those constructions were "unauthorized" was firmly disputed by the Jewish Agency and by the Ministry of Housing. Attorney Shlomo Ben-Elyahu, for instance, wrote on behalf of the Jewish Agency that the outposts labeled "unauthorized" by Talia Sasson had in fact been built with Government approval and according to the law.

The dispute over whether or not some of constructions in Judea and Samaria were "unauthorized" stems from a legal loophole. In March 1999, the Israeli Government passed a decision that required government approval for the expansion of existing settlements. Since then, many settlements have been expanded without formal government approval but with the government's full knowledge as well as funding. What the Levy Report is saying is that technically and on paper there was no government decision to expand some settlements, but that in fact the government was actively involved in expanding and funding settlement expansions. Therefore, the Government should take full responsibility for its actions (or for those of its predecessors) and authorize *de jure* what it has authorized *de facto*.

Since 1999, Israeli governments have refrained from officially approving settlement expansions for fear of international criticism, but they did expand settlements "under the radar." Both the Sasson and the Levy reports point out to this contradiction (if not hypocrisy) and are basically telling the Government that it should decide what it wants. But while the Sasson Report concludes that all constructions that were not formally approved since 1999 should be demolished, the Levy Report concludes that they should be officially approved *a posteriori*, as they should have been in the first place. Moreover, the Levy Report says that if the Government is going to build or expand a settlement, it should pass a formal decision so that new constructions approved by the government cannot be declared "unauthorized" by the High Court of Justice and be demolished.

Demolishing entire neighborhoods is precisely what the High Court of Justice has recently ordered, and the Court's orders are based on laws and practices that discriminate against the Jews. While international law recognizes the rights of Jews to live in Judea and Samaria, Jordanian law forbids them from buying land there. A Jordanian law from 1953 (by which Israel absurdly still abides), states that only citizens or residents from the Hashemite Kingdom of Jordan are allowed to buy land in Jordan. Because this law is still valid in Judea and Samaria, Arabs are allowed to buy land there but Jews are not (Jews circumvent this limitation by buying land via corporations registered in Judea and Samaria).

In property disputes between Jews and Arabs, the latter tend to be believed and the former dismissed —as Colonel Moti Almoz testified to the Levy Commission. In the case of the Ulpana neighborhood in Beit-El, for instance, an Arab resident petitioned the High Court of Justice, claiming that he was the owner of the land on which the neighborhood was built. This property claim was never proven in the District Court where the case is still pending, and yet the High Court accepted the unproven claim of the Arab petitioner and ordered the demolition of five buildings. Even if the property claim had been proven, the Court should have ordered the compensation of the owner and not the demolition of the buildings. Indeed, this is precisely what the European Court of Human Rights ruled in March 2010 regarding a property dispute in Cyprus.

The Levy Report rightly argues that citizens who lawfully bought a house or an apartment built by the Government should not be expelled from their home by the High Court of Justice just because the Government did not abide by its own decisions (i.e. not to expand settlements without a formal and official decision). The Report also states that the High Court of Justice should not order the demolition of houses because of a property claim that has not yet been proven in a District Court.

I fail to understand why the simple legal facts and the healthy common sense that emerge from the Levy Report should be a source of concern. Why on earth should Israel's prestige be imperiled for respecting more carefully the rule of law, as the Levy Report recommends? I wonder if those who condemn the Levy Report actually read it. But if saying the truth imperils our prestige, then the lack of prestige is a badge of honor.

Chapter 44:

The Two-State Religion: Reassessing the "Demographic Threat"

The main rationale of the Oslo Accords was that establishing a 23rd Arab state ten miles away from Tel-Aviv would bring peace to Israel and stability to the Middle-East. This theory no longer passes the laughing test. Besides the bloody mess engendered by Oslo, the so-called "Arab Spring" has brought the European-inspired model of Arab nation-states to its knees. So why resuscitate a failed and dying model for a fictitious "Palestinian people" that has embraced Islamism like the rest of the Arab world?

Because of demography, of course. A Palestinian state might not bring peace, we are told, but it is nonetheless a necessity to save Israel from turning into a bi-national or a segregationist country.

Since proponents of the "two-state solution" were so wrong about peace, why assume that they are so right about demography?

The two-state solution has become a two-state religion, so let me indulge in blasphemy.

For a start, Gaza is now out of the equation. The "demographic threat" must therefore be gauged in pre-1967 Israel as well as in Judea and Samaria, i.e. in what is known as "the area between the River and the Sea" (referred to as "the area" in this chapter).

The case for the "demographic threat" is based on a census conducted in 1997 by the "Palestine Central Bureau of Statistics" (PCBS). According to that census, there were 2.78 million Arabs in Judea and Samaria in 1997. This figure surprised many at the time because a similar census conducted by the Israeli Central Bureau of Statistics (ICBS) in 1996 had revealed that the number of Arab residents in Judea and Samaria was 2.11 million. How could the Arab population have increased so rapidly within a year?

The answer is that the PCBS included 325,000 overseas residents and double-counted the 210,000 Arab residents of Jerusalem. In 2011, there were about 400,000 Arab residents of Judea and Samaria living overseas. They are still included in the PCBS demographic count. According to internationally accepted demographic standards, overseas residents who are abroad for over a year are not counted demographically. The PCBS does not abide by this international standard (Israel does). Yet Israel's public discourse on the "demographic threat" is based on the PCBS' flawed census.

The PCBS also assumed, back in 1997, that there would be an annual net Arab immigration to Judea, Samaria and Gaza of 45,000. In reality, there has been an annual net Arab emigration from Judea, Samaria and Gaza of 25,000 on average.

In 2012, Jews constitute a two-third majority in the area. When Israel declared its independence in 1947, there was an opposite ratio (one third of Jews). In 1900, Jews were an 8% minority. So far, therefore, time has been on the Jews' side. The question is whether time will continue to be on our side. Recent demographic trends suggest that the answer is positive.

Since 1992, the Arab fertility rate in Judea and Samaria has decreased significantly and consistently (it is now of 3.2 births per woman). Within pre-1967 Israel, the Arab fertility rate has decreased from 9.23 in 1964 to 3.5 today. This decrease has been constant. Jewish fertility rates have also decreased since 1964, but very slightly: from 3.39 in 1964 to 3.0 today. But, more significantly, the Jewish fertility rate started increasing in the late 1990s (it was 2.62 in 1999, 2.71 in 2004, and 3.0 in 2011). The fertility gap between Jews and Arabs went from 5.84 in 1964 to 0.5 today. So the gap is closing, to the Jews' advantage.

The constant increase of the Jewish fertility rate since the late 1990s is not only due to traditionally high rates among Orthodox Jews. Indeed, this rate has been increasing among secular Israelis.

The ICBS has consistently overestimated Arab fertility rates and underestimated Jewish fertility rates. Yet the "demographic threat" discourse is based on the ICBS' mistaken predictions.

Then there is immigration and emigration. While there have been constant waves of Jewish immigration ("Aliya") since Israel's independence, there has been a net annual emigration of Arab residents from Judea and Samaria and from Gaza in recent years: 10,000 in 2004, 25,000 in 2006, and 28,000 in 2008.

So the claim that Israel would turn into a bi-national state were it to annex Judea and Samaria is unfounded. Jews would still constitute a two-third majority, and that majority would continue to increase according to the latest demographic trends. Whether it is desirable for Israel to have a one-third minority of Arab citizens is admittedly a question that deserves to be asked, but the "bi-national threat" is groundless.

Future demographic trends must also take immigration and emigration into account. During the National Unity Government of Yitzhak Shamir and Shimon Peres (1984-1988), both leaders disagreed on the likeliness of massive Aliya from the Soviet Union. Peres claimed that bringing Jews from the Soviet Union was completely fanciful and that Shamir was advocating this idea only to provide a demographic rationale for his "annexationist ambitions in the West Bank." Yet Shamir was right and Peres was wrong: a million Jews immigrated to Israel from the Soviet Union and from Ethiopia under Shamir's watch.

Today, the main reservoirs of potential Aliya to Israel are in North America and in Western Europe (5.27 million in the United States; 375,000 in Canada; 483,000 in France; 292,000 in Britain). Aliyah from English-speaking countries has increased significantly in the past decade partly thanks to the wonderful work done by *Nefesh BeNefesh*. Many French Jews are on their way out.

Those who say today that bringing even half a million Jews from America and Europe in the next decade is fanciful should remember that the same claim was made two decades ago about Soviet Jewry.

Last but not least is the issue of economic incentives to encourage emigration. On that issue I just want to ask a question: why is it acceptable to suggest economic incentives for Jews to leave Judea and Samaria, but unacceptable to suggest the very same idea for Arab residents?

In 1947, Prof. Roberto Bachi implored Ben-Gurion not to declare independence. Bachi, a Professor of Statistics at the Hebrew University and the founder of Israel's Central Bureau of Statistics, claimed at the time that with a population of 600,000 the Jews would become a minority by 1967. Bachi did not take into account the massive waves of Aliya, in which he did not believe. His predictions were grossly mistaken but his spirit of doom was carried on by his student and follower Sergio Della Pergola (an Italian Jew like Bachi himself).

Had Ben-Gurion listened to statisticians and demographers in 1947, there would never have been a Jewish state. Contrary to what the same statisticians and demographers say today, Israel's future as a Jewish and democratic state would not be undermined by the annexation of Judea and Samaria –provided that Israel actively encourages Aliyah from the West in the coming years. As Ben-Gurion said after declaring independence: "A Jewish government whose concerns and actions will not be predominantly geared to the enterprise of aliya and settlement ... will betray its foremost responsibility and will endanger the great historical achievement gained by our generation."

Chapter 45:

So, is there a "Palestinian State?"

Since the signature of the Oslo Agreements, the Palestine Liberation Organization (PLO) has often threatened to unilaterally declare statehood, even though it did just that in 1988 in Algiers. Abbas himself never formerly declared independence. In his speech at the UN General Assembly in September 2011, he clarified that a Palestinian state had already been declared by Arafat in Algiers in 1988. After the vote of the UN General Assembly on 29 November 2012, Abbas claimed that an independent Palestinian state now exists. It doesn't.

For a start, General Assembly resolutions are mere recommendations. Resolution 181 recommended the partition of the British Mandate but it did not establish the State of Israel. Likewise, the General Assembly's November 2012 resolution did not establish a State of Palestine. The General Assembly does not and cannot establish states.

According to international law, an entity must meet four criteria in order to claim statehood: 1. It must exercise effective and independent governmental control; 2. It must possess a defined territory over which it exercises such control; 3. It must have the capacity to freely engage in foreign relations; 4. It must have effective and independent control over a permanent population.

The Palestinian Authority (PA) meets none of the above criteria.

Independent Government Control:
Under the Declaration of Principles ("DOP") on Interim Self-Government Arrangements, signed between Israel and the PLO on September 13, 1993, the parties agreed that the PA would only have limited powers. The PA does not possess the independent, effective and sovereign governmental control that is required to satisfy the definition of statehood. It has no jurisdiction over significant areas of responsibility which are essential to an effective and independent government, such as control over borders –an area of responsibility which was not transferred to the Palestinian Authority, and which continues to be exercised exclusively by Israel. Even in Area A, where more extensive powers and responsibilities have been transferred, the PA does not exercise the powers of a sovereign government. The absence of the requisite degree of control is all the more evident in Areas B and C, where the PA's jurisdiction is of a more limited nature and Israel continues to exercise significant authority. Finally, there is not one Palestinian government but two: A Hamas government in Gaza, and a PLO government in Ramallah. The last election in the PA was in 2006. It was won by Hamas, and Abbas is hardly representative of a population that hasn't been allowed to vote for eight years.

Defined Territory:
The lack of legitimate title over territory has in the past been the basis for denying recognition to such entities as Manchukuo and the Turkish Republic of Northern Cyprus. The 1988 PLO "Declaration of Independence" did not specify the borders of the "State of Palestine." There never existed

such a state in the past, and therefore the PA cannot claim any legal title over the West Bank, as if this territory had been under the control of a Palestinian state in the past (it was conquered and annexed by Jordan in 1949 and remained under the Hashemite Kingdom's control until 1967). By contrast, there is a recorded history of Jewish national sovereignty and presence. Israel's legal rights stem from the Treaty of Sèvres (1920) and from the League of Nations Mandate (1922). The PLO disputes the legality of both documents. But if it was illegal for the League of Nations to recognize the Jews' national and historical rights over their original country, then all the nation-states that emerged from the dismembering of the Ottoman and Austro-Hungarian empires are illegal as well (such as Austria and Lebanon for instance). The League of Nations did not grant national rights to some "Palestinian people" because no such people had ever been heard of at the time, and because it had never been recorded in the annals of history. Indeed, the United Nations Special Commission on Palestine (UNSCOP) dismissed the Arab claim that the League of Nations Mandate was illegal. The Report says that the Arabs "have not been in possession of it [Palestine Mandate territory] as a sovereign nation," and that there were "no grounds for questioning the validity of the Mandate for the reason advanced by the Arab states." The territory claimed by the PA is not defined. It is fragmented and disputed, and is not based on any past or legal sovereignty.

Foreign Relations:
The DOP specifies that the PA does not have powers and responsibilities in the sphere of foreign relations. True, the PA has been conducting foreign relations in practice, but this has been done in violation of the DOP.

Permanent Population:
The PA has no control over the population of Gaza, which is run by Hamas. Its control over the population in Areas A and B is partial. And

as the U.S. Court of Appeals has held, where there are doubts as to the territorial scope of a putative state, its claim to a permanent population is in doubt.

Those countries that voted at the UN General Assembly in favor of recognizing the PA as a state ignored the most basic rules of international law. While the EU is keen to lecture on legality, it breached international law by recognizing as a state an entity that doesn't meet the criteria of statehood. Worse, the EU ignored its own standards and requirements on statehood. The EU conditioned in the past the recognition of the former republics of Yugoslavia and of the Soviet Union not only on the traditional criteria of statehood, but also on other requirements, such as a commitment to abide by international law, the proof of being a viable entity. The EU did not make such demand with regard to the PA.

The EU let the PA get away with breaching the Oslo Agreements. The DOP states clearly (Art. XXXI [7]) that "Neither side shall initiate or take any step that will change the status of the West Bank and the Gaza Strip pending the outcome of the permanent status negotiations." Declaring the West Bank and Gaza a state clearly changes, or aspires to change, the status of those territories. As for the PA's claim that such a unilateral move (and breach of the DOP) is inevitable in light of the failure to reach an agreement with Israel, it reminds one of this well-known anecdote: a man murders his parents, is prosecuted in court, and asks the judge for mercy because he's an orphan. The PA was unwilling to reciprocate Israel's compromises and concessions at Camp David (July 2000), at Taba (December 2000), and during the Annapolis negotiations (2008).

The PA's claim that there is no self-determination without statehood is plainly wrong. In international law, self-determination does not necessarily mean statehood. The Yugoslavia Arbitration Commission, for instance, determined that the self-determination right of Serbians in Bosnia and Croatia should amount to a minority protection but not to statehood. The unilateral declaration of statehood by the Turkish minority of Northern Cyprus was rejected by the international community, which claimed at the time that Turkish Cypriots could enjoy self-determination without statehood.

Moreover, the principle of self-determination cannot be applied in an absolute or one-sided way. In international law, the exercise of self-determination must take other rights into account. The PA's statehood bid denies the rights of the Jews for three reasons: a) The PA continues to incite its population against Israel and to teach its children that the ultimate goal is the elimination of Israel; b) Mahmoud Abbas has declared more than once that the Palestinian state will not tolerate the presence of a single Jew in its midst (and therefore that Jews will be denied access to their holy sites such as Hebron and the Tomb of Rachel); c) By continuing to insist on implementing the ill-named "right of return" to Israel proper, Abbas is denying the Jews their right to self-determination by demanding that they become a minority in their own country.

The General Assembly vote on 29 November 2012 did not establish a "Palestinian state." It did confirm, though, that the "peace process" is a sham and that there is no point negotiating with the PLO what it will eventually obtain at the UN.

Chapter 46:

Which Intifada are we up to?

The death of Palestinian prisoner Arafat Jaradat in an Israeli jail in February 2013 raised the fear of a "third intifada." If a new intifada were indeed to erupt, however, it would not be the third. It would be the sixth.

Historically, intifadas have always followed the same pattern: a. the Palestinian leadership comes-up with a lie and deliberately inflames its population; b. once the violence turns lethal, the Palestinian leadership claims it had nothing to do with it; c. the international community steps in, explaining that in order to stop the violence Israel must address the Palestinians' justified anger and legitimate claims; d. the Palestinian leadership obtains from Israel what it failed to obtain at the negotiation table. It always works.

The first intifada erupted in 1929, when Hadj-Amin al-Husseini spread the lie (with doctored pictures) that the Jews were planning to overtake the Al-Aqsa mosque in order to rebuild their temple. Al-Husseini used violence because he had failed to convince the British to halt Jewish immigration and land purchases. The violence he ignited was lethal: 133 Jews were killed, and the Jewish community of Hebron was decimated. But the strategy worked: in October 1930, Sir John Hope Simpson's report agreed to curb Jewish immigration. Al-Husseini realized that this was the way to go, so he kept going.

Al-Husseini launched a second intifada in 1936. He wanted the British to repeal the League of Nations mandate and establish an Arab state instead of a "Jewish National Home." This time, some 400 Jews were killed. Again, it worked: the Peel Commission (1937) recommended the de facto cancellation of the League of Nations mandate, and the establishment of a mini Jewish state in the Galilee as well as on a narrow strip between Tel-Aviv and Haifa. Al-Husseini rejected the offer, however, and intensified the violence. The British made him a better offer still with the 1939 White Paper, which further curbed Jewish immigration and purchasing rights.

Yasser Arafat, who more than once described al-Husseini as his hero and his model, used the very same tactics. On December 8, 1987, an Israeli truck driver accidentally killed four bystanders in Gaza. Although this was a road accident, the PLO decided to spread the lie that it was a deliberate murder. This is how the third intifada (generally and inaccurately known as the "first intifada") started. Some 200 Israelis were killed. As a result, Israel agreed (in the Oslo Accords) to give the PLO a foothold in the Gaza Strip and in Jericho. Within twenty years, Arafat had managed to implement the PLO's "phased plan" adopted in Cairo in 1974.

After the 1996 Israeli elections, Arafat decided to launch a fourth intifada in order to have the international community twist the arm of Israel's new government. This time, the lie spread by Arafat was that Israel was causing the Al-Aqsa Mosque to collapse. In September 1996, the Israeli government opened the northern exit of the Hasmonean tunnel so that visitors wouldn't have to walk back to the entrance at the end of their tour. The opening had been coordinated with the Waqf, which was given permission to build a huge mosque in Solomon's Stables. In spite of this deal, Arafat decided to spread violence by calling upon the Palestinians to "protect the Al-Aqsa Mosque" (he claimed that Israel had dug a tunnel under the Al-Aqsa Mosque, when in fact Israel had only opened another exit to a tunnel that had been there for 2000 years and that does not run under the Al-Aqsa Mosque). Again, it worked: President Bill Clinton intervened and decided to meet Arafat's political demands. The result? The 1997 Hebron Agreement, in which Israel agreed to withdraw from the City of the Patriarchs.

Then came the fifth intifada in September 2000, which killed over 1,000 Israelis. This intifada was not ignited by one lie, but two: Ariel Sharon's visit on the Temple Mount was a provocation (in fact, Prime Minister Ehud Barak had informed Arafat of the visit and had coordinated the timing with him), and Israel had assassinated a child at the Netzarim junction in Gaza (in reality, the "killing" of Mohamed al-Dura had been staged and filmed by Palestinian cameraman Talal abu-Rahmah). Arafat and Bargouti had planned the fifth intifada for a long time, and when it became clear at Camp David in July 2000 that Israel was not going to give in on the "right of return," Arafat played the old "Al-Husseini trick." It worked, as always. The PLO obtained more Israeli concessions at the Taba Talks and with the Clinton parameters. Most significantly, the fifth intifada achieved two major goals: for the first time, a US president (George W. Bush) and an Israeli prime minister (Ariel Sharon) openly declared that they agreed to the establishment of a Palestinian state (Road Map, 2003), and for the first time Israel dismantled settlements in an area claimed by the PLO (Disengagement plan, 2005).

If it always works, why not keep going?

Chapter 47:

Does the Israeli Left Have a "Plan B"?

The 2013 annual conference of the Institute for National Security Studies (INSS), a leading Israeli think tank, had a clear agenda: to promote the idea of unilateral disengagement from Judea and Samaria. INSS's suggestions were summarized in a paper authored by Gilead Sher and his team: "The Palestinian Issue: Toward a Reality of Two States." Unilateralism is not the authors' favorite option: such a strategy, they claim, should only be implemented if and when the Palestinian Authority rejects another Israeli peace offer —an offer that should be based on Olmert's proposal to Mahmud Abbas in 2008.

None of the new government's coalition partners are ready to endorse the Olmert proposal. Even Tzipi Livni (a minority partner in the current government) criticized Olmert's proposal while she was serving as his Foreign Minister, because she disagreed with Olmert on the refugee issue. Yair Lapid has said that Olmert went too far with his proposal to Abbas. For Likud, Israel Beitenu and the Jewish Home, the Olmert proposal is a non-starter. So expecting the newly elected Israeli government to resubmit the Olmert proposal to Abbas is not only unrealistic but also strange: why should the government implement a policy for which it was not elected and which was rejected at the polls?

For the record, the Olmert proposal consisted of an Israeli withdrawal from 99.5% of Judea and Samaria (with minor land swaps); of a safe passage route from Hebron to the Gaza Strip; of the forced evacuation of tens of thousands of Israelis (including from Hebron, Ofra, and Bet-El); of the transfer of sovereignty over Jerusalem's "holy basin" (including the Temple Mount and the Western Wall) from Israel to an international custodial regime composed of the United States, Saudi Arabia, Jordan, Israel, and the Palestinian State; and of the acceptance by Israel of the return of 5,000 Palestinian refugees to Israel proper, with financial compensation for the rest.

But suppose, for the sake of the argument, that Olmert was Prime Minister again and that his coalition was backing him on the 2008 proposal. Would Abbas, this time, accept it? One theory (promoted among others by Israeli journalist Raviv Drucker) claims that Abbas rejected Olmert's 2008 proposal because Olmert was already a lame duck at the time. This theory flies in the face of historical evidence. Condoleezza Rice writes in her memoirs *No Higher Honor* that Olmert submitted his proposal in May 2008, and that Abbas told her that he couldn't tell five million "refugees" that only five thousand would return home. In May 2008, Olmert was no lame duck: only on 30 July 2008 did he announce that he would not run for his party's leadership. Abbas mentioned to Rice the so-called "right of return," not Olmert's legal troubles, to justify his rejection of the proposal. Al-Jazeera's "Palestine Papers" revealed that, in September 2008, the Palestinian leadership decided not to react officially to the Olmert proposal so as not to be blamed for its failure. No mention was made of Olmert being a lame duck.

Did Abbas just stay mum about Olmert's proposal or did he reject it? Abbas himself answered this question in his interview with Jackson Diehl in *The Washington Post* on 29 May 2009. Abbas said in the interview that he *turned down* Olmert's proposal. Not because Olmert was a lame duck, but because, in Abbas' own words, "the gaps were wide" between what Olmert offered and what Abbas was willing to accept. Then there is another theory according to which it is Tzipi Livni who told Abbas not to pocket Olmert's offer because the latter was a lame duck. But Abbas himself says that this is not the case. In an interview with *Asharq Al-Awsat* on 22 December 2009, Abbas said the following about the Livni theory: "This did not happen. No intervention by Tzipi Livni took place."

So the lame duck theory doesn't wash. Abbas rejected the Olmert proposal because of the "right of return."

Therefore, Gilead Sher and his acolytes have good reasons to assume that Abbas "might" reject the Olmert proposal again in the theoretical and unlikely scenario of a historical replay. This is why, according to the INSS paper, Israel should act unilaterally. Aware of the disastrous security consequences of the 2005 unilateral withdrawal from Gaza, INSS does not suggest a military withdrawal from Judea and Samaria but only a civil one. In other words, most Israelis living beyond the 1949 armistice line would be deported, but the IDF would retain its presence beyond that line. According to INSS, such a move will achieve two goals: a. it will preserve Israel's Jewish majority; b. it will improve Israel's international image and standing.

Let's start with the second goal. As a result of the 2005 unilateral withdrawal from Gaza, Israel was compelled to go to war in December 2008 to stop the shelling of its citizens. Images of that war were a PR disaster —a disaster that was dwarfed by the ensuing Goldstone Report. The military naval blockade of Gaza (itself an inevitable consequence of the 2005 withdrawal) caused an international outcry that led to the

Marmara incident –another PR waterloo. So Israel's international image and standing *worsened* as a result of the 2005 "disengagement" simply because blockades and bombardments (the side effect of retreating when you live in the Middle East) are more ruinous to your image than military occupation. Those side effects might be averted by the continuous military presence advocated by INSS in Judea and Samaria. But then the Palestinians and the world will still accuse Israel of maintaining its "occupation." So what's the point? Indeed, Israel is still accused of occupying Gaza even though it withdrew its army from there (the military naval blockade is enough for ill-wishers to accuse Israel of being an occupier).

The first rationale of INSS's proposed disengagement is that, without it, Israel will turn into a bi-national state. This claim, however, is groundless. Since 2005, Gaza is out of the demographic equation. Without Gaza, there is a two-third Jewish majority between the Jordan River and the Mediterranean Sea. The demographic trends of the last decade (declining Arab birthrates, increasing Jewish birthrates, Jewish immigration, Arab emigration) suggest that this Jewish majority is stable if not growing. Whether or not Israel can afford to increase its Arab minority from 20% to 33% is admittedly a question that deserves to be asked and debated, but the "bi-national threat" is a sham. Indeed, the *Sunday Times* Middle East correspondent Uzi Mahnaimi recently declared in an interview with *Makor Rishon* (3 May 2013) that Israel would retain a stable 70% Jewish majority were it to annex Judea and Samaria.

Chapter 48:

Does the Israeli Right Have a "Plan B"?

When John Kerry announced the renewal of final status negotiations between Israel and the Palestinian Authority (PA) in July 2013, he specified that the parties had nine months to solve their 100 year-old conflict. Had Kerry made his announcement on July 1st instead of July 18, the set deadline would have been April 1st and Kerry could have claimed authorship for an unbeatable Fools' Day prank. Four months ahead of the Kerry deadline, both Israel and the PA had already started the blame-game for the expected failure of the talks.

I cannot name a single Palestinian who openly blames his government for the current deadlock, but Israel has no shortage of politicians, academics and journalists who are busily blaming Netanyahu for the lack of peace. Instead of wasting their time and energy with the blame-game, Israelis should think about the "day after."

There are three potential scenarios for the post-April 18 deadline: unilateral disengagement, annexation or permanent status-quo.

The rationale of unilateral disengagement is that it enables Israel to extricate itself from a demographic trap despite the absence of an unachievable peace agreement. The precedent set by the Gaza disengagement in 2005, however, has made this option a non-starter. Missiles would rain on Israel, while the prospect of more Goldstone Reports would tie Israel's hands in its ability to respond (which was the purpose of the Goldstone Report in the first place). Moreover, because Israel would not unilaterally withdraw to the 1949 Armistice Lines but from, say, 80% of the West Bank, it would still be accused of "occupation" (as it is still accused of "occupying" Gaza).

The annexationist model would only apply to the West Bank, as Israel already pulled-out from Gaza. While there are diverging figures on the exact number of Arab residents in the West Bank, Israel would retain a two-third Jewish majority were it to annex Judea and Samaria and grant Israeli citizenship to its all residents. In light of the increasing Jewish birthrates and declining Arab birthrates in the past twenty years, the Jewish majority would likely remain stable. The wisdom of increasing Israel's Arab minority from its current 20% to about 33%, however, is highly debatable at best.

The third, and most likely option, is the perpetuation of the status quo with minor changes that will entrench the physical separation between Israel and the Palestinians while preventing the militarization of the West Bank and not impede its economic development. In this scenario, however, the PA will redouble its "lawfare" (legal warfare) against Israel at the UN and at other international organizations.

The PA committed to suspend its "lawfare" while negotiations are taking place, but it is still acting against Israel in international institutions via third parties. In May 2013, shortly before the talks resumed, the Comoros Islands (as small archipelago state near Madagascar) filed a complaint against Israel with the ICC because the *Mavi Marmara* ship raided by Israel in 2010, was registered in the Comoros. Turkish lawyers representing Comoros claim that under Article 12 of the ICC Statute, Comoros has a legitimate claim in bringing Israel under the court's jurisdiction because the *Mavi Marmara*, on which nine Turkish activists were killed, was technically under Comoros' jurisdiction.

It is obvious that Comoros is acting on behalf of the PA (and of Turkey). The PA is trying to get the ICC to indict Israeli officers via a third country, while it is officially refraining from such actions during the negotiations with Israel. After the PA was granted its "non-member observer status" at the UN General Assembly in November 2012, it announced its intention to use this new status to bring legal action against Israel at the ICC. It will obviously do so openly after April 2013.

While Israel will have to continue battling "lawfare" if it chooses to maintain the status quo, it might be the least of three evils. Unilateral disengagement would relieve Israel of its demographic angst but it would also require military operations whose consequence will be international condemnations and opprobrium. Annexation may not turn Israel into a bi-national state as critics suggest, but it would still generate an undesirable demographic makeup.

Hence the refusal of "peace processors" to contemplate an alternative to a peace that they failed to achieve at Camp David (in July 2000), at Taba (in December 2000), and with Olmert (in 2008), and which they would be unable to achieve today even if Labor were to replace the Jewish Home in the coalition, and even if Netanyahu were to endorse the Olmert proposal.

"Peace processors" claim to be realists, but in truth they are no less irrational than their ideological foes. Alternatives to the two-state model all have serious shortcomings, but the greatest shortcoming of that model is that it keeps working in theory and failing in practice.

Chapter 49:

Mahmoud Abbas' Minority Opinion: Why Can't there be Minorities in an Arab State?

Shortly after negotiations between Israel and the Palestinian Authority (PA) resumed in July 2013, PA Chairman Mahmoud Abbas declared that he wouldn't tolerate the presence of a single Jew in a future Palestinian state. Imagine if Scotland, which is supposed to hold a referendum on its independence in 2014, would declare that it shall not tolerate any Englishman (or Jew, for that matter) on its sovereign territory. While Abbas' declared intolerance for minorities is plainly anti-Semitic, Western leaders let him get away with it.

The partition (or two-state) model has been applied to partially solve conflicts in other parts of the world, but nowhere does this model entail the absence of minorities. The Indian sub-continent was divided between India and Pakistan in 1947. Although this partition engendered a tragic mutual population transfer (about 7 million Muslims left India for Pakistan, and about 7 million Hindus and Sikhs left Pakistan for India), both countries retained minorities: there is a 14% Muslim minority in India, and a 2% Hindu minority in Pakistan.

In Cyprus, where there has been a de facto partition following the Turkish invasion and occupation since 1974, there are minorities on both sides of the divided island. Even though Turkey has expelled an estimated 200,000 Greeks Cypriots from the occupied North and has transferred Turkish settlers to take their place, minorities are to be found on both sides of the separation fence (the village of Pyla in the Turkish-occupied North has a mixed Greek and Turkish population). In March 2010, the European Court of Human Rights ruled over a property dispute in Cyprus that even when a property claim is proven, the occupying power should compensate the original owner of the land and not order the demolition of the settler's house.

When Czechoslovakia dissolved into two separate states in 1993, neither the Czech Republic nor Slovakia got rid of the other side's minorities: there is a 1.5% Slovak minority in the Czech Republic, and a 0.5% Czech minority in Slovakia.

Since the Second World War, there have been many cases of partition and of territorial withdrawal. But in most cases, settlers stayed and were not asked to leave as part of a peace deal.

When Saarland decided in 1955 to become part of Germany, the French population was not asked to leave.

With the collapse of the Soviet Union in 1991, former Soviet republics became independent. Newly independent countries such as Estonia, Latvia, and Lithuania asked the Russian settlers to leave, but Russia refused and the EU took the side of the Russian minorities, claiming that their forced transfer to Russia would constitute a human rights violation. In the end, the Russian minority was allowed to stay.

When Cambodia reached a peace agreement with Vietnam in 1991 after 13 years of Vietnamese occupation, the Vietnamese settlers were allowed to stay in Cambodia. When East Timor gained its independence in 2002 after 27 years of Indonesian occupation, the Indonesian settlers were not asked to leave as part of the peace deal.

So why should the Arab-Israeli conflict be an exception? If there is true peace, why shouldn't Jews be allowed to stay as a minority in a Palestinian state? Why should there be an Arab minority in the Jewish state, but no Jewish minority in the Arab state? According to the 1947 United Nations Partition Plan for Palestine, there was to be a 1% Jewish minority in the Arab state and a 45% Arab minority in the Jewish state. Even though there was a wide gap between those two percentages, no one suggested at the time that partition entailed the absence of minorities. With over half a million Jews living in Judea and Samaria and in the eastern part of Jerusalem, a major population transfer is not only immoral but also unrealistic.

This is why Prime Minister Netanyahu first suggested in 2011 the idea of having Jews remain as a minority in a Palestinian state. In his address to the US Congress in May 2011, he said the following: "I'm saying today something that should be said publicly by all those who are serious about peace. In any real peace agreement, in any peace agreement that ends the conflict, some settlements will end up beyond Israel's borders."

The Institute for National Security Studies (INSS) published a paper on April 8, 2013 ("Jewish Enclaves in a Palestinian State") in which it was suggested that "The residents of some 65 small and isolated settlements with a total population of 36,000 who decide to remain in their homes will be able to retain their Israeli citizenship and also receive Palestinian citizenship. These settlements will be under the full sovereignty of the Palestinian state...Those who remain in these settlements will be subject to the sovereignty and the laws of the Palestinian state, as Israeli Arabs are subject to the sovereignty of the State of Israel."

So the fact that Abbas is rejecting the idea of retaining a Jewish minority in a Palestinian state is not only anti-Semitic. It would also turn the resolution of the Israeli-Palestinian conflict into the only case of a two-state solution in which only one state retains a minority belonging to the other state. Abbas' "minority opinion" not only says a lot about his liberal credentials; it also says a lot about the West's double-standards.

Chapter 50:

The "Right of Return" as an Obstacle to Peace

In his 2013 address to the United Nations General Assembly (UNGA), Palestinian Authority (PA) Chairman Mahmoud Abbas called for a solution to the Palestinian refugee problem in accordance with UNGA Resolution 194.

In the Palestinian narrative, Resolution 194 grants a legal right to the Palestinian refugees and their descendants to settle in Israel and to reclaim the real estate and land they lost in 1948. It is time to set the record straight.

For a start, General Assembly resolutions are mere recommendations. As opposed to Security Council Resolutions, they are not binding in international law. UNGA Resolution 194 is no exception: it is a non-binding recommendation. So even if this resolution recognized the right of Palestinian refugees and their descendants to return to Israel (which it doesn't) such recognition would neither be binding nor enforceable.

Article 11 of Resolution 194 says inter alia that "the refugees wishing to return to their homes and live at peace with their neighbors should be permitted to do so at the earliest practicable date, and ... compensation should be paid for the property of those choosing not to return."

The resolution doesn't talk about "Palestinian refugees" but about "refugees" as it refers to both Arab and Jewish refugees that were displaced as a result of war in the former British Mandate. It mentions both return and compensation as possible solutions. But, mostly, it only refers to the refuges themselves and certainly not to their future descendants. This central point touches to the core of the refugee problem: the Palestinians claim that the refugee status and the "right of return" allegedly recognized by the UN applies not only to the 1948 refugees but also to their descendants. This claim is groundless in international law and has no precedent in 20th century history.

In the 20th century, refugees were unfortunately a common phenomenon in international relations. There was a population transfer of 2 million people between Greece and Turkey in 1923. In 1937, the Peel Commission proposed a population exchange between Jews and Arabs in the framework of a territorial partition of British Palestine. After World War II, some 14 million Germans were expelled from Eastern Europe and became refugees. The partition of India in 1947 created a double refugee problem: over 7 million Hindu refugees and over 7 million Muslim refugees (with the breakup of Pakistan in 1971, some 10 million Bangladeshis became refugees as well). So did the partition of British Palestine, though with different proportions: some 600,000 Arab refugees from the newly established State of Israel, and some 900,000 Jewish refugees expelled from Arab and Muslim countries in the wake of the 1948 Arab-Israeli war and its aftermath. All in all, there were about

60 million refugees in the world in 1948, and the Palestinian Arab refugees represented 1% of world's refugee population.

These Palestinian refugees could have been integrated in Arab countries with which they shared a common ethnicity, culture, language and religion. Instead, they were kept in camps and discriminated against by Arab leaders who cynically used them as pawns against Israel. Rather than trying to solve the Palestinian refugee problem, Arab leaders did everything to maintain it. While the United Nations High Commissioner for Refugees (UNHCR) was established to solve the global refugee problem, the United Nations Relief and Works Agency for Palestine Refugees in the Near East (UNRWA) was created to maintain the Palestinian refugee problem.

Even though Palestinian refugees only represented 1% of the world refugee population in 1949, they were the only refugees for whom a special UN agency was established. The rest of the world's refugees were (and still are) dealt with by UNHCR. This unjustified institutional duality has far reaching implications because of how UNHCR and UNRWA define refugees. While UNHCR defines refugees as forcibly displaced persons, UNRWA applies this definition to the refugees' descendants too. Hence has the world's global refugee population decreased from 60 million in 1948 to 15 million in 2012, while the Palestinian "refugee" population has increased from 600,000 in 1948 to 5 million today.

It is time to put an end to this absurd and unjustified double standard. There is no reason why UNHCR's definition and jurisdiction shouldn't apply to Palestinian refugees. Incidentally, that would "reduce" the actual number of Palestinian refugees to about 50,000 (most of them are elderly by now). Alternatively, were the world to universalize the UNRWA algorithm, Poland would have to reintegrate the descendants of German refugees, and millions of Hindus and Muslims would have to re-cross the border between India and Pakistan.

The true meaning of UNGA Resolution 194 is that the actual Arab and Jewish refugees of 1948 should be compensated or allowed to reintegrate their lost homes. Israel should publicly offer to implement that resolution in order to expose the truth: the actual number of Palestinian refugees is 50,000, and the roughly equal number of Jewish refugees must be compensated as well.

Once the truth is told and internalized about the refugee issue, the Israeli-Palestinian conflict might actually become solvable.

Chapter 51:

John Kerry, an Innocent Abroad

Former US President Richard Nixon once joked with Israeli Prime Minister Golda Meir that both leaders had a Jewish foreign minister (Henry Kissinger and Abba Eban). To which Golda replied with her legendary wit: "Yes, but mine speaks English without an accent." She was referring to Kissinger's heavy German intonation and to Eban's Shakespearean oratory. But accent was not the only difference between the two diplomats. Kissinger was a Bismarck-type cynic who pushed Realpolitik to its limits, while Eban was an idealist who abandoned a promising career in England to be "the voice of Israel" after the Holocaust. Too polished for Israeli politics, Eban was dubbed by Prime Minister Levy Eshkol "der gelernter naar" – the erudite fool.

Forty years later, the foreign ministers of Israel and America have traded roles. Not only does Avigdor Lieberman speak English with a Russian accent, he is also the quintessence of a political realist. John Kerry, on the other hand, would fit the "erudite fool" formula if it weren't for his lack of erudition. In his first trip overseas as Secretary of State in February 2013, Kerry declared in Germany that "In America you have a right to be stupid."

Luckily for him, John Kerry lives in a free country. In August 2013, he compared the victims of the Boston terrorist attack to the IHH terrorists aboard the Mavi Marmara who died after trying to kill IDF soldiers. After that, he called the military coup against the democratically elected President of Egypt "a restoration of democracy." Kerry's impromptu remark at the height of the Syrian crisis that America wouldn't storm Assad were he to dismantle his chemical weapons is what enabled Vladimir Putin to hold the US back.

Kerry's remarks during his last trip to Israel, however, are not a mere addition to a fool's anthology. They ruined the meek chances of reaching an agreement between Israel and the Palestinians, and they encouraged the Palestinians to resort to violence. By blaming Israel and absolving the PA for the possible failure of the current negotiations, and by threatening only Israel of the consequences of such failure while justifying Palestinian violence and media warfare if and when the talks collapse, Kerry has convinced the Palestinians that they don't need to show any flexibility and that they will not be blamed by America for setting the region ablaze once again.

The fact that Kerry could only think of Israel for the failure of the "peace process" makes one wonder where he has been for the past 20 years. It is the PLO that rejected the groundbreaking peace offers of Ehud Barak in July 2000, of the Clinton Proposal in December 2000 and of Ehud Olmert in 2008. The rejection of those proposals was mostly due to the Palestinians' insistence on a "right of return" –the implementation of which would turn Israel into a bi-national state. Yet Kerry did not call upon the Palestinians to forfeit this fantasy for the sake of peace. Nor did he castigate them for the endless anti-Semitic incitement, glorification of terrorists, and calls for the liberation of all of Palestine in their media. Kerry did not warn the Palestinians that they would pay a price for ruining the chance of peace by insisting on invading Israel with five million Arabs and by teaching their children that "peace" with Israel is just a temporary ploy for the "liberation" of Jaffa and Nazareth.

After such declarations, why should the PA make compromises? John Kerry has effectively become a major and additional obstacle to achieving peace between Israel and the Palestinians. And yet, Kerry is widely perceived as a peacemaker, while his newly installed Israeli counterpart Avigdor Lieberman is accused of ruining the "peace process."

Lieberman, however, is not responsible for the Palestinians' rejection of the above mentioned peace offers. Nor are his positions on the Palestinian issue more hawkish than those of his Prime Minister. On the contrary: Lieberman's political platform includes a readiness to make concessions over Jerusalem, as well as land swaps between Israel and a future Palestinian state.

The true reason why Lieberman is reviled is that he is a party-pooper among delusional and politically correct academics, diplomats and journalists. And this is precisely why his return to the Foreign Ministry is good news. Had Lieberman been in the Government from its inception, Israel would not have issued an apology to Erdogan, nor would it have agreed to the release of Palestinian terrorists for the mere "privilege" of renewing pointless negotiations with the PA.

I am no fan nor friend of Lieberman. His authoritarian tendencies and closeness to Austrian businessman Martin Schlaff (who was suspected of issuing bribes to the sons of former prime minister Ariel Sharon) are not my cup of tea, and I strongly and publicly criticized his political machinations with the leader of the Orthodox Shas party Aryeh Deri to unseat Jerusalem's successful mayor Nir Barkat. But the outrageousness of John Kerry, Catherine Ashton and Mahmoud Abbas have reached such levels that Lieberman's irreverence and straightforwardness are called for to restore Israel's self-respect.

Lieberman's realism and spine are dearly needed to remind advocates of the "right to stupidity" that your liberty to swing your fist ends where my nose begins.

Chapter 52:

The Challenge to Israel's Sovereignty in the Negev: Historical Background

Sixty-six years ago, on 29 November 1947, the United Nations General Assembly voted to divide the British Mandate between a Jewish State and an Arab State (Resolution 181). There are many myths around this resolution, as well as a particular side effect that Israel did not expect at the time but which has recently become more palpable.

After the vote's results were announced, members of the Jewish delegation at the UN fell on each other in tears and, across the pre-state mandate, Jews burst into celebrations. By contrast, Arab League Chairman Azzam Pasha was enraged and vowed that "any line of partition drawn in Palestine will be a line of fire and blood."

In truth, however, Resolution was 181 legally meaningless. Like all General Assembly resolutions, it was a non-binding recommendation. The claim that the UN "created" Israel on 29 November 1947 is absurd.

The General Assembly has no authority to "create" states. The Syrian ambassador to the UN was 100% right when he declared after the vote that "The recommendations of the General Assembly are not imperative on those to whom they are addressed. I fail to find in this charter any text which implies, directly or indirectly, that the General Assembly has the authority to enforce its recommendations by military force."

A second myth around Resolution 181 is that the Arabs were justified to reject it because it was unfair to the Palestinians. For a start, the UN Partition Plan did not mention the Palestinians, nor did it recommend the establishment of a Palestinian state. There was a reason for this: nobody had ever heard of such a people at the time. Resolution 181 recommended the partition of the British Mandate between an "Arab State" and a "Jewish State." But if anyone got discriminated against it was the Jews, not the Arabs.

"Palestine" did not exist in the Ottoman Empire. There were administrative districts called "Sanjaks" (such as the Sanjaks of Jerusalem, of Gaza, and of Nablus). The British revived the Latin word "Palestina" and re-created an administrative entity that had ceased to exist with the demise of the Roman Empire. In July 1922, Great Britain was entrusted by the League of Nations to implement "the establishment in Palestine of a national home for the Jewish people." What the League of Nations meant by "Palestine" was the legal entity created by the Treaty of Sèvres (which covers today's Israel and Jordan). In September 1922, Britain informed the League of Nations that it had decided to exclude the East bank of the Jordan River (otherwise known as "Transjordan") from its legal commitment to the Jewish People.

This was a de facto partition of the League of Nations Mandate, a partition that amputated from the Jews 77 percent of the territory on which the Jewish national home was supposed to be established. The 1947 UN partition plan was an additional partition on the remaining 23 percent. In the second partition, the Jews were granted 56 percent of Western Palestine and the Arabs 43 percent –hence the claim that the 1947 partition was unfair to the Arabs (the remaining one percent was the Jerusalem region, which was to become a "corpus separatum"). But, in fact, the 1947 partition plan left the Jews with 12 percent of Mandatory Palestine – hardly an unfair deal to the Arabs.

The reason why the second partition plan attributed 56 percent of Western Palestine to the Jews was because it included the Negev Desert. Chaim Weizman, who later became Israel's first president, fought very hard to have the Negev included in the Jewish state, even though it was a bare and uncultivable area. The United Nations Special Committee on Palestine accepted his argument that the Jewish state needed enough space to absorb Holocaust survivors and Jewish immigrants.

Israel's sovereignty over the Negev, however, was challenged in the 1950s by the US and British governments. The 1955 "Alpha plan," promoted by the Eisenhower Administration, advocated territorial contiguity between Egypt and Jordan, and hence Israeli territorial concessions in the Negev.

Today, Israel's sovereignty over the Negev is being challenged by European NGOs and elected officials, who deny Israel's sovereign right to implement the Prawer Plan dealing with the resettlement of the region's Bedouin population. In July 2012, the European Parliament passed a bill calling upon Israel to stop the Prawer Plan. On October 17, 2013, the "Group of the Progressive Alliance of Socialists and Democrats" in the European Parliament took part in a seminar in Brussels on the Bedouins in the Negev. The event displayed a large poster that read: "Stop Prawer-Begin Plan, no ethnic cleansing of Palestinian Bedouins."

When Chaim Weizman finally obtained the Negev's inclusion into the proposed Jewish state, he did not imagine that Israel's sovereignty over that desert would be challenged six decades later. And today's Israeli leaders, who seem to believe that Israel will be left alone once it retreats to the 1949 armistice lines, would be well-advised to take note of the fact that Israel is being accused of "occupation" within its pre-1967 borders.

Chapter 53:

The Challenge to Israel's Sovereignty in the Negev Desert: The Case of the Bedouins

How did a domestic Israeli issue (a government program to solve land litigations in the Negev desert) become international news with harsh condemnations from the European Parliament? Why did demonstrators against the Israeli policy in the Negev wave PLO flags? And what to make of the fact that Benjamin ("Benny") Begin, a former cabinet minister and a so-called "Likud prince," who co-authored the "Prawer-Begin Plan," has provided anti-Israel NGOs with a dream scenario to smear Israel in the international media?

The word "Bedouin" comes from the Arabic *badawi*, which means "nomad." The Bedouins originated in the Arabian Peninsula, from where they spread out to the surrounding deserts in search of water and food. They were converted to Islam in the 7th century. Most Bedouins living in the Negev today arrived in the early 19th century. In the late 19th century, the Ottoman authorities started the forced sedentarization of the Bedouins. After WWII, with the emergence of independent nation-states throughout the Middle East and North Africa, the nomadic seasonal migrations of the Bedouins were halted. In most countries, forced sedentarization came with a price. In Syria, Bedouin tribalism was outlawed by the Baath party in 1958, and in Egypt the government bulldozed Bedouin-run tourist campgrounds in the Sinai in 1999.

There were an estimated 12,000 Bedouins in Israel's Negev desert after the 1948 War of Independence. They were all granted Israeli citizenship and many serve in the army's elite tracking units. The Bedouin population has grown to about 200,000, a huge growth that has generated serious issues of urban development and of land ownership. Nearly half of Israel's Bedouins live in settlements that were built illegally on state lands, without government approval and without proper urban planning. According to the Interior Ministry, and as anyone can witness on Google Earth, the Bedouins build about 2,000 new illegal structures in the Negev every year.

The Israeli government does not recognize those oriental favelas because they are illegal and because those who built them are unable to provide verifiable property rights. Indeed, most Bedouin land property claims have been dismissed by the courts for lack of evidence and based on aerial photos from pre-state days, which show that there were no cultivated lands back then in the Negev.

Israel's Bedouins kept building illegal settlements despite the government's investment in Bedouin towns in the Negev (such as Rahat, the largest Bedouin city in the world). As a result, nearly half of Israel's Bedouins live in shantytowns built on public property. Funds for illegal Bedouin building in the Negev come from the Gulf states, which funnel money through the northern branch of the Islamic Movement in Israel.

The Israeli government could and should enforce the rule of law in its lawless desert. Instead, it went for a compromise with the Bedouins over their massive land theft and crude disregard for zoning laws. This is what the "Prawer-Begin Plan" is all about.

The Prawer-Begin Plan is both immoral and delusional. It is immoral because it waives national sovereignty, rewards theft and lawlessness, and undermines the rule of law. It is delusional because the Bedouins themselves reject it, and because they are happy to pocket the land and money that the government is offering them but they have no intention to abide by the law, in return.

The Prawer-Begin Plan calls for recognizing claims to 63% of Bedouin land, attributing 54,000 acres of land to the Bedouins, and offering generous financial compensation for stolen land that will be handed back to the state (the state is paying money to get back its stolen property). In return, the land grabbing will cease and all land disputes between the Bedouins and the State will be considered settled.

Privately, the Bedouins admit they can't believe their luck. But they reject this sucker's deal, encouraged by NGOs whose agenda is to delegitimize Israel and are therefore more than happy to challenge Israel's sovereignty in the Negev.

An entire army of NGOs funded by the New Israel Fund (NIF) has been orchestrating a smear campaign against Israel in order to depict the Bedouins as helpless natives, victims of "ethnic cleansing." These NGOs include Adalah, the Association for Civil Rights in Israel (ACRI), the Negev Coexistence Forum for Civil Equality (NCF), Bimkom, and Rabbis for Human Rights (RHR). RHR went as far as to produce a movie ("Fiddler with no Roof") that compares the Bedouins to the Jewish victims of the anti-Semitic Tsarist regime.

The ultimate tragedy of the Prawer-Begin Plan is that a former "Likud Prince" has become the "useful idiot" of anti-Israel NGOs. In fairy tales, frogs turn into princes; in the Likud, the process is reversed.

Chapter 54:

Time is on Israel's Side

In its 18 January 2014 edition, *The Economist* claimed that Israel will not remain Jewish if it does not evacuate the West Bank ("demography," it says, is heading to "a Palestinian majority"). Interestingly, *The Economist*'s argument is no longer about peace but about demographics. With the Oslo Agreements having brought war and bloodshed, and with the European-imposed Arab state model crumbling under the weight of political Islam, the idea that establishing a 23rd failed Arab state is what will bring peace to this war-torn region does not even pass the laughing test. Hence has the justification for Palestinian statehood switched (at least among rational people) from peace to demographics.

But if *The Economist* and other proponents of the two-state theory have been so wrong about peace, why assume that they are so right about demographics?

For a start, Gaza is now out of the equation, and therefore calculations only apply to pre-1967 Israel and to the West Bank. The binational scare is based on a census conducted in 1997 by the "Palestine Central Bureau of Statistics" (PCBS). According to that census, there were 2.78 million Arabs in the West Bank in 1997. This figure surprised many at the time because a similar census conducted by the Israeli Central Bureau of Statistics (ICBS) in 1996 had revealed that the number of Arabs in the West Bank was of 2.11 million. How could the Arab population have increased so rapidly within a year?

The answer is that the PCBS included 325,000 overseas residents and double-counted the 210,000 Arab residents of Jerusalem. In 2011, there were about 400,000 Arabs from the West Bank living overseas. They are still included in the PCBS demographic count. According to internationally accepted demographic standards, overseas residents who are abroad for over a year are not counted demographically. The PCBS does not abide by this international standard (Israel does). The PCBS also assumed, back in 1997, that there would be an annual net Arab immigration to the West Bank and Gaza of 45,000. In reality, there has been an annual net Arab emigration from the West Bank and Gaza.

According to Israeli demographer Sergio della Pergola, Jews constitute a 62% majority between the Jordan River and the Mediterranean Sea, excluding the Gaza Strip. When Israel declared its independence in 1947, there was a one-third Jewish minority. In 1947, Roberto Bachi (a professor of statistics and founder of Israel's Central Bureau of Statistics) implored Prime Minister David Ben-Gurion not to declare independence. Bachi claimed at the time that with a population of 600,000 the Jews would become a minority by 1967. Bachi did not take into account the massive waves of "Aliya" (Jewish immigration), and his predictions turned out to be mistaken.

The Jewish population has grown so far, mostly thanks to Aliya. How does the trend look for the coming years?

Since 1992, the Arab fertility rate in the West Bank has decreased significantly and consistently (it is now of 3.2 births per woman). Within pre-1967 Israel, the Arab fertility rate has decreased from 9.23 in 1964 to 3.5 today. This decrease has been constant. Jewish fertility rates have also decreased since 1964, but very slightly: from 3.39 in 1964 to 3.0 today. But, more significantly, the Jewish fertility rate started increasing in the late 1990s (it was 2.62 in 1999, 2.71 in 2004, and 3.0 in 2011). The fertility gap between Jews and Arabs went from 5.84 in 1964 to 0.5 today. So the gap is closing The increased Jewish fertility rate since the late 1990s is not only due to traditionally high rates among Orthodox Jews, but also among secular Israelis.

Then there is immigration and emigration. While there have been constant waves of Aliya since Israel's independence (thus ensuring the growth of the Jewish population), there has been a net annual emigration of West Bank Arabs.

So to claim, as *The Economist* does, that "demography" is heading "to a Palestinian majority" is factually wrong. This does not mean, of course, that a two-third Arab minority (as opposed to the current 20%) is a good idea (it isn't). But considering the odds of a failed and hostile state surrounding Jerusalem and overlooking Tel Aviv, and considering the actual demographic trends between the Jordan River and the Mediterranean Sea, there is no reason to panic about the current deadlock's demographic consequences. The Palestinians have their own government. They admittedly don't enjoy full freedom, but then again freedom and Arab statehood have proven to be a contradiction in terms.

As for the assertion that time is not on Israel's side, it defies logic. Israel is a success story, while our Arab neighbors are plagued by civil wars, cultural decline, and economic contraction. If time is their friend, they surely don't need enemies.

Chapter 55:

What the PLO Learned from Vietnam

In January 2014, Israel's Defense Minister Moshe Ya'alon was asked to retract his accurate diagnosis of US Secretary of State John Kerry ("obsessive and messianic"), but Kerry himself keeps getting away with being outrageous and embarrassing. Kerry has referred to Vietnam as a possible model for solving the Israeli-Palestinian conflict. If Vietnam is what Kerry has in mind, Israel has good reasons to worry.

In January 1973, the Paris Peace Accord officially partitioned Vietnam into two states: North Vietnam and South Vietnam. The agreement was immediately violated by the Communists, who attacked South Vietnam and conquered it within two years. Embattled in the Watergate scandal and driven from office in 1974, President Richard Nixon abandoned the South to its fate. At least one million South Vietnamese were sent to "reeducation camps," an estimated 200,000 were executed, and millions fled their country on boats, with hundreds of thousands dying at sea.

Obviously, Kerry wasn't thinking (for a change). But he should be thanked for accidentally reminding us that the Vietnamese precedent is precisely what the PLO means by "two-state solution."

After Yasser Arafat took over the PLO's leadership in 1969, he went to North Vietnam to study the strategy and tactics of guerrilla warfare waged by Ho Chi Minh. This is also when the PLO started translating the writings of North Vietnam's General Nguyen Giap into Arabic. Arafat was particularly impressed by Ho Chi Minh's success in mobilizing sympathizers in Europe and in the United States. Giap explained to Arafat that in order to succeed, he, too, had to conceal his real goal and should use the right vocabulary: "Stop talking about annihilating Israel and instead turn your terror war into a struggle for human rights," Giap told Arafat. "Then you will have the American people eating out of your hand."

What Giap taught Arafat is that, in asymmetric struggles, the militarily weaker side can win thanks to what became an integral part of warfare in the 20th century: the media. Ultimately, Vietnam defeated both France and the United States because Giap knew how to brilliantly manipulate the media in order to convince the French and the Americans that they were sacrificing their sons for an unjust and hopeless war. This is how Giap summarized his strategy: "In 1968 I realized that I could not defeat 500,000 American troops who were deployed in Vietnam. I could not defeat the 7th Fleet, with its hundreds of aircraft, but I could bring pictures home to the Americans which would cause them to want to stop the war." It worked.

Giap not only taught Arafat the wonders of propaganda in the age of modern media. He also introduced him to the idea of "phased strategy." What the Communist Vietnamese meant by "two-state solution" was the conquest of the south in phases: first sign a "two-state" agreement with the US, and then repeal it unilaterally by invading the south after the withdrawal of US forces.

This is how Arafat endorsed the phased "two-state" strategy. In June 1974, the PLO adopted the "Phased Plan." It called for the establishment of a "Palestinian National Authority" in the West Bank and Gaza as a first step toward the "liberation of Palestine." The Phased Plan was adopted in light of the Arab failure in the 1973 Yom Kippur War and in light of the success of the "two-state" strategy in Vietnam.

In an interview with Egyptian TV *Orbit* on April 18, 1998, Arafat confirmed that the Oslo Agreements with Israel were meant to implement the 1974 Phased Plan. In an interview published on June 24, 2001 in the Egyptian newspaper *Al Arabi*, Faisal Husseini declared that the Oslo Agreements were a "Trojan Horse," the true purpose of which was the phased and total "liberation of Palestine" (the interview was published shortly after Husseini's death). On September 23, 2011, PLO official Abbas Zaki declared on Al Jazeera that the PLO's strategy is still to eliminate Israel in stages, but that saying so openly is unwise.

Mahmoud Abbas and other PLO leaders never pronounce the phrase "two states for two peoples." They only use the expression "two-state solution." What they mean by this "solution," however, is not the end of the conflict after the establishment of two distinct nation-states, but a "two-state solution" Vietnam-style. This is why Abbas refuses to recognize Israel as the nation-state of the Jewish people, this is why he insists on invading Israel with the descendants of the 1948 Arab refugees, and this is why he flatly rejects the idea of a Jewish minority in a Palestinian state.

There is really no reason for Mr. Kerry to apologize. Rather, he ought to be thanked for reminding us of the Vietnam "peace agreement" and of what the PLO means by the "two-state solution."

Chapter 56:

Tales from Palestinian Mythology

Chief Palestinian negotiator Saeb Erekat claims to be a descendant of the Canaanites. "I am a proud son of the Canaanites who were there 5,500 years before Joshua bin Nun burned down the town of Jericho" he said in Munich in February 2014.

Ah yes. For a start, the biblical figure of Joshua did not burn Jericho down, rather he caused its walls to collapse. And since the conquest of the city is estimated to have taken place some 3,300 years ago, the "Canaanites tuned Palestinians" would be, according to Erekat, 8,800 years old. Historically, the Canaanites vanished around the 8th century BCE, i.e. way before the Arab conquest of the Land of Israel in the 7th century CE.

The 1947 UN Partition Plan recommended dividing the British Mandate between a "Jewish" and an "Arab" state: it did not recommend the establishment of a "Palestinian state" because no one had ever heard of such a people at the time (as Awni Abd al-Hadi testified to the

1937 Peel Commission: "There is no such country as Palestine ... Our country was for centuries part of Syria.") As for Erekat, he comes from the Huwaitat Arab tribe, which migrated from Medina (in today's Saudi Arabia) to the Levant.

Erekat's nonsensical statements are far from being isolated: they faithfully express Palestinian mythology. The denial of facts and the re-writing of history constitute an integral part of the PLO's strategy. Back in December 1998, Dr. Yussuf Alzamili (then chairman of the history department at the Khan Yunis College) instructed Palestinian historians to re-write the "history of Palestine" so as to erase any Jewish presence.

As revealed by Eldad Pardo, a Hebrew University professor who extensively reviewed Palestinian Authority schoolbooks in 2011, Alzamili's instructions were faithfully followed. In one of the books reviewed by Pardo, the Jewish Quarter does not appear on the map of Jerusalem's Old City, and the Hebrew inscription was erased from a trilingual (English, Hebrew, and Arabic) post stamp from the British Mandate period. Other textbooks describe the Canaanites as an Arab-speaking people whose land was stolen by Jews.

At the Camp David conference in July 2000, PLO chief Yasser Arafat claimed that King Solomon's Temple had not been built in Jerusalem but in Shechem (Nablus). Arafat later changed his version and said that the Temple never existed at all. He also claimed that the Western Wall is not a remnant of the Jerusalem Temple, that it is a Muslim site called Al-Buraq and the Koran says so (it doesn't). Arafat said that the Western Wall is part of the Al Aqsa Mosque (in fact, the Western Wall is a remnant of the Second Temple, a remnant that stood 635 years before the construction of the mosque in the year 705). Those absurd claims are constantly repeated in Palestinian media, such as the PA's official daily *Al-Hayat Al-Jadida*.

As for Erekat's "Canaanite-Palestinian" theory, it is in fact a widespread Palestinian myth. Erekat himself called Jesus "Palestine's first

martyr" on 31 December 2012. On 24 December 2013, regular columnist Adel Abd Al-Rahman wrote in *Al-Hayat Al-Jadida* that Jesus is the
"son of the Palestinian people" and that "he laid the foundation of the
Canaanite identity." Al-Rahman wrote in the same newspaper on 6 May
2013 that Jesus was a "Canaanite Palestinian." On 23 June 2013, *Al-
Hayat Al-Jadida* wrote that "the Canaanite Arabs were the first to settle
and build Jerusalem. They named it Jebus and lived there uninterruptedly for thousands of years." Back in 2005, on 18 November, *Al-Hayat
Al-Jadida* wrote that "Jesus is a Palestinian, son of Mary the Palestinian."

Erekat's latest "historical" theory exposes the depth and absurdity of
Palestinian mythology.

What is the value of the PA officially recognizing the fact that Israel
is the nation-state of the Jewish people if, at the same time, it teaches
its children that the Palestinians have been living on this land for 9,000
years, that Jesus himself was Palestinian, and that the Western Wall is a
Muslim site?

An old Jewish joke says that there are three proofs that Jesus was
Jewish: He inherited his father's business; he thought his mother was a
virgin; and his mother thought he was God.

Palestinian "history" makes the joke fall flat.

Chapter 57:

Palestinian Refusal to Recognize the Jewish State leaves Israel with Few Choices

In case there still was any doubt about what Israel means by being recognized as a Jewish state, Palestinian Authority (PA) Chairman Mahmoud Abbas has made things crystal clear.

Speaking on March 6, 2014 on PA television, Abbas declared: "We shall never agree to recognize the Jewish state." He explained that he would not give up what he called the "right" of the alleged 5 million descendants of the 1948 refugees to become Israeli citizens, if they so wish. And he announced that any deal with Israel would be submitted to a referendum among the "5 million Palestinians around the world, from Canada to Japan." So, recognizing Israel as the Jewish state means waiving the implementation of the Palestinian "right of return" to Israel.

This is why Netanyahu is demanding such recognition - and why Abbas keeps rejecting it.

Abbas' most recent refusal to recognize Israel as the Jewish state because such recognition would constitute a waiver of the "right of return" was endorsed by the "Revolutionary Council" of the PA, as well as by the Arab League. Clearly, what Abbas means by a "two-state solution" is an Arab/Palestinian state without a single Jew, and a State of Israel with an Arab majority (as a result of the implementation of the "right of return" to Israel). As in the Vietnam precedent, and in line with the PLO's 1974 "phased plan," the idea is to eliminate Israel progressively by using demographic pressure and political deceit.

What Abbas means by "two-state solution" is, therefore, significantly different from the "two states for two peoples" formula. Those who refuse to give up on the "two states for two peoples" formula, however, pooh-pooh Abbas's statements by arguing that: a. Abbas doesn't really believe that the Palestinian "right of return" will apply to Israel; b. Abbas has no choice but to say what his constituents want to hear; c. The PLO already recognized Israel anyway, so this "Jewish state" recognition issue is a dud. All three arguments are demonstratively false.

If Abbas weren't serious about the "right of return," he would not have rejected the 2008 peace offer of then-Israeli Prime Minister Ehud Olmert. Abbas apologists claim that he rejected the proposal because Olmert was a lame duck. This theory flies in the face of historical evidence. Condoleezza Rice writes in her memoirs *No Higher Honor* that Olmert submitted his proposal in May 2008, and that Abbas told her that he couldn't tell four million refugees that only 5,000 would return home. In May 2008, Olmert was no lame duck: only on 30 July 2008 did he announce that he would not run for his party's leadership. Abbas mentioned to Rice the so-called "right of return," not Olmert's legal troubles, to justify his rejection of the proposal.

As for the "he has no choice but to say it" explanation, it is reminiscent of the anecdote about the man who kills his parents and then begs for the court's mercy because he is an orphan. Abbas' state-controlled media and schoolbooks keep hammering that the "right of return" is sacred and non-negotiable. If Abbas were serious about abandoning this fantasy, he would get out the message through his state-controlled media and schoolbooks. Abbas has only himself to blame for the fact that the myth of the "right of return" is alive and kicking.

The third argument is flawed, as well. In his letter to Prime Minister Yitzhak Rabin on 9 September 1993, PLO chief Yasser Arafat did recognize "the right of the State of Israel to exist in peace and security" (though not Israel's Jewishness). More significantly, however, Arafat committed in his letter to repeal the articles of the Palestinian Covenant that deny Israel's right to exist. Those articles, however, were never repealed.

In April 1996, the Palestinian National Council (PNC) announced its decision to amend the Palestinian Covenant and to appoint a commission to amend it - but the amendment was not carried out.

Abbas's firm insistence on the "right of return" will inevitably lead the current negotiations to another dead end. This is why leading Israeli figures are calling for a "Plan B." Former Israeli ambassador to the US, Michael Oren, and former IDF Chief of Intelligence, Amos Yaldin, advocate unilateral withdrawal. *Jerusalem Post* columnist Caroline Glick, in her newly released book *The Israeli Solution*, calls for full annexation.

Both disengagement and annexation are unilateral acts. Both have serious drawbacks. But in light of Abbas's words and deeds, unilateralism seems to be Israel's only way out. Israel admittedly has a choice of bad options. A negotiated two-state solution is no longer one of them.

Chapter 58:

Releasing Barghouti: Immoral and Counter-Productive

Israel's controversial scheduled release of convicted Palestinian murderers has become more controversial, still, because of the demand by Palestinian Chairman Mahmoud Abbas to release Marwan Barghouti. During the negotiations about Gilead Shalit's release, Prime Minister Netanyahu firmly rejected the demand to release Barghouti. Former *Meretz* Chairman Yossi Beilin, by contrast, called for Barghouti's release in October 2011, and again in March 2014.

By Yossi Beilin's own admission, Barghouti is no Dalai Lama, no Gandhi, and indeed no Nelson Mandela. Beilin does not go into details of his understatement. Barghouti was the leader of the military wing of the Al-Aqsa Brigades, which carried out thousands of deadly attacks (including suicide bombings) against Israeli civilians. These deadly attacks included the murder of a Greek Orthodox monk on June 12, 2001;

the murder of six Israelis during a bar-mitzvah celebration on January 7, 2002; the murder of three Israelis in a shooting spree at a Tel-Aviv restaurant on March 5, 2002. Barghouti was also directly responsible for operating the terrorist cell of Raed Karmi in Tulkarem, which carried out many deadly terrorist attacks.

As Beilin was pleading for Barghouti's release in March 2014, Alan Bauer, the victim of a terrorist attack masterminded by Barghouti, sent the following letter to President Obama: "Tomorrow will mark 12 years since our oldest son, then seven years old, and I were wounded in a suicide bombing in downtown Jerusalem. Yehonathan had the head of a screw pass fully through his right brain, while I had two screws pass through my left arm. The role of Marwan Barghouti in this attack was revealed in indictments against the heads of the Fatah terror cell behind the attack ... We cannot re-wind the clock and make the injuries and suffering disappear; the one thing we can do is to pursue justice and to do everything in our power to prevent terrorists from striking again."

Beilin advocates Barghouti's release because he believes that Barghouti is one of the rare Palestinian leaders who can "sell his people on a peace agreement with Israel." Beilin does not even bother to address the moral issue of pardoning a murder for the sake of reaching a hypothetical peace agreement. Neither does he provide any evidence that Barghouti would be able and willing to "sell his people on a peace agreement with Israel."

Beilin's contention that Ariel Sharon's visit to the Temple Mount "sparked the second intifada" is factually wrong. This claim was dismissed by the Mitchell Report of April 2001, which unequivocally stated: "The Sharon visit did not cause the Al-Aqsa Intifada." On 6 December 2000, PA minister Imad Faluji declared in *Al-Ayyam* that "the Palestinian Authority began preparing the present intifada and bracing for it since the return from Camp David at the request of President Yasser Arafat, who envisaged the intifada as a complementary measure to the Palestinian steadfastness in the negotiations and not as a protest over Sharon's visit to al-Haram al-Sharif."

Beilin is also wrong when he writes that Barghouti got "caught up in the violent escalation of the second intifada." On March 4, 2000 (four months before the Camp David summit), Barghouti declared in an interview to *Akhbar al-Khalil*: "Whoever thinks that the issues of the final-status agreement ... can be resolved by negotiations alone is deluding himself ... The negotiations over these issues must be accompanied by a campaign on the ground, that is, a confrontation. We need dozens of campaigns like the 1996 al-Aqsa tunnel." Beilin claims that Barghouti sees in an agreement with Israel "a paramount Palestinian interest." But which kind of agreement? For Barghouti, such agreement must include the "return" of all Palestinian refugees and their descendants to Israel (interview on Israel's Channel 2 TV, 18 October 2000).

Beilin's wrong assessments and unsubstantiated claims were proven disastrous with the Oslo Accords. But at least, Beilin himself expressed his own doubts when those agreements were signed. In an interview he gave the *Maariv* daily on November 26, 1993, Beilin declared that "should it transpire that [the Palestinians] fail to stem terrorism, then [Oslo] will have to be regarded as a temporary agreement, and with all the difficulty involved, we will have no choice but to renege on it."

Beilin never acted on his own warning after the Oslo agreement produced a massive wave of terrorism (including during the 1992-1996 Labor government). Instead, Beilin has spent the past two decades blaming his blunder on technicalities.

In his book *Touching Peace* Beilin explains that the Yom Kippur War shattered his faith in Israel's leaders. With the passing of time and with the tragic outcome of his political theories, Beilin has come to incarnate, and even to surpass, the hubris and dogmatism of leaders he rightfully criticized as a youngster.

Chapter 59:

Israel is Giving in to a Hollow Palestinian Threat

The 20-year-old circular "negotiations" between Israel and the PLO, and Israel's acquiescence to release murderers for the mere sake of pursuing those negotiations, are perhaps best summarized by a famous scene from the 1964 James Bond movie *Goldfinger*. Tied to a table by Dr. Goldfinger, Bond helplessly watches the approaching laser beam about to cut him in half. "Do you expect me to talk?" asks Bond. "No Mister Bond," answers Goldfinger. "I expect you to die. There is nothing you can talk to me about that I don't already know."

Admittedly, Israel does not wish to be blamed for the failure of the current negotiations. Recent history, however, provides ample evidence that Israel will be blamed, regardless of its concessions and that the Palestinians will be absolved, regardless of their intransigence.

We have already seen this movie. It had the same ending after the Camp David conference of July 2000, after the Clinton parameters of December 2000, and after the Olmert proposal of May 2008. In each case, Arafat and Abbas simply got away with saying "no" and could even rely on countless apologists in Israel and in the US to justify their obstructiveness. The hope for a different outcome of a fourth attempt defies logic. In fact, President Obama made sure to clarify in advance, via his March 2014 interview with columnist Jeffrey Goldberg, which side the United States intends to blame for the present talks' expected failure.

Another possible, and unconvincing, explanation for Israel's insistence on maintaining the negotiations is the Palestinian "threat" to initiate unilateral moves at the UN and to "ask membership in all UN agencies" as PA official Mustafa Barghouti warned and as Mahmoud Abbas actually did in April 2014 when he announced that the Palestinians were applying for acceptance to 15 UN agencies. This also is a movie that Israel has seen many times.

In December 1988, the UN General Assembly recognized the "State of Palestine" proclaimed by Yasser Arafat in Algiers a month earlier. Since the signature of the 1993 Oslo Agreement, the PLO has threatened many times to unilaterally declare statehood, even though it did just that in 1988 in Algiers. In November 2011, the virtual "State of Palestine" became a member of UNESCO. On November 29, 2012, the General Assembly granted non-member observer state status to the virtual "State of Palestine." Full UN membership, however, requires the Security Council's approval (Russia's veto has been blocking Kosovo's membership just as the US veto has been blocking Palestine's).

Would it be that terrible if the virtual "State of Palestine" were to become a member of additional UN agencies such as the World Meteorological Organization? Obviously, the PA's threat is about obtaining membership at the International Criminal Court (ICC) and about pressing cases against Israel. That "threat," however, is hollow, as well.

PA Chairman Mahmoud Abbas has more than once threatened to "go to the ICC" to challenge Israeli settlements in the West Bank, as well as Israeli retaliatory military actions in the Gaza Strip. In January 2009, the PA formally accepted the jurisdiction of the ICC, but in April 2012, the ICC Prosecutor declared himself unable to determine whether "Palestine" is a state for the purpose of the Court's jurisdiction. Theoretically, the General Assembly's vote from November 2012 defines "Palestine" as a state for the purpose of the ICC's jurisdiction. But since Israel is not a member of the ICC, the Court can only have jurisdiction over the territory of "Palestine" – a territory that is not defined, since there never was a Palestinian state in the past. Even the General Assembly's November 2012 decision did not determine the borders of "Palestine." The resolution does refer to the former armistice lines between Israel and Jordan, but those temporary lines, drawn more than 60 years ago, were not an international border.

In any case, the General Assembly has no authority to determine the borders of states. Nor does it have the authority to supersede Security Council Resolutions (according to Security Council Resolution 242, the future borders between Israel and its neighbors shall be negotiated). Moreover, since the Oslo Accords grant Israel exclusive criminal jurisdiction over Israelis in the West Bank, the PA cannot delegate to the ICC a territorial jurisdiction that it does not possess.

Finally, the use of the ICC by Palestinian "lawfare" is a double-edged sword. Israel could give the Palestinians a taste of their own medicine by joining the ICC and suing the "State of Palestine" for its deliberate targeting of, and incitement against, Israeli civilians.

Israel's decision to free convicted murderers for the sake of renewing negotiations is not only morally abject but it is also strategically misguided as well, since the Palestinians will undoubtedly "go to the ICC" the moment negotiations fail, and because the "threat" of adding the ICC to the repertoire of Palestinian "lawfare" is hollow.

Chapter 60:

John Kerry Should Have Learned from Dennis Ross

When US Secretary of State John Kerry coerced Israel and the Palestinian Authority (PA) into renewing negotiations in July 2013, Israel was supposedly given a choice between a settlement freeze and the release of Palestinian prisoners. The Israeli government chose (wrongly in my opinion) the second option. And yet, Kerry is now partially blaming the failure of the talks on Israel's decision not to implement a settlement freeze which never was part of the deal.

Kerry also mentioned Israel's refusal to release the fourth batch of Palestinian prisoners. He did not mention the fact that, on 19 March 2014, Fatah spokesman Ahmad Assaf publicly declared that the PA successfully blackmailed Israel into releasing prisoners (by "threatening" to pursue membership at UN bodies) and that the only purpose of negotiating (or pretending to negotiate) with Israel is to complete the release of prisoners.

One wonders where Kerry has been for the past two decades, and whether he ever consulted with US diplomats who learned one or two things about previous botched attempts to reach an agreement between Israel and the PA.

In his book *The Missing Peace,* former Middle East envoy Dennis Ross rebuts Arafat's claim that he had been promised 90% of the West Bank by the late Yitzhak Rabin: "In an earlier briefing I told the president that this was one of Arafat's mythologies; Rabin had never done that, and, in fact Rabin had envisioned only going to between 70 and 80 percent."

Not only did Rabin envision relinquishing no more than 80 percent of the West Bank (without territorial "compensations"), but his vision of an agreement with the Palestinians was not as far-reaching as what subsequent Israeli prime ministers agreed to, in vain. Two weeks before his assassination, Rabin spelled out in the Knesset his vision of a final agreement. He said that, in the end, there would be a "Palestinian entity" that would be "less than a state." Rabin also pledged that Israel will "not return to the June 4, 1967 lines" and that it would retain control over the Jordan Valley "in the broadest meaning of that term." Rabin also pledged never to release convicted Palestinian murderers.

In August 2000, Arafat told Dennis Ross that Prime Minister Ehud Barak had gone "further" than Yitzhak Rabin would have agreed. "Much further," Ross corrected him. At Camp David, Barak agreed to the establishment of a Palestinian state on 92 percent of the West Bank and to Palestinian sovereignty over the Arab neighborhoods of Jerusalem. Before the Camp David conference, Osama Elbaz (President Hosni Mubarak's diplomatic adviser) said that the dream of the Palestinians was to obtain 91 percent of the West Bank. Asked by Dennis Ross why, then, they had rejected Barak's offer of 92 percent, Elbaz candidly replied: "They raised their expectations."

President Clinton's "parameters" of December 2000 went even further than Barak's offer. The Palestinians would have ended-up with between 94 and 96 percent of the West Bank (with a 1 to 3 percent land swap with pre-1967 Israel). East Jerusalem (including the Temple Mount) would have become the capital of a Palestinian state. Israel would have recognized the Palestinian "right of return" while retaining the right to decide which Palestinians would be entitled to Israeli citizenship. Israel accepted the Clinton parameters. Arafat rejected them.

As Dennis Ross writes: "Rabin and Peres had made a historical choice; Arafat made only a tactical move ... Arafat went to Oslo after the first Gulf War not because he made a choice but because he had no choice ... Oslo was his salvation. As such, it represented less a transformation than a transaction."

Mahmoud Abbas is no better. In May 2008, he rejected Ehud Olmert's offer, which went further than the Clinton parameters. Together with the land swaps, the Palestinians were now getting the totality of the West Bank (and of the Gaza Strip). Olmert also agreed to relinquish the Temple Mount and to accept thousands of Palestinian refugees. But, as Abbas explained to US Secretary of State Condoleezza Rice, that wasn't good enough because "five million refugees," and not only a few thousand, should be allowed to become Israeli citizens.

Benjamin Netanyahu was ready to go much further than Yitzhak Rabin in the current talks with the Palestinians. As opposed to Rabin, Netanyahu accepted the establishment of a Palestinian state. As opposed to Rabin, Netanyahu agreed to free convicted murderers. And, contrary to Rabin, Netanyahu seems to have accepted the principle of land "compensation."

It is a fact that in the past two decades Israel has made significant concessions, while the Palestinians have made none.

Dennis Ross concludes in his book *The Missing Peace* that the Palestinians should "learn from the past and not simply deny it or reinvent it." John Kerry would be well advised to learn that lesson, as well.

Chapter 61:

Failure of Two-State Solution will not make Israel an Apartheid State

Once again, US Secretary of State John Kerry has caused an uproar with his thoughtless remarks, this time by claiming that Israel will turn into an apartheid state and will not remain Jewish without a two-state solution. The most generous explanation for Kerry's serial blunders is that he is a simpleton. Whatever the explanation, Kerry's last claim actually deserves discussion.

His argument is factually wrong.

Israel and the Palestinians do not need a peace agreement in order to get out of each others' hair. Israel pulled out of the Gaza Strip in 2005 without a peace agreement, and it can repeat a unilateral pullout from most of the West Bank, while completing the unfinished separation fence along the 1949 armistice lines. In such a scenario, the West Bank would turn into a missile launching pad, just like the Gaza Strip, and the IDF would deter rocket firings by aerial bombardments, as it does in Gaza. Israel will be relieved of the so-called "demographic threat," it will face two manageable security nuisances (from the West Bank and from Gaza), and the conflict with the Palestinians would revolve around the Palestinian claims to areas that Israel would retain and annex in the framework of a unilateral pullout.

I am not advocating such a policy (as opposed to a growing number of Israeli academics and journalists). I am just stating the obvious fact that Israel does not need a peace agreement with the Palestinians in order to preserve its Jewish majority. In the case of a unilateral Israeli pullout, there would be no apartheid in Israel, just as there is no apartheid in Israel today. Israel's Arabs would continue to be the only free Muslims and Christians of the Middle East.

Israel will not become an apartheid regime in the scenario of a "unitary state," either. What is meant by a "unitary state" is the full annexation of the West Bank and the granting of Israeli citizenship to West Bank Arabs. Since Israel's unilateral pullout from the Gaza Strip in 2005, this territory with its 1.7 million Arabs is now outside the demographic equation.

What would be the actual demographic consequence of a full and formal annexation of the West Bank?

The cliché that people are entitled to their own opinions but not to their own facts does not seem to apply to Middle Eastern demographics. Experts and self-proclaimed experts cannot agree on the actual number of Arabs in the West Bank. The figures of the Palestinian Central Bureau of Statistics (PCBS) are contested by former Israeli diplomat Yoram Ettinger and by the American-Israel Demographic Research Group (AIDRG). Their findings have, in turn, been rejected by Sergio DellaPergola (a statistics professor at Hebrew University) and by Ian Lustick (a political science professor at the University of Pennsylvania).

Guy Bechor, a Middle East expert who teaches at the Interdisciplinary Center Herzliya (IDC), recently claimed that, based on the latest data of the Israel Central Bureau of Statistics and of the CIA, there is a stable and even growing Jewish majority between the Mediterranean Sea and the Jordan River (excluding the Gaza Strip). According to Bechor, there has been a sharp drop in Muslim birthrates throughout the Middle East in recent years (including among Palestinian Arabs: the average Palestinian birthrate went down from 5 in 2003 to 2.7 in 2013), and a significant increase in Jewish birthrates in Israel (including among secular Israelis, for whom the average birthrate is now 4).

Even by a conservative estimate, there is a nearly two-thirds Jewish majority between the Jordan and the Mediterranean (excluding Gaza), a majority that will stabilize and grow even without taking into account a likely increase in Jewish immigration to Israel. Were Israel to grant full citizenship to West Bank Arabs, Israel would still have a two-thirds Jewish majority, and there would be no apartheid. I am not advocating that policy either, but full annexation would not make Israel an apartheid state. It would significantly increase Israel's Arab population (admittedly to different degrees, depending on whom you ask), but there would still be a Jewish majority.

A peacefully negotiated two-state solution has failed once again. This paradigm was based on the delusional assumption that Israel should expect Palestinian cooperation for the preservation of a secure and democratic Jewish state. Unilateralism is the only way out. It is for Israelis to decide which kind of unilateralism they wish to implement: unilateral withdrawal or annexation. Both options have serious drawbacks, but the choice between them must be discussed. Indeed, this discussion will likely redefine Israel's right-left divide and replace the defunct and irrelevant debate about the two-state paradigm.

Chapter 62:

Israel's Hierarchy of Error

Gilad Shaar, Eyal Yifrach and Naftali Frankel were kidnapped five kilometers away from my home. When news of the kidnapping reached my family, the same thought crossed our mind: it could have been us. My teenage children study in the Gush Etzion area and they sometimes hitchhike to get home. On Fridays, I jog on our beautiful Judean hills, often passing a parked car of Arab farmers who tend their vineyard and could ambush me. Why then, many ask, expose yourself and your children to such danger? Indeed, "settlers" are not only accused of being irresponsible toward their children but also toward their country: they prevent Israel from enjoying peace, they take away precious public funds, and they bring international isolation upon Israel.

When I made *aliyah* (i.e., immigrated to Israel) from Paris as a young man, I was asked why I was putting my life in danger by joining a war-torn country (Israel had recently gone through the trauma of Saddam Hussein's Scuds). When cafés and buses exploded on a nearly daily basis in Israel's cities at the beginning of the millennium, I felt safer in my "settlement" of Efrat than on the streets of Tel Aviv. When Hezbollah rockets rained down on northern Israel in the summer of 2006, Haifa residents found a safe haven in our "settlement." When Prof. Zeev Sternhell wrote in May 2001 that Arab terrorists should spare him and focus instead on the "settlers," he expressed his personal wish but ignored that of the Arabs themselves. Neither Hamas nor the PLO draw a demarcation line between "good" and "bad" Israelis.

Arab terrorism indiscriminately targets Jews on both sides of the "Green Line" and the cause of that terrorism is not Israel's presence beyond that line. The three kidnapped teens are believed to be in Hebron, a city where 67 Jews were massacred by Arabs in August 1929 (38 years before Israel captured the West Bank). Between 1949 and 1967 (when all Israelis lived on the "right" side of the Green line), thousands of Israelis were targeted and killed by infiltrators from the Gaza Strip and from the West Bank. Nachshon Wachsman was kidnapped in October 1994 near Ben Gurion airport. When Israel removed all its settlements from the Gaza Strip, it was "rewarded" with thousands of rockets. When Prime Ministers Ehud Barak and Ehud Olmert offered (in July 2000 and in May 2008 respectively) to remove most Israeli settlements in exchange for peace, they were rebuffed.

So, no, I do not expose myself and my children to extra danger and I do not prevent the advent of peace. Nor do I feel like a burden to my country: I work hard and pay taxes as do my neighbors. Efrat has one of the most educated and productive populations in Israel, as well as an unusual high number of young IDF officers.

The theory that settlements isolate Israel doesn't wash, either. Historically, Israel's worst period of international isolation was in 1953: the Soviet Union had cut diplomatic relations with Israel; in the United States, the new Eisenhower Administration embarked on an openly pro-Arab policy; France and Israel had not yet developed their military relationship. Israel renewed its diplomatic relations with the Soviet Union in 1991 and established diplomatic relations with China and India in 1992: all this happened under the "pro-settlement" government of Yitzhak Shamir and before the Oslo process. The occupation of northern Cyprus does not isolate Turkey and the occupation of Western Sahara does not isolate Morocco. International relations are governed by interests, not by feelings.

So the Israeli left is both delusional and dishonest when it tries to create a "moral hierarchy" between Israelis on both sides of the green line. What was more "kosher" about expelling the Arabs of Lydda (today's Lod) in 1948 and destroying their houses than about building villages on the bare hills of Judea? My house in Efrat is built on an empty hill. My office at Tel Aviv University is built on the destroyed Arab village of Sheikh Muwannis. As argued by *Haaretz* columnist Ari Shavit in his book *My Promised Land* (2013), the Zionist left tries to obliterate the fact that, for the Arabs, the true historical scar, the "Naqba," is the exodus and destruction of 1948, not the mere change of sovereignty of 1967. Amos Oz castigates "settlements" but his kibbutz Hulda is named for the Arab village of Hulda that was destroyed by Israel in 1948. As Shavit writes: "It's Hulda, stupid."

Exactly. It is perfectly legitimate to argue that Israel should withdraw to the green line. But to say that doing so will bring us tranquility and moral vindication is silly and dishonest. Freedom, especially when you are Jewish, comes at a price regardless of where you live.

Chapter 63:

Why Does Israel Supply Gaza with Electricity and Cement?

When my children ask me why Israel supplies Hamas with the cement and electricity used to build tunnels for the storage of rockets and the kidnapping of Israelis, I refer them to an unforgettable scene from the movie *Ice Age 4*. In it, terrified prehistoric animals flee the apocalypse but two of them keep laughing. "Doesn't it weigh on you?" asks a puzzled co-traveler, "that the world might be ending?" Trying to give a serious answer, the two merry fellows reveal their secret: "We are very, very stupid."

Is Israel just being stupid, or does it have a legal obligation to supply the Gaza Strip with cement and electricity? As explained by Prof. Avi Bell from Bar-Ilan University in a recent paper published by the Kohelet Policy Forum, a think-tank, Israel is under no legal obligation to provide Gaza with electricity.

Article 23 of the Fourth Geneva Convention states, inter alia, that the contracting parties shall allow the free passage of food, clothing and medicine to children under 15 and to pregnant women (the article mentions neither electricity nor cement). The Gaza Strip is not a contracting party to that Convention, nor is it occupied by Israel. Israel, for its part, is not a party to the First Protocol Additional to the Geneva Conventions of 1977, whose Article 70 imposes wider duties upon belligerents (though it doesn't mention electricity and cement, either). Even if these articles were to apply to the conflict between Israel and Gaza, Israel would still be under no obligation to supply electricity to Gaza because the parties are required "to allow the free passage" of goods (Article 23) and to "allow and facilitate" their "rapid and unimpeded passage" (Article 70) - but not to supply them.

On the specific issue of electricity, targeting electric plants during wartime is a widespread and accepted practice. How can a country be allowed to destroy its enemy's electric supply but be required to guarantee that supply? This is why Prof. Yoram Dinstein, a renowned expert on international law and on the laws of war, writes in his book *The Law of Belligerent Occupation:*

"The notion that a Belligerent Party in wartime is duty bound to supply electricity and fuel to its enemy is plainly absurd."

Israel is accused of imposing a blockade on Gaza but, in truth, Israel only maintains a maritime military blockade, whereas the Gaza Strip is landlocked because of Egypt. Israel prevents the entry of Iranian weaponry to Gaza by sea, while Egypt does not want Gazans to enter its territory. A 2011 UN panel chaired by Sir Geoffrey Palmer concluded that Israel's naval and military blockade of Gaza is both justified and legal under international law. Indeed, even Palestinian Authority Chairman Mahmoud Abbas said in June 2010 that Israel's military maritime blockade was necessary in order to prevent Hamas from obtaining more weapons. Four months ago, in March 2014, the Israel Navy intercepted a shipment of missiles sent by Iran to the Gaza Strip.

While Israel supplies the Gaza Strip with electricity, water, food, medicine, and all non-military items, Egypt prevents the entry of such goods into Gaza. In January 2008, Gazans forced their way through the Egyptian border, only to be pushed back. In June 2010, the Arab Physicians Union asked Egypt to allow the entry of 400 tons of food, blankets and electric generators into Gaza, but the Egyptian government rejected the request. Israel's Security Cabinet, on the other hand, approved, also in June 2010, the entry of non-military material into the Gaza Strip.

Once Operation Protective Edge is over, Israel will have to decide what to do about Gaza. Admittedly, the Israel Defense Forces have not been able to deter Hamas the way they have been deterring Hezbollah. Should Israel reoccupy Gaza or, instead, repeat its military operations every two years? A "political solution" is obviously impossible with Hamas. As for the PLO, it was toppled by Hamas in Gaza in 2007. Were Israel to reinstall the PLO there, it would likely be toppled again. Justice Minister Tzipi Livni said that the Gaza Strip must be demilitarized. This statement doesn't even pass the laughing test. Who will keep Gaza demilitarized? The PLO? The Blue Helmets? Or the French Foreign Legion, maybe?

The US should use its economic leverage over Egypt so that Cairo ends its land blockade of Gaza and partially retakes control of that enclave (at it did between 1949 and 1967). Egypt would rather keep Gaza sealed, but that policy is inhumane and counter-productive. There are no ethnic, religious, and language differences between Arabs on both sides of the border between Egypt and Gaza. With massive economic aid from donor countries, Egypt could and should re-integrate the Gaza Strip.

Chapter 64:

Losing the Battle, Winning the War

"Palestine makes you dumb" wrote Bret Stephens, the *Wall Street Journal*'s foreign affairs columnist. This is because of the "Palestine Effect" which Stephens defines as "the abrupt and total collapse of logical reasoning, skeptical intelligence and ordinary moral judgment." *The Economist*'s latest cover story on Israel ("Winning the Battle, Losing the War") confirms Stephens' diagnosis. When it comes to Israel, this otherwise insightful British magazine makes a selective use of reason (not least because its articles are levelheaded while its caricatures are bigoted: this week's "KAL's cartoon" depicts Benjamin Netanyahu furiously smashing miniaturized Gazans with an oversized and blood-soaked hammer).

The Economist's editorial on the 2014 Gaza war recognizes that Hamas is anti-Semitic and barbaric, and that Israel is both a true democracy and a successful economy. It admits that Israel's critics apply double standards to Israel and to other democracies at war; that the BDS (Boycott, Divestment and Sanctions) campaign is not only about occupation but also about undoing Israel as a Jewish nation state; and that anti-war demonstrations in France degenerated into anti-Semitic vandalism. By British standards, this reads like a Zionist manifesto.

Then the "Palestine Effect" begins. "The destruction is driving support towards Hamas and away from the moderate Palestinians who are Israel's best chance for peace" goes the editorial. How does *The Economist* know that the war boosted Hamas' popularity rather than the opposite? In fact, Hamas won the 2006 Palestinian elections after Israel pulled out of the Gaza Strip and after Israel's acting Prime Minister Ehud Olmert publicly stated that Israel was ready to pull out of the West Bank as well were the Palestinians to choose "moderate leaders." At the time, the only destruction was that of Jewish villages (by Israel) and of the greenhouses left in Gaza by the Jews (which the Arabs could have preserved to their own benefit, but which they chose to destroy instead).

As for the "moderate Palestinians," who and where are they? Is that the PLO, which never repealed its charter, and which recently formed a unity government with Hamas before the war in Gaza erupted? The PLO, which posted on its Facebook page on 21 January 2014 (half-a-year before the current destruction that supposedly threw "moderate Palestinians" to the arms of Hamas) that "we shall turn Tel-Aviv into a ball of fire?" The PLO, which posted on its Facebook page two weeks ago (on July 22) that "Mahmoud Abbas concluded his brief speech with the first verse of the Quran that permits Muslims to wage war for Allah" and on July 23 that "the land is forbidden for the enemy, and all Shabiba (Fatah's student movement) members are potential Martyrs (Shahids) for our beloved Palestine?"

The Economist is correct when it argues that Israel should not ignore criticism simply because many critics of Israel are unfair and ignorant. But how does it expect to be taken seriously when it claims that the so-called two-state solution "remains the only one that will work" and that "time is not on Israel's side?"

The two-state solution keeps working in theory and failing in practice. The 1937 and 1947 partition plans were accepted by the Jews and rejected by the Arabs. In 2000 and in 2008, Israel agreed to the establishment of a Palestinian state in the West Bank and in Gaza, but both Yasser Arafat (in 2000) and Mahmoud Abbas (in 2008) rejected the Israeli offer because it did not include the "right of return" (which would undo Israel's Jewish majority and is therefore incompatible with the "two-state solution").

As for the claim that "time is not on Israel's side" it sounds fantastic given the fact that Israel is a success story surrounded by failed states. Obviously, what *The Economist* means is that demographics is not on Israel's side. That is highly disputable. The Gaza Strip is out of Israel's demographic equation since 2005. Even if Israel were to fully annex Judea and Samaria, it would retain a two-third Jewish majority. That majority would not only be stable but would likely grow because Arab birthrates have been declining since the early 1990s, because Jewish birthrates are on the rise since the late 1990s, and because Jewish immigration to Israel keeps growing (especially from Europe).

So it is not that Israel won the current battle but is losing the war. Actually, the very opposite is true. Israel lost the Gaza battle because a small democracy closely scrutinized by the world media cannot crush its enemies as America did in Afghanistan and as France did in Mali. But Israel is winning the war because its population is more resolute than ever, because our enemies are busy killing each other, and because more and more people in the West (though admittedly not *The Economist*) realize that Israel is the first, but not the last, target of Jihad.

Chapter 65:

Back to the Iron Wall

When Ariel Sharon announced his "disengagement plan" at the 2003 Herzliya Conference, he claimed that "the purpose of the disengagement plan is to diminish terrorism and to provide security to Israel's citizens," and that his plan "would improve our quality of life and boost our economy." Since the plan's implementation in August 2005, over 12,000 rockets have been fired into Israel and more than 5 million Israelis are living under threat of rocket attacks. Around the Gaza Strip, Israelis live in constant fear of a missile landing on their house and of terrorists popping out of their living room from an underground tunnel.

Israel has had to fight three wars to tackle the effects of the 2005 retreat (Operation Cast Lead in 2008, Operation Pillar of Defense in 2012, and the ongoing Operation Protective Edge). As for the economy, Hamas has proved its ability to shut down Ben-Gurion airport and to bring Israel's tourist industry to its knees. Operation Protective Edge is estimated to have cost $3.6 billion (direct military expenses and indirect damages to the Israeli economy). When Sharon submitted the disengagement plan to his Likud constituents in a referendum (whose results he ignored), he claimed that "after disengagement, the international community will no longer be able to assert that the Gaza Strip is occupied." This also proved to be delusional.

Israel left Gaza, but Gaza never left Israel. In fact, Gaza is more lethal from without than from within.

Sharon came up with his disengagement plan to surprise his enemies from their rear, just as he did three decades earlier when he crossed the Suez Canal. In 2003, Sharon was under criminal investigation and his forced resignation had become a foregone conclusion. In addition, the Geneva Initiative put him on the defensive. His cynical tactical move proved masterful: the state prosecutor suddenly and mysteriously dropped all charges against him, and Israel's left-leaning media re-branded its bête noire to Israel's greatest statesman since Ben-Gurion.

But Sharon's disengagement plan also expressed the zeitgeist of the Herzliya Conference, reflecting an emerging consensus among Israelis. After Arafat had rejected the Camp David proposal in July 2000 and the Clinton parameters in December 2000, even Israel's most starry-eyed peaceniks were altogether horrified and disillusioned. In October 2000, Shlomo Avineri, an enthusiastic supporter of the Oslo process, published an open letter to Edward Said in *The Jerusalem Post* saying: "You were right, Edward: compromise doesn't work ... Thank you again for your honesty." Benny Morris, who started his academic career as a "new historian" on the far left of Israel's political spectrum said in an interview with *Haaretz* in 2004: "When the Palestinians rejected the proposal of [prime minister Ehud] Barak in July 2000 and the Clinton proposal in December 2000, I understood that they are unwilling to accept the two-state solution. They want it all. Lod and Acre and Jaffa."

Unilateral disengagement was meant to solve a two-variable equation: A= Reaching a peace agreement between Israel and the PLO has proven to be impossible; B= Maintaining the status quo might spell Israel's demographic doom. In theory, unilateral disengagement was clever. In practice, it was a disaster. With the recent failed attempt, once again, to reach an agreement with the PLO, some have been floating the idea of unilaterally withdrawing from Judea and Samaria. As the Gaza precedent has proved beyond a doubt, a unilateral withdrawal from Judea and Samaria would bring Jihadists, rockets and tunnels to the immediate vicinity of Jerusalem, Tel-Aviv, and Ben-Gurion international airport. With psychotic Jihadists taking over Iraq and Syria and heading toward Jordan, and with Iran about to reach the nuclear threshold, the idea of repeating disengagement just to relieve Israel's demographic concerns is tantamount to treating a headache with a guillotine.

The realistic left acknowledged the conceptual error of Oslo in 2000. It now recognizes that the unilateral plan-B must also be shelved.

In the 1930s, the Arab-Revolt incited by Hadj Amin al-Husseini, Britain's betrayal of Zionism, and the rise of Hitlerism in Germany convinced David Ben-Gurion that the Jews could not mortgage their self-determination on the Arab's impossible consent. This was the underlying idea developed by Zeev Jabotinsky in his 1923 article "The Iron Wall" –an idea that Ben-Gurion ended-up endorsing. Today, even the former "new historian" Benny Morris espouses the "Iron Wall" ethos for lack of better options.

"For a left-winger, you sound very much like a right-winger, wouldn't you say?" Morris was asked by Ari Shavit in the above mentioned *Haaretz* interview. "I identify with Albert Camus" said Morris. "He was considered a left-winger and a person of high morals, but when he referred to the Algerian problem he placed his mother ahead of morality. Preserving my people is more important than universal moral concepts."

Chapter 66:

Mahmoud Abbas Cannot Rewrite International Law

Palestinian Authority (PA) Chairman Mahmoud Abbas announced in August 2014 that he was about to unveil a diplomatic initiative involving the United Nations (UN). Unnamed officials in Abbas' entourage claimed that the PA would ask the UN Security Council to set a deadline for a total and unconditional Israeli withdrawal from Judea and Samaria (the "West Bank").

This is not the first time that Abbas "threatens" to go to the UN. In September 2011, he submitted to the UN Secretary General an official membership application from the "State of Palestine" (the Security Council announced two months later that it was unable "to make a unanimous recommendation" on the application). In November 2012, the UN General Assembly upgraded the status of the PLO from "observer entity" to "non-member observer state." That vote, however, did not establish a "Palestinian state."

UN General Assembly resolutions are not binding (as opposed to Security Council resolutions). They are mere recommendations. The General Assembly does not, and cannot, establish states. Contrary to a widespread misconception, the UN did not establish the State of Israel. On November 29, 1947, the General Assembly only approved the recommendation of UNSCOP (the United Nations Special Committee on Palestine) to divide the British Mandate between a Jewish state and an Arab state. This approval was a non-binding opinion, which became moot the moment it was rejected by the Arab states, in any case. What established the State of Israel were seven decades of Jewish immigration and hard labor and a war for independence which the Jews fought by themselves without any help from the UN (though with the military help of a Soviet satellite –Czechoslovakia). Likewise, the General Assembly resolution from 29 November 2012 did not establish a "State of Palestine."

What Abbas is trying to do, therefore, is to involve the Security Council by creating an artifice that would supposedly metamorphose the West Bank into the legal equivalent of Kuwait in 1991 or of South Korea in 1950 – when the Security Council allowed the use of force to liberate those two violated and conquered sovereign states. Abbas' initiative, however, is legally groundless.

Israel is not occupying a formerly sovereign state, and therefore its status is not comparable to that of Iraq in Kuwait or that of North Korea in South Korea. When Israel conquered Judea and Samaria in a war of self-defense in June 1967, it did not cross an international border but a temporary armistice line defined as such by the 1949 Rhodes Agreements. Israel did not conquer a sovereign country but a territory that had been illegally conquered and annexed by Transjordan for 18 years (from 1949 to 1967) and that had been approved by the League of Nations for the self-determination of the Jewish people. The League of Nations did not grant national rights to some "Palestinian people," because no one had ever heard of such a people back then.

Indeed, UNSCOP dismissed the Arab claim that the League of Nations Mandate was illegal. Its report said that the Arabs "have not been in possession of it [Palestine Mandate territory] as a sovereign nation," and that there were "no grounds for questioning the validity of the Mandate for the reason advanced by the Arab states." If it was illegal for the League of Nations to recognize the Jews' national and historic rights over their original country, then all the nation-states that emerged from the dismembering of the Ottoman and Austro-Hungarian empires are illegal, as well.

It is precisely because Israel did not conquer a sovereign country in June 1967 but recovered, in a war of self-defense, a territory that that been assigned to the Jewish people by the League of Nations and that had been illegally controlled by Transjordan for 18 years, that UN Security Council Resolution 242 (of November 1967) did not demand an unconditional and total Israeli withdrawal from the territories conquered in 1967. Had it been so, Resolution 242 would have been adopted under Chapter 7 of the UN Charter (which allows the use of force to impose the respect of international law, and which was applied against North Korea in 1950 and against Iraq in 1991). Rather, Resolution 242 was adopted under Chapter 6 of the UN Charter, which calls upon belligerents to settle their disputes peacefully.

Resolution 242 determines the guidelines for a peaceful resolution of the Arab-Israeli conflict, such as an Israeli withdrawal "from territories" (and not "from the territories") it conquered in 1967, in exchange for peace and defensible borders. Not only does 242 not require an Israeli withdrawal from the former and temporary armistice lines delineated by the Rhodes Agreements, but it also sets as a condition for an agreed-upon Israeli withdrawal full peace agreements and defensible borders. It is undisputable that the 1949 temporary armistice lines cannot constitute defensible borders. As for Abbas, he wants an Israeli withdrawal but without peace.

Mahmoud Abbas can rewrite history in Palestinian schoolbooks and even believe in his own propaganda, but he cannot rewrite international law.

Chapter 67:

Palestinian Mythology is Keeping Jerusalem United

In the Hebrew calendar, the 28th of the month of Iyar marks the 47th anniversary of the reunification of Jerusalem in the Six Day War. "Jerusalem Day," as it is called in Israel, is mostly celebrated today by religious Zionists. Some Israelis reject the celebration altogether, sharing the Arab view that East Jerusalem is "occupied." Those contrasting views among Israelis are not new. Right after Israel liberated its capital 47 years ago, the Chief Rabbi of the IDF, Rabbi Shlomo Goren, blew the shofar at the Western Wall and on the Temple Mount, and proclaimed that the Jewish people had recovered their holiest site for the first time since the destruction of the Second Temple by Titus in 70 CE. By contrast, then Defense Minister Moshe Dayan asked himself, while contemplating the Old city after Israel's victory: "What do I need all this Vatican for?"

The Jewish "clash of civilizations" is powerfully retold by Yossi Klein Halevi in his book *Like Dreamers: The Story of the Israeli Paratroopers Who Reunited Jerusalem and Divided a Nation* (2013). Halevi follows the story of the Israeli paratroopers who liberated Jerusalem. On one side of the spectrum is Yoel Bin-Noun, a Zionist Rabbi who was a student at the "Merkaz Harav" yeshiva (Talmudic academy) and who became one of the founders of the "Gush Emunim" settlement movement. On the other side of the spectrum is Udi Adiv, an anti-Zionist Marxist radical who secretly traveled to Syria in the 1970s to join the PLO guerilla.

Since the Six Day War, successive Israeli governments have been ambivalent about Jerusalem. Israel formally applied Israeli law to all of Jerusalem but let the Islamic Waqf administer the Temple Mount. It passed and enforced a law guaranteeing freedom of worship for all religions and the preservation of all holy places, but it does not let Jews pray on the Temple Mount.

Yet even secular Israelis who would otherwise willingly part from "that Vatican" have to admit that only under Israeli sovereignty have Jerusalemites of all faiths been free and have all holy places been preserved.

When the Old City of Jerusalem was under Jordanian control from 1949 to 1967, 58 synagogues were destroyed (including the landmark "Hurva" synagogue), and the Jewish cemetery on the Mount of Olives was desecrated, with gravestones being used to pave roads. After the Palestine Liberation Organization (PLO) took partial control of the Jerusalem Waqf with the 1993 Oslo Agreements, the Waqf undertook massive digging and building activities on the Temple Mount, destroying countless Jewish relics from the First and Second Temple periods. As a result, even staunchly secular public figures such as novelists A.B. Yehoshua and Haim Guri joined the Committee for the Prevention of Archeological Destruction on the Temple Mount.

The archeological vandalism of the Muslim Waqf has had the unexpected and ironic effect of turning iconic figures of Israeli secularism into the defenders of the Holy of Holies. Similarly, the PLO's official denial of the existence of the Jerusalem Temples has put Israel's Laborite old guard on the defensive. Thus, former Labor Prime Minister Ehud Barak replied to Arafat's "Temple denial" that the Temple Mount is "the Archimedes point" of Israel's existence.

"Temple denial," however, is a recent phenomenon that stands in stark contrast with Islamic tradition.

During the early Muslim period (between the 7th and 11th centuries), the Arabs used to call Jerusalem and the Temple Mount, interchangeably, Bayt Al-Maqdis, an Arabic transliteration of the Hebrew Beit Hamikdash (Temple). A 1924 tourist guidebook published by the Supreme Muslim Council says the Temple Mount is the site of the Jerusalem Temple. Araf al-Araf, a Palestinian Arab historian who, as a close friend of Haj Amin al-Husseini could hardly be suspected of pro-Zionist sympathies, wrote in his 1951 book "Tariah Al-Quds" that the Temple Mount "was bought by David to build the Temple, but it is Solomon who built it in 1007 BCE."

Not only is "Temple denial" a recent phenomenon; so is Islam's interest in the Temple Mount. Muhammad made a point of eliminating pagan sites of worship and of sanctifying only one place: the Kaaba in Mecca. In the 14th century, Islamic scholar Taqi al-Din Ibn Taymiyya ruled that sacred Islamic sites are to be found only in the Arabian Peninsula. The Koran does not mention Jerusalem, and Muslim Jerusalemites pray toward Mecca. They do not take off their shoes in the space between the Dome of the Rock and the al-Aqsa Mosque.

Without Zionism, there would have been no Muslim sanctification of the Temple Mount and no Arab denial of the existence of the two Jerusalem Temples.

Israelis may still be divided about their reunited city; but their ideological divide is thankfully being narrowed by modern Palestinian mythology.

Part Three:

International Challenges – Israel on the World Chessboard

Chapter 68:

Palestine is the Promised Land of Western Nihilism

Is it a coincidence that the last flotilla that desperately tried to reach Gaza in July 2011 set sail from Greece? While the Greek economy was imploding at the time, Gaza's was booming. Those angry Hellenes trying to break the blockade (and to fix their ships) looked more like boat people than like freedom fighters.

Crowds were protesting daily (and violently) in Athens in 2011. At the time, the Greek government passed an austerity plan through parliament to get a bailout from the EU, but the rescue plan will only temporally keep afloat a bankrupt economy incapable of paying its debts and of reforming itself. Greece is insolvent: its debts amount to 160% of its GDP. The government cannot finance its own budget deficit, and it would run out of money without help from the EU and the IMF.

Gaza, by contrast, enjoyed a two-digit (16%) GDP growth in 2010. The *New York Times* reported at the time that a new mall and two luxury hotels had just opened in Gaza. Imports are unrestricted except, of course, for weapons and ammunition.

So those European citizens of bankrupt countries kept afloat by German and US taxpayers (via the EU and the IMF respectively) seem to have figured out that moving to Gaza is really what the "audacity of hope" was all about. In reality, of course, the "flotillas" have a sinister agenda.

One of the key organizers of the "second flotilla" to Gaza was Muhammad Sawalha, a Hamas activist living in Britain who is among the signatories of the "Istanbul Declaration." This document states, among other things, that "the Islamic nation" has an obligation to provide weapons to the Palestinians "so that they are able to live and perform the jihad in the way of Allah Almighty." Other flotilla organizers included Walid Abu al-Shewarib, a member of Hamas as well as of the German branch of the Muslim Brotherhood, and Amin Abu Rashid, a Hamas leader from Holland.

Hamas' strategy to end the maritime arms embargo imposed by Israel on Gaza is simple: create a clash with the IDF, portray Hamas as the victim and Israel as a bully, and gather international support for the "liberation" of Gaza. This strategy partially worked with the 2010 "Gaza Flotilla" (French daily *Libération* called Israel a "pirate state"). As the delightful "We Con the World" satire put it: "We'll make them all believe that the Hamas is Momma Theresa… We'll make them all believe the IDF is Jack the Ripper."

That Hamas-Europe is organizing a flotilla to help Hamas-Gaza makes sense. They are, after all, co-workers and brothers-in-arms. It is the support of self-proclaimed progressive Jews and Western liberals for those medieval anti-Semites and misogynists that seems unexplainable. Actually, there is an explanation.

Among the flotilla crusaders were people like Adam Shapiro and Dror Feiler. The former is a Brooklyn Jew who says he doesn't consider himself Jewish, who married an Arab girl, and who visited Arafat in his compound in March 2002 at the height of the PA's terror war against Israel. The latter was raised on a Communist Kibbutz, moved to Sweden, and renounced his Israeli citizenship. If people like Shapiro and Feiler care so much about freedom and human rights, how come they don't organize flotillas to Syria and Libya where people are being butchered by their tyrants? The answer is that Shapiro and Feiler have an obsession with Israel because Israel acts as a mirror of what they want to bury: their Jewish identity.

As for European and American leftists, Israel is a painful reminder of their failed attempt four decades ago to rid Western society of its Judeo-Christian basis. "Palestine" has become the mythical promised land of Western nihilism. Unlike the real boat people, those freedom fighters wannabes from Europe and America are not fleeing massacres and starvation. But they, too, hope that wandering on the sea in front of cameras will salvage them from misery.

Chapter 69:

Erdogan's Dhimmi Problem: Can Islam come to terms with Jewish Sovereignty?

Under Islamic law ("Shariah"), non-Muslims (such as Christians and Jews) are mostly free to practice their religion in private but are discriminated and treated as second-class citizens, or "dhimmis." When the Jews regained their independence in 1948, they not only rebelled against "dhimmitude."[16] They also regained and freed, like the Spaniards after the Reconquista, a land once ruled by Islam. To Muslims, this was - and still is- a double offence.

Turkey's Islamist Prime Minister, Recep Erdogan, has taken upon himself to make Israel a "dhimmi state." Edorgan was raised as a Sufi Muslim and was imprisoned in 1998 for singing out loud that "The mosques are our barracks, the domes our helmets, the minarets our

---

[16] The word "dhimmitude" was coined by author Bat Yeor to describe the life of dhimmis.

bayonets and the faithful our soldiers." While mainstream Western media are at pains to describe Turkey's Islamist AKP Party as "moderate," Erdogan himself declared on Kanal D TV in August 2007 that describing Islam as moderate "is offensive and an insult to our religion." Erdogan has been embracing the presidents of Iran and Sudan. While Sudan's president is accused of genocide by the International Criminal Court, and while Turkey has been asked to apologize for the Armenian genocide, Erdogan has declared that "No Muslim can perpetuate genocide."

Erdogan comes from an anti-Jewish tradition. His political mentor Necmettin Erbakan was an anti-Semite. As soon as he became Prime Minister in 2003, Ergodan adopted a hostile policy toward Israel. In March 2004, Erdogan called Israel a "terrorist state" following the elimination of Hamas founder Ahmad Yassin. In February 2006, he received Hamas leader Khaled Mashal in Ankara. In January 2009, Erdogan publicly humiliated Shimon Peres at the Davos conference. In October 2009, the Turkish state television started airing fiction series showing Israeli soldiers intentionally murdering Palestinian children. In November 2009, Erdogan declared that he would rather meet Sudanese President Omar al-Bashir than Israeli Prime Minister Benjamin Netanyahu. In March 2010, Erdogan claimed that the Temple Mount, Hebron and Rachel's Tomb in Bethlehem were never Jewish sites.

While Erdogan's hatred of Israel is authentic, his public outbursts at Israel are opportunistic. Those outbursts are the easiest way for him to be acclaimed as a hero by Islamists both in Turkey and around the world. The Israeli government made the right decision by refusing to behave as a "dhimmi state." The attitude of the Obama administration, by contrast, is irresponsible and scandalous. Instead of making Erdogan pay the price for his foreign policy choices, the Obama administration has been hopelessly trying to appease him.

Erdogan is ultimately responsible for the death of his co-citizens aboard the "Mavi Marmara." He is the one who sent out the jihadist organization Insani Yardim Vakfi (or IHH) to militarize Gaza and arm Hamas. Yet, President Obama called Erdogan after the Marmara incident to express "his deep condolences for the loss of life and injuries resulting from the Israeli military operation." The Palmer Report recently released by the UN (an organization not known for its pro-Israel bias) says unambiguously that Israel's naval blockade of Gaza was legal, that Turkey should have done more to stop the flotilla, and that Israeli soldiers were brutally attacked and had to use force in self-defense. And yet the Obama administration is still asking Israel to apologize instead of scolding Turkey for its troublemaking.

Rather than stopping Erdogan from bullying Israel and from destabilizing the Middle East with his irresponsible policies, the Obama administration has adopted an appeasing stance, which in turn is encouraging Erdogan who is now threatening to go to war in order to lift the siege of Gaza.

It is precisely because the Obama administration has opted for appeasement that Israel must show steadfastness. As Churchill has said, an appeaser is someone who feeds the crocodile hoping he will be eaten last. Israel cannot afford to play that game. But steadfastness is not enough. Israel should go on the offensive by exposing Erdogan's hypocrisy to the world.

Doing so is no rocket science. While scolding Assad for shooting at Syrian demonstrators, Erdogan recently ordered air strikes in Kurdistan, killing over 100 Kurds. While saying that Israel should accept the establishment of a Palestinian state, Erdogan is adamant not to allow an independent Kurdish state to emerge. While Erdogan urges Israel to negotiate with Hamas, he himself recently declared that Turkey "considers it a disgrace to sit down at the negotiating table with [the Greek Cypriots] at the United Nations" as Turkey just celebrated its 37 year-old occupation of Cyprus. And in 2006, after obtaining Syria's capitulation to Turkey's occupation and annexation of the Alexandretta Province,

Erdogan offered Israel to broker a peace deal with Syria based on Israeli, not Syrian, capitulation over the Golan.

While Erdogan must be made to understand that Jews are no longer dhimmis, we Israelis have to realize that the end of dhimmitude does not only mean the end of humiliation. It also provides the ability, and perhaps even the duty, to make our enemies get a taste of their own medicine.

Chapter 70:

Why Do European Socialists Like Hanukah?

Hanukah, as we know, commemorates a miracle. In November 2010, I witnessed one firsthand.

I delivered a lecture in Toulouse, France, on "The Political Ideology of Israel's De-Legitimization." On the conference's panels were French intellectuals and public figures who refuse to write and talk in Newspeak, such as Richard Prasquier (President of CRIF), Yvan Rioufiol (*Le Figaro*'s least politically correct columnist), Philippe Karsenty (a media analyst who's been fighting, with guts and resilience, the French state TV channel France 2 on the Al-Dura blood libel), Robert Redecker (a French philosophy professor who lives under permanent police protection because of a fatwa issued against him for a critical article he once wrote on Islam), and Jacques Tarnero (a French author and filmmaker who argues that European opinion makers are trying to absolve Europe from the Holocaust by accusing Israel of behaving like its former torturers).

There was also a French Senator, Jean-Pierre Plancade. Originally a member of the French Socialist Party, he is now an independent.

Plancade ended his talk by begging the Jews to bring light to the world, and he referred to the upcoming Hanukah holiday to make his point. Coming from a politician who rose within a party that is both staunchly secular and sympathetic to the Palestinian narrative, those were striking words indeed.

Why do these people side with Israel and the Jews? Because they realize that their own freedom is threatened by Israel's enemies. As Jacques Tarnero explained during the conference, he feels like France is going through another Dreyfus Affair: The France 2 channel knows and privately admits that it is lying about the Al-Dura Affair, but the media and the Government are circling the wagons around Charles Enderlin because Raison d'État and corporate solidarity come before the truth. Who cares if Daniel Pearl was beheaded to "avenge" the blood of Muhammad Al-Dura, and if Al-Dura has become an icon to justify the murder of Jews?

The panel I attended in Toulouse was not an isolated event. More and more Europeans are speaking out against the assault on truth and freedom, against the appeasement of Islamism, and against the demonization of Israel. Former Spanish Prime Minister José María Aznar says that if Israel is vanquished, the West is finished. His "Friends of Israel Initiative" is gaining new recruits by the day. German Chancellor Angela Merkel recently declared that "multiculturalism in Germany has failed" –a polite way of saying that most of Germany's Turkish immigrants never integrated into German society. More and more political parties in Europe are gaining ground on platforms that call for a restriction of Muslim immigration and for the defense of Western values.

Merkel's comments came in the wake of a new book that is both hugely popular and controversial: *Deutschland Schafft sich ab* ("Germany Does Away with Itself") by German politician Thilo Sarrazin. Like Plancade, Sarrazin is a left-winger who, because he is speaking out his mind about Islam and the West, is being vilified and ostracized.

For what did Sarrazin write, after all? That Germany's immigrant Muslim population is reluctant to integrate and tends to rely more on social services than to be productive, and that the Muslim population growth may well overwhelm the German population within a couple of generations at the current rate. True, Sarrazin also made silly comments on gene and intelligence, but that's not why he is under attack. He is under attack for addressing a topic that is unofficially but effectively banned from public discourse.

The fact that Sarrazin's book sold out after a few days says a lot about what many Germans want to hear and about what their elites want to silence.

As Matthias Matussek from *Der Spiegel* wrote: "Political correctness is silencing an important debate … Sarrazin's findings on the failed integration of Turkish and Arab immigrants are beyond any doubt. He has been forced out of the Bundesbank. The SPD wants to kick him out of the party, too. Invitations previously extended to Sarrazin are being withdrawn. The culture page editors at the German weekly *Die Zeit* are crying foul and the editors at the *Frankfurter Allgemeine Zeitung* are damning Sarrazin for passages he didn't even write. But what all these technicians of exclusion fail to see is that you cannot cast away the very thing that Sarrazin embodies: the anger of people who are sick and tired—after putting a long and arduous process of Enlightenment behind them—of being confronted with pre-Enlightenment elements that are returning to the center of our society."

Instead of trying to please Europe's appeasers, Israel should assist Europe's *résistants*. As more and more Europeans are showing courage and moral clarity, let us do what they expect from us: lead the struggle of the Maccabees and dissipate darkness with the lights of Hanukah.

Chapter 71:

Vive le Québec libre !

In March 2011, the French University of Montréal (l'Université du Québec à Montréal, or UQÀM) made me feel good: After I delivered my lecture there, I was surrounded by four bodyguards that rushed me through a backdoor and then into a car that drove off speedily. What fun: I felt like a head of State kept away from the mob or like James Bond narrowly escaping a Soviet trap. Alas for my ego, the true reason for this drama is that I am Israeli.

Although I was invited to give a talk on a non-controversial issue (the geopolitics of energy), what made my presence controversial is that I am Israeli. Some students and their representatives demanded the cancellation of my invitation on the grounds that hosting an Israeli would be an affront to the University, since Israel is "committing genocide in Palestine." The faculty did not reject the demand outright. Rather, it organized a vote on the issue (a majority of professors rejected the cancellation of my lecture).

Those students who unsuccessfully tried to prevent me from speaking at UQÀM posted around the campus a picture and a quote of mine with the purpose of discrediting me. But both the picture and the quote they picked actually made me proud. The picture (downloaded from my website) shows me in my IDF uniform. As for the quote (also taken from my website), it goes like this: "Saying that you are anti-Zionistic but not anti-Semitic is like saying that you have nothing against the Jews as long as they are vulnerable." As a Jew, I am proud to be a reserve soldier in the IDF. And as a public speaker and author, I like it when people quote my favorite punch lines.

After I finished my talk, the "questions" from the audience were mostly hysterical (and long) tirades on the "crimes of Zionism." One student accused me of being a "war criminal" because of my affiliation with Bar-Ilan University (I'm a fellow at BIU's Center for International Communication). Since BIU runs a couple of programs at the Ariel Academic College, that makes me a war criminal. To which I replied that the Ariel Academic College, as opposed to the Tel-Aviv University campus (where I teach), is not built on the ruins of an Arab village, and that as opposed to my Arab colleagues in Israeli universities, I as a Jew cannot become a professor in an Arab country.

I kept going on with more embarrassing facts that made my accusers look silly. To the point, indeed, that they simply left the room —only to come back later on to scream out "Zionists, Murderers!" with loudspeakers.

"Anti-Semitism is the snobbism of the poor" wrote Jean-Paul Sartre in his *Réflexions sur la question juive*. Today, anti-Zionism is the snobbism of the ignorant. On many campuses, all you need in order to acquire "respectability" without knowledge is to adopt an outraged attitude toward Israel.

The audience at UQÀM was not only composed of Arab inciters and of native local simpletons. In fact, a few people came to me at the end of my talk (and Q&A session) to shake my hand and say thank you. Some were Jews, many were Christians. They all said the same thing to me: "Thank you for saying the truth, thank you for restoring our pride, thank you for giving us hope."

Those people know that their freedom is at stake. So do more and more Europeans and Americans. They realize that the intellectual terrorism, irrationality and hypocrisy that characterize the treatment of Israel in the West are ultimately a threat to the West itself.

The list of *résistants* is growing by the day. It includes Canadian Prime Minister Stephen Harper who declared recently that "those who threaten the existence of the Jewish people are a threat to all of us;" Former Spanish Prime Minister José Mariá Aznar, who says that "Israel's struggle is our struggle;" Spanish liberal journalist Pilar Rahola, who has written that "if Israel is destroyed, our freedom, modernity and culture will be destroyed;" Italian member of parliament Fiama Nirenstein, who has declared that "the libelous accusations against Israel are an embarrassment to the world;" French Socialist senator Jean-Pierre Plancade, who implores Israel to win for the sake of his freedom; former German Social-democrat senator Thilo Sarrazin, who claims that Islam is overtaking Germany; and British journalist Melanie Philips who shows how Britain is sinking into irrationality

When de Gaulle exclaimed « Vive le Québec libre! » from a balcony at the Montréal City Hall on July 24, 1967, he meant « freedom » from Anglo-Saxon cultural supremacy. Today, Québec's freedom, and indeed the freedom of the West, is once again threatened by the hatred and irrationality of which the Jews are always the first, but not last, victims in line. Now that we Jews are sovereign and free, our former oppressors expect us to prevail for their own sake. What an irony —and what a responsibility.

Chapter 72:

The Sheep, the Wolf, and the Village's Idiot

The ideological divide between idealists and realists stems from two sets of assumptions about human nature and reality. Realists are wary of men's real intentions, while idealists rely on human goodwill: the state of nature is heaven to Rousseau and hell to Hobbes because the former believes that man is naturally good and socially perverted, while the latter assumes that man is 'solitary, poor, nasty, brutish and short.' Realists and idealists also see reality from two different viewpoints: to the realist, reality is a given to which man needs to submit and adapt his will; to the idealist, reality is man-made and can therefore be subjugated to man's will. Machiavelli teaches the Prince how to adapt to reality, while Kant implores him to change and adapt it to his ideals.

These two different sets of assumptions – Is man good or bad? Is reality stronger than human will or the other way round? – are at the core of the ideological divide between Right and Left in open societies, and this debate applies to foreign policy.

This debate is ideological precisely because one cannot prove scientifically whether man is intrinsically good or bad, and whether reality is amendable to human will. History, however, provides a useful list of examples that can help make a reasonable guess. So does the gauging of failed and successful policies. In that regard, President Obama has made a remarkable contribution (albeit inadvertently) to an age-old philosophical inquiry.

In his Cairo speech (June 2009), Barack Obama tried to sweet-talk the Muslim world into abandoning its animosity toward America. A year-and-a-half later, it would be an understatement to say that his overtures have been rebuffed. Turkey, once a close ally of the US and Israel, has become Iran's foremost apologist. Iran continues to defy the United States by pursuing its nuclear program and by progressively overtaking Iraq and Lebanon. The Talibans are as determined as ever in Afghanistan and in Pakistan. Syria keeps deepening its ties with Iran and Hezbollah despite (or because of) America's gestures (such as resending a US Ambassador to Damascus). And now, the pro-Western and anti-Islamist regime of Ben-Ali has been overthrown in Tunisia, while Hezbollah is about to effectively run Lebanon's next government.

It would be admittedly unfair to focus on President's Obama's failure. For his confidence that Islamists would be tamed with a good speech is hardly different from Woodrow Wilson's assumption that the League of Nations would keep German militarism in check, or from Jimmy Carter's belief that Khomeini was a human rights activist.

Wilson, Carter and Obama failed to recognize that some ideologies are based on the need for a sworn enemy. As Professor Emmanuel Sivan explains in his book *The Clash within Islam*, jihad creates a dichotomy "between Muslim and all external, heretical groups, which are fundamentally evil ... Thus coexistence over time is certainly not a plausible political option." Indeed, no amount of goodwill or elevated rhetoric can appease ideologies that make the eternal struggle against "The Enemy" a divine commend or the founding principle of collective identity.

Naïveté has a price –a price that America has been able to afford thanks to its power and geography. Israel, by contrast, has no strategic tolerance for silliness (though it certainly has a political attraction to it). A popular Israeli joke offers the ultimate answer to the realism vs. idealism debate in foreign policy: Isaiah prophesizes that one day the sheep will lie down peacefully next to the wolf; yet even when the dream comes true it will be safer to be the wolf.

Especially, the joke could have added, if the sheep is being watched by the village's idiot.

Chapter 73:

Europe's Favorite Occupation

For the European Union (EU), labeling Hezbollah as a terrorist organization amounts to a tough philosophical question. But labeling Israeli products from Judea and Samaria as non-Israeli entails no such travails.

While there is no question that Hezbollah is a terrorist organization, defining Judea and Samaria as "occupied territory" is debatable at best.

In international law, a territory is considered occupied after being conquered from a sovereign country. Judea-Samaria was neither a sovereign country nor part of a sovereign country when it was conquered by Israel in June 1967. During the 1948 War, and as a result of the 1949 Armistice Agreements, the Hashemite Kingdom conquered and annexed the hilltops of what was supposed to become part of an Arab state according to the 1947 Partition Plan. This annexation was never recognized by the international community (with the exception of Britain and Pakistan). So Israel did not seize a territory from a recognized and legal sovereign country. Rather, Israel recovered a territory that had been granted to the Jewish people for self-determination by the Balfour Declaration (1917), by the Sèvres Treaty (1920), and by the League of Nations Mandate (1922) which was confirmed by the UN Charter in 1945. Those are binding international documents, as opposed to the 1947 Partition Plan, which was a mere recommendation (like all UN General Assembly resolutions) and which became moot the moment it was flatly rejected by the Arab League. The "West Bank" is thus a disputed, not an occupied, territory.

There are many disputed or occupied territories in the world. Yet the EU does not discriminate against products from those disputed or occupied areas.

China rules over Tibet and Xinjiang against the will of those territories' populations. Xinjiang's indigenous Uighurs used to constitute 90% of the province's population sixty years ago; today they are a mere 60%. More and more Tibetans are rebelling against Chinese rule over their country: since March 2011, over 100 Tibetans have torched themselves. Uighurs and Tibetans can hardly count on the West to gain independence. China holds over one trillion dollars of US Government bonds, and its army constitutes a credible military threat to US allies in East Asia, such as Japan and Taiwan. As for France, President Sarkozy did speak out about Tibet and even met with the Dalai-Lama. But at the G20 Summit in London in April 2009, Chinese President Hu Jintao refused to meet his French counterpart and demanded a French declaration "recognizing" that Tibet belongs to China. Sarkozy duly complied.

In 1979, Morocco conquered all of Western Sahara, a country that was supposed to become independent after the end of Spanish rule. The Moroccan government ruthlessly represses the Polisario Front and transfers settlers to its southern colony. But the West and the UN couldn't care less.

In 2008, Russia conquered Abkhazia and it actively promotes Russian settlement there. The US and the EU, however, feel that the last thing they need is to pick a bone with Russia over its settlers in Abkhazia.

In 2009, the Sri-Lanka government decimated in a bloody war the Tamil independence movement. The world has mostly been relating to this massacre as an internal issue.

I am not suggesting that Israel should be left alone just because the above undemocratic regimes are ruthless. The West rightfully expects Israel to live up to its own democratic standards and to abide by international law. But then the West should apply the same principle to itself.

In June 2013, the UN renewed the status of French Polynesia as a "non-self-governing territory" and it asked France to set Polynesia on the path to full independence. Altogether, there are 16 territories in the world defined by the UN as "non-self-governing territories." The French typically claim that their overseas territories prefer their present status to full self-determination and independence. That claim certainly doesn't wash with New Caledonia.

Since 1986, the United Nations Committee on Decolonization has included New Caledonia on its list of non-self-governing territories. Following secessionist unrest and military repression, the French Government agreed in 1988 to hold a referendum on Caledonian independence within ten years. In 1998, the French Government convinced the pro-independence Kanaks to push off the referendum by another fifteen to twenty years. Since 1998 plus 15 equals 2013, Kanaks have been inquiring lately about their referendum. France's reply is that independence will mean the end of all economic aid —undoubtedly a powerful deterrent.

France denies independence from far-away subjects, but people are denied their independence in the European Union itself. Cyprus, an EU member, has been partially occupied by Turkey since 1974. The Turks have displaced about 200,000 Greek Cypriots to the south. They have brought in Turkish settlers and built a separation fence. The EU has given-up on solving this conflict and it has come to terms with the status-quo.

Spain will not let the Basques and Catalonians secede, and Britain has been fighting to keep Northern Ireland within the UK. There is no philosophical debate in Europe about whether or not IRA, ETA or FLNC fighters should be labeled terrorists or militants.

True, Catalonians have Spanish citizenship and Caledonians are French nationals. The comparison with the Palestinians can therefore not be stretched. Still, there are in the European Union disputed territories and peoples whose independence is denied.

After the EU announced its decision to discriminate against Israeli products that come from a disputed area, the Israeli Foreign Ministry tried to convince the EU to back down by claiming that discriminating against those products would affect the income of Arabs employed in factories located beyond the Green Line. Hence is the Israeli Foreign Ministry depicting Israel as a convicted criminal asking the Court not to jail him so that he can keep supporting his beaten wife and children.

Rather than using this pitiful argument, Israel should give Europe a taste of its own medicine: if the EU has a new policy of discriminating against products coming from disputed areas, Israel should reciprocate with products coming from New Caledonia, Catalonia, and the Basque Region. After all, there might be Israelis who care about the Kanaks' right to full self-determination, and they should be allowed to express their displeasure at France by not buying products coming from that colonial relic.

That Israel's diplomatic establishment would regard so logical and reasonable a step as excessively aggressive, if not insolent, is a scandal in itself.

Chapter 74:

The EU is entitled to its own Opinions, not to its own Facts

The European Commission announced in July 2013 that Israeli institutions operating beyond the 1949 Armistice Lines shall no longer be allowed to apply for "grants, prizes and financial instruments" from the European Union (EU). The practical implication of this decision is that Ariel University, as well as Israeli companies operating beyond the 1949 line, will be barred from participating in the next European R&D program to be launched in 2014.

In 1996, Israel became the first non-European country to be associated with the EU's "Framework Program for Research and Technical Development." Nearly 1,500 Israeli companies and universities received funding in recent years, making the EU Israel's largest source of public research funding.

Theoretically, the Hebrew University might also be affected, having one of its two campuses in the eastern part of Jerusalem ("Mount Scopus"). Israel was granted access to Mount Scopus in the 1949 Rhodes Armistice Agreement, but Jordan refused to allow Israel access to the enclave within its territory. Does the EU consider Mount Scopus within the 1949 Armistice Lines? Will the new European decision discriminate in grant allocations between Hebrew University researchers working at the Givat Ram campus in the western part of Jerusalem and those working from the Mount Scopus campus? And what about the student dorms on Mount Scopus? Some are built within the 1949 enclave, some outside. Will doctoral students applying for an EU grant have to specify in which dorms they lodge? One wonders if the European Commission is aware of these intricate legal technicalities.

Besides those technicalities, the Commission's decision raises two fundamental legal issues.

The first has to do with the very legality of the decision itself. Trade and scientific relations between Israel and the European Union are regulated by the 1995 Association Agreement that entered into force in 2000. Article 77 of the Agreement states that the EU "shall not give rise to discrimination between Israeli nationals or its companies or firms." Clearly, the Commission's decision does create such discrimination. At the time of the document's signature, the EU did not state or clarify that the Association Agreement was not valid beyond the 1949 Armistice Lines. The Commission's decision, therefore, constitutes a post-facto breach of the 1995 Agreement.

The second legal issue has to do with the Commission's declared stance that any Israeli presence beyond the 1949 Armistice Lines constitutes illegal occupation. The demarcation line that separated Israel from Jordan between 1949 and 1967 was never an internationally recognized border. It was a temporary armistice line, defined as such by the 1949 Rhodes Agreement. In international law, a territory is considered occupied when conquered from a sovereign country. Such was not the status of the West Bank in June 1967. There was no sovereign country there when Britain abandoned its mandate in 1948. As for the conquest and annexation of the West Bank by the Hashemite Kingdom in 1949, it was never recognized by the international community (except for Britain and Pakistan). As for UN Security Council 242, it clearly does not consider the 1949 line a permanent future border, nor does it require Israel to withdraw to that line. So why does the EU define as illegal a situation that is not considered as such by international law?

Finally, the European Commission's decision to discriminate against institutions operating from disputed territories can potentially backfire against the EU itself. For there are, within the EU, territories that are disputed and populations whose full independence is denied. Cyprus, an EU member, has been partially occupied by Turkey since 1974. The EU and the international community have been unable to resolve the conflict between Greek and Turkish Cypriots, just as they have been unable to resolve the dispute between Israelis and Palestinians. Yet the EU does not penalize Turkey over the deadlocked situation in Cyprus.

Then there are the overseas French territories, the full independence of which is still denied. Since 1986, the United Nations Committee on Decolonization has included New Caledonia on its list of non-self-governing territories. In June 2013, the Committee renewed the status of French Polynesia as a "non-self-governing territory" and it asked France to set Polynesia on the path to full independence. Should the European Commission exclude France's possessions in the Pacific from applying for EU grants and funding?

Clearly, the European Commission's decision stands on a shaky legal ground and applies different standards to Israel and to the EU itself. As the saying goes, people are entitled to their own opinions but not to their own facts. The EU seems to feel immune from that principle.

Chapter 75:

The EU is an Obstacle to Peace in the Middle East

The claim that Israeli "settlements" constitute "an obstacle to peace" has become a self-evident European dogma. The truth, of course, is that there was no peace between Israel and its Arab neighbors when none of those "settlements" existed (between 1949 and 1967); that the Palestinian leadership rejected twice Israel's offer to dismantle most of its settlements (by Ehud Barak in July 2000 and by Ehud Olmert in September 2008); and that when Israel unilaterally dismantled all its settlements in Gaza in 2005, it was "rewarded" by thousands of rockets.

Rather than settlements, one of the major obstacles to peace between Israel and the Palestinians is the so-called "right of return." By this euphemism, the Palestinians want to flood Israel with about five million immigrants who are the descendants, or alleged descendants, of the 600,000 Arabs who left their homes during Israel's War of

Independence. This would turn Israel into a bi-national state with an Arab majority. Except for a minority of post and anti-Zionist Israelis, even the most dovish members of the Israeli Left consider the "right of return" a non-starter.

While the Zionist Left generally pooh-poohs the "right of return" as a mere rhetorical tool in which the Palestinians themselves don't actually believe, the fact is that the Palestinian refusal to give in on that issue is what caused the rejection of Barak and Olmert's peace proposals. Moreover, neither Arafat nor Abbas ever tried to educate their people into admitting that the "right of return" is unrealistic; on the contrary: both leaders have made the "right of return" a central tenet of Palestinian nationalism and an issue whose abandonment is an act of high treason.

The fantasy of the "right of return" is kept alive and indeed nurtured by UNRWA, the United Nations Agency created in 1949 to handle the issue of Palestinian refugees. There are two main reasons why UNRWA perpetuates and even aggravates the "Palestinian refugee problem." First, the mandate of UNRWA (as opposed to the mandate of the United Nations High Commissioner for Refugees, or UNHCR) is not to integrate refugees into their host countries but to support them and to subsidize their lives as second-class citizens in camps. Second, UNRWA applies the definition of "refugees" to the descendants of the refugees, while UNHCR limits this definition to the refugees themselves. Hence has the world's number of refugees decreased from 60 million in 1947 to 17 million today, while the number of "Palestinian refugees" has increased from 600,000 in 1948 to five million today.

UNWRA is thus a major obstacle to peace. Had UNHCR been in charge of Palestinian refugees (UNHCR handles all the world refugees except Palestinian refugees), the issue would have been solved a while ago. First, were Palestinian refugees defined as such according to UNHCR criteria, about 50,000 Palestinian refugees would still be around today, most of them elderly. Second, UNRWA collaborates with the discriminatory policies of countries such as Lebanon and Jordan by subsidizing the confinement of Palestinian refugees in camps instead of integrating them into countries with which they have no language, ethnic, and religious differences.

Dismantling UNRWA and transferring the fate of the remaining actual Palestinian refugees to UNHCR would thus remove a major obstacle to peace.

The EU has just decided to do the very opposite by granting UNRWA a €72 million donation. This decision is not only an affront to the Palestinian refugees themselves, since it contributes to the perpetuation of their status of segregated and pauperized minorities among their Arab brothers. It is also an affront to the cause of peace. The EU, in effect, has just signed a big check that will fund a major obstacle to peace.

While the EU did somewhat realize the Kantian vision of democratic peace within its borders (although with a little help from the United States, whose army protected Europe from the Soviet Union during the Cold War), Europe's contribution to peace outside of the Old Continent's borders has been dismal. From Rwanda to the former Yugoslavia, the EU has been powerless at best and part of the problem at worst. The EU (formerly EEC) promoted the PLO in the 1970s and did not welcome the Camp David Agreements of 1979. Although the Oslo Agreements were technically not made in the EU (Norway is not an EU member), the European recipe for peace in the Middle East has failed miserably and tragically.

The EU's recent decision to fund UNRWA belongs to a long history of counter-productive efforts. But, mostly, it confirms the fact that the EU is an obstacle to peace in the Middle-East.

Chapter 76:

Mali, An Opportunity for Israel

For years, al-Qaeda has been trying to overtake the countries of the Sahel region, and Mali was its main target. Without the French military intervention in January 2013, Mali would have become the first Islamic state of the Sahel region, followed by neighboring Niger, a country on which France heavily depends for its uranium imports. Yet, by defending its interests, France has opened a diplomatic opportunity for Israel.

Mali's interim President Dioncounda Traoré had very harsh words for the Arab members of the African Union on the closing day of the organization's summit in Addis Ababa on January 27, 2013. Addressing the Arab states that had condemned France's air attacks against the Islamists – such as Egypt and Tunisia – Traoré questioned their refusal to condemn the horrific actions inflicted by the Islamists on the people of Mali, but willingness to express outrage against a French intervention.

Mali's political leaders and opinion-makers openly express their feeling of betrayal by the Arab countries, especially those run by Islamist regimes; after cutting ties with Israel under Arab pressure, they expected those same Arab states to aid them in their fight against the Islamists. Instead, the Arab countries condemned France, not the Islamists. A recent article in the Malian daily *Le Matin* directed its critique specifically at the Palestinians and their ambassador to Mali, Abu Rabah. In addition to being the PLO's ambassador, Abu Rabah is the head of Mali's diplomatic protocol. He is ubiquitous in the media and has managed to put the "Palestinian cause" on top of Mali's national agenda – including the naming of a public square in Bamako, Mali's capital, after the "Palestinian Martyr" Mohamed al-Dura. Yet Abu Rabah did not have a single word to say against the Islamists. *Le Matin* not only lashed out at Abu Rabah, it claimed that the Islamists are backed by the Arab and Muslim countries. Since Mali has been duped by its so-called Muslim brethren, *Le Matin* concluded, it should change its foreign policy.

Mali's feeling of betrayal is reminiscent of Africa's disappointment in the Arab and Muslim world in the 1970s, when Libya and Saudi Arabia used financial incentives to convince African countries to cut ties with Israel. After the Yom Kippur War, the Arab League threatened to apply its oil embargo to Africa. As a result, all African countries (except Lesotho, Malawi, Mauritius, and Swaziland) severed their ties with Israel. African countries, however, soon realized that their move brought no benefits, and that the Arab League was willing to share its enemies but not its oil. More and more African leaders and opinion-makers openly accused the Arabs of racism, reminding them of their past slavery trade in Africa. They were also concerned by Muammar Gaddafi's expansionist and destabilizing policies.

In the 1980s, Israel proactively re-engaged Africa under the leadership of Defense Minister Ariel Sharon and Foreign Ministry Director-General David Kimche. Most African countries restored their ties with Israel in the 1980s and 1990s. However, some African states changed course in the following decade. Niger severed its diplomatic relations with Israel in 2000 at the outbreak of the Second Intifada, and Mauritania in 2009, after Israel's military operation in Gaza. Both countries are Muslim, and both were influenced by Iran.

In 2008, Iranian President Mahmoud Ahmadinejad declared that his country intended to develop ties with Africa. One year later, he visited many African countries with Iranian diplomats and generals, signing commercial, diplomatic, and defense deals. Israel lost a project of water sewage in Senegal after Iran promised to carry out the same work at lower cost. Iran's influence in Africa also relies on Lebanon's rich and influential Diaspora in countries such as Congo, Guinea, and Senegal, which donates money to Hezbollah.

However, with the electoral victory of Islamists in Egypt and Tunisia, and with the near takeover of Mali by al-Qaeda, more and more African countries are becoming fearful of Iran and of its Islamist allies. Ethiopia, forced to confront Islamist militias backed by nearby rebels in Somalia, has become one of Israel's closest allies in Africa, as well as a major buyer of Israeli defense equipment. Kenya, which also faces Islamist terrorism from neighboring Somalia, is interested in strengthening its military ties with Israel. Even Nigeria reportedly spent about $500 million on Israeli military equipment in the past few years.

Mali's anger at Arab countries, especially Egypt, is part of a wider African fear of Islamic influence and of Iranian meddling on the continent. Even though France's military intervention in Mali is only meant to serve French interests, it opens a window of opportunity which Israel should seize to improve its relations with Africa and with France itself.

French military strikes against Mali's Islamists are in stark contrast to France's backing of the Muslim rebels in Côte d'Ivoire during that country's civil war in 2002-2011. There, President Laurent Gbagbo, a Christian, started challenging France's strong economic grip over his country. His defiant policy created a community of interests between France and Côte d'Ivoire's Muslim rebels led by Alassane Ouattara. Hence did France support the Muslim rebels from Côte d'Ivoire's northern region against Gbagbo and the Christian south. The embattled Ivorian president, a close friend of Israel, sought and obtained Israel's logistical help. France and Israel ended up confronting each other by proxy in Côte d'Ivoire. In April 2011, then-French President Nicolas Sarkozy ordered a French military commando to oust Gbagbo from his bunker, allowing Ouattara to take the presidency. Alassane Ouattara is admittedly no Islamist and should not be compared to the Al-Qaida forces in Mali. Nevertheless, France did support Muslims against Christians in Côte d'Ivoire.

While France and Israel collided in Côte d'Ivoire, the policy of President François Hollande in Mali creates a new community of interests since France is now fighting forces that are hostile to Israel. Thus, the Malian crisis constitutes an opportunity for Israel to improve its relations with France and with former French colonies in Africa.

Chapter 77:

A Diplomatic Opportunity for Israel in the Sahel

France has been successful in breaking the alliance of Tuareg separatists with Jihadists linked to al-Qaeda, whose declared purpose is to establish an Islamist state. Six months after the launching of the French military operation, the Tuareg separatists were willing to trade their secessionist policy for political autonomy within Mali. Jihadists, on the other hand, were still fighting. One of their targets was neighboring Niger.

The Jihadist presence in Niger was confirmed in June 2013 by suicide attacks at a military base in Agadez and at a French uranium mine in Arlit. Those attacks were carried-out by the Movement for Unity and Jihad in West Africa, a terrorist organization linked to al-Qaeda. Both France and Niger have good reasons to be nervous. About 75% of France's electricity is produced from uranium-fed nuclear plants, and most of France's uranium is imported from Niger. As for Niger's weak economy, its main source of income is uranium production.

The United Nations has stepped in, announcing in July 2013 that it was sending a 12,000-strong peacekeeping mission to Mali. The blue helmets will consist of French, West African and Chinese troops. The fact that China is now militarily involved in Africa is telling. China is Africa's largest trading partner: it buys and sells about $200 billion a year – double the amount of US trade with Africa. China has 41 embassies in Africa and its new president, Xi Jinping, visited Africa on his first foreign trip.

The United States and China are competing for economic and political influence in Africa – and Africa's oil resources. This competition now has a military dimension. After the terrorist attacks in Agadez and Arlit, Niger's government was so shocked and helpless that it accepted military aid from the United States and France in order to face the Jihadist threat. The Chinese blue helmets in Mali and the dispatch of US military equipment to Niger will create a double US and Chinese military presence in the Sahel. This new phenomenon is noticeable, because the US and China have conflicting policies over Iran, a country that has significantly boosted its diplomatic and economic activity in Africa in recent years.

In 2008, then Iranian President Mahmoud Ahmadinejad declared that his country intended to develop ties with Africa. One year later, he visited many African countries with Iranian diplomats and generals, signing commercial, diplomatic, and defense deals. Israel lost a project of water sewage in Senegal after Iran promised to carry it out at a lower cost. Iran's influence in Africa also relies on Lebanon's rich and influential Diaspora in countries such as Congo, Guinea and Senegal, which donates money to Hezbollah.

While China has been protecting Iran at the UN Security Council, the United States is trying to torpedo Iran's diplomatic offensive in Africa. This is where Israel's role and interests in Africa enter the fray.

With the electoral victory of Islamists in Egypt and Tunisia, and with the Jihadist threat in Mali and Niger, more and more African countries were becoming fearful of Iran and of its Islamist allies. According to foreign media reports, Ethiopia, forced to confront Islamist militias backed by nearby rebels in Somalia, has become one of Israel's closest allies in Africa, as well as a major buyer of Israeli defense equipment. Kenya, which also faces Islamist terrorism from neighboring Somalia, is interested in strengthening military ties with Israel. Even Nigeria reportedly spent about $500 million on Israeli military equipment in recent years.

Shortly after France's military intervention in January 2013, Mali's President publicly expressed anger at Arab countries, especially Egypt, for condemning France but not the Jihadists. Mali's president was expressing a wider African fear of Islamic influence and of Iranian meddling on the continent.

Africa's growing concerns over the Jihadist threat and over Iran's influence open a window of opportunity for the United States and Israel. President Obama's 2013 visit to Africa was a clear indication that his administration is aware of its pivotal role in Africa's complicated geopolitics. Israel should follow suit and meet the expectations of its African friends.

Chapter 78:

Netanyahu, Groucho Marx and Machiavelli: Why Freeing Terrorists is Wrong

Benjamin Netanyahu seems to have endorsed Groucho Marx's definition of political flexibility: "These are my principles. If you don't like them, I have others." Netanyahu has written extensively on terrorism, espousing the view that terrorists should never be freed. Yet Netanyahu did just that in October 2011, when he freed hundreds of terrorists for the liberation of Gilead Shalit, a soldier held in Hamas captivity for five years. Having put aside his principle once, Netanyahu could hardly argue with US Secretary of State John Kerry when the latter told him: "You freed hundreds of Hamas prisoners to release Gilead Shalit but won't do a similar gesture for Mahmoud Abbas? You're basically encouraging the PLO to abduct an Israeli soldier in order for Abbas to get his boys home."

Like every statesman, Netanyahu is faced with the eternal dilemma between Realpolitik and principles. For this dilemma, Machiavelli provided a clear-cut recommendation: "Where the very safety of the country depends on the resolution to be taken, no consideration of justice or injustice, humanity or cruelty, nor of glory or of shame, should be allowed to prevail. The only question should be: What course will save the life and liberty of the country?" Netanyahu seems to have endorsed Machiavelli's recommendation. By doing so, he is missing, like Machiavelli himself, an important point: opting for Realpolitik and putting all moral considerations aside can end up undermining a country's very life and liberty.

The late Israeli diplomat Abba Eban once wrote: "Writers who have described the ideal society have usually contrived to situate their Utopias on desert islands or on the peaks of inaccessible mountains, thus avoiding the two conditions that make Utopia impossible: boundaries and neighbors." The Zionist movement aspired to build a Jewish state neither on a desert island nor on a mountain, but in the heart of the Middle East. As early as 1903, the British government offered Uganda for the establishment of a sovereign Jewish state. The Zionist leadership had to choose between immediate sovereignty and a return to Zion. A similar dilemma emerged again with the 1937 and 1947 partition plans, which entailed a tough choice between ideology (recovering Jerusalem and the Land of Israel) and pragmatism (sovereignty here and now).

With independence came new foreign policy dilemmas. The 1952 Reparation Agreement between Israel and West Germany was a case in point: should Israel turn the page with Germany just because its economy was desperate for cash? After the 1967 Six Day War, Prime Minister Levy Eshkol captured Israel's dilemma when he quipped that he liked the dowry but not the bride: Israel had recovered its historical homeland but inherited a demographic burden. After the 1973 Yom Kippur War, Israel tried to bypass its international isolation by cooperating with the apartheid regime in South Africa and with militaristic regimes in Latin America: this was pure Realpolitik, but hardly a policy that suited the aspiration of being "a light unto the nations."

The list is longer but the dilemma described by Machiavelli is always the same: when faced with the choice between interests and principles, what should a statesman do? In the case of Israel, the tension between idealism and realism is even sharper because Israel lives in a permanent state of war and, at the same time, has declared ideals such as the sanctity of life, Jewish solidarity, and the ingathering of exiles.

In Western historiography, national heroes are generally remembered as statesmen who didn't give up on their principles even in the face of mortal danger. Abraham Lincoln could have ended the Civil War earlier had he not insisted on abolishing slavery. Yet Americans consider him a hero precisely because he decided to fight to the end in the name of the ideal for which he went to war in the first place. Winston Churchill could have reached an agreement with Hitler after the collapse of France in June 1940, but he took the risk of fighting to the end because he understood the war was about Western civilization, not about power politics.

In Israel, though, pragmatism is considered sacrosanct. Israel's first prime minister, David Ben-Gurion, was wise to accept the UN partition plan. Former premier Menachem Begin was brave to relinquish the Sinai to Egypt. Yitzhak Rabin was a hero because he recognized the PLO. Indeed, most Israeli commentators have only good things to say about politicians willing to free terrorists, to make territorial concessions and to give in to international pressure.

Netanyahu has endorsed this narrative and psyche. Unlike national heroes in the West, but like Machiavelli, Netanyahu has become blinded by Realpolitik and no longer sees that when a country abandons justice and honor, its liberty becomes meaningless. He also seems to have forgotten that, like Groucho Marx's principles, leaders themselves are interchangeable.

Chapter 79:

Israel does not owe its Start-Up Nation Status to the EU

"Horizon 2020" is the eighth "Framework Program" (FP) of the European Union (EU). Framework Programs are European research and development (R&D) funds that function like an investment fund: member states contribute according to the size of their GDP, and their return on investment (ROI) depends on how many of their companies and research institutes successfully applied for FP grants.

Israel was the first and only non-European country admitted as a full participant in the fifth FP (1998-2002). Subsequently, it took part in FP6 (2002-2006) and in FP7 (2007-2013). Israel owes its FP membership to its scientific excellence, which benefits European R&D. So far, Israel's participation has made perfect sense. Israel invested €152.1 million in FP5 and got €166.8 million in return. With FP7, Israel invested €535 million and was awarded €698 million. Israel's stake does more than deliver

impressive figures. Its participation fosters valuable scientific cooperation between Israeli and European universities, companies, and research
institutes.

Those facts, however, are not accurately reported by Israel's mainstream media. *Yediot Aharonot*, for instance, claimed in August 2013 that
Israel gets €1.5 for every Euro it invests in FP. In fact, Israel got €1.09 per
invested Euro in FP5 and €1.3 per invested Euro in FP7. *Yediot Aharonot*
also mislead its readers by presenting this inaccurate 1.5 figure as guaranteed in "Horizon 2020." There is no such guarantee. It is fairly reasonable to assume that Israel's participation will be a fruitful one yet again.
Yet claiming, as *Yediot Aharonot* does, that Israel would invest €600 million and will get €900 million in return is simply wrong. Israel won't lose
€300 million by not participating in "Horizon 2020". It will lose valuable
scientific partnerships and a likely profitable investment. However, those
€600 million can be directly invested into Israel's own R&D.

In her *Times of Israel* blog, Naomi Chazan even claimed that by not
joining "Horizon 2020", Israel "will bring about the collapse of the
foundation stones that have made Israel into a start-up nation". That is
absurd. Israel does not owe its "start-up nation" status to the European
Union. Not participating in "Horizon 2020" will not bring about the
"collapse" of Israel's R&D.

The real question is whether or not the undisputable benefit of joining "Horizon 2020" justifies Israel's acceptance of the new conditions
set by the European Union.

On July 19, 2013, the European Commission issued a Directive for-
bidding any European funding and cooperation with Israeli entities located beyond the 1949 Armistice Lines, requiring that any agreement
signed by an EU member state with Israel should include a clause stating
that any territory beyond the 1949 Armistice Lines is not part of the
State of Israel. Since the Western Wall and Mount Zion, for example,
are beyond the 1949 Armistice Lines, Israel would have to publicly state

the "illegality" of its control of those two Jewish historical sites before applying for EU grants. The EU's demand is not just groundless in international law. It is also deeply offensive.

The EU also applies double standards to Israel, when compared to other countries that also hold agreements with the EU. For instance, the EU did sign a customs union with Turkey in 1995. Yet the EU never announced that Turkish products, produced or manufactured in occupied northern Cyprus, shall be excluded from this customs union.

Also in 2005, the EU signed a fisheries agreement with Morocco. This agreement applies to Western Sahara, even though the EU does not recognize Moroccan sovereignty over the region. The EU has been negotiating a free-trade agreement with India. Still, the applicability of such a deal over the disputed territory of Kashmir is not discussed.

Chapter 80:

When it comes to the Middle East, Europe must Practice what it Preaches

The European Union (EU) may well be the modern incarnation of Immanuel Kant's "democratic peace" theory, for it confirms that democracies that abide by common rules do not go to war against one another. Yet the EU is far from being a dispute-free zone. And the way European countries deal with their own conflicts stands in sharp contrast with what they preach to others about conflict resolution. Indeed, the EU's credibility and influence in our region would increase were it to dissipate the strong impression that we are expected to do as Europe says, but not as it does.

In August 2013, Spanish fishermen sailed into disputed waters off Gibraltar to protest the construction of a reef by the Government of the British-controlled territory. The British Royal Navy intervened to stop the fishermen from entering the area, and London is even dispatching the HMS Westminster warship. By way of retaliation, Spain tightened its border with Gibraltar.

This fishery feud, however, was but a symptom of a sovereignty dispute between Great Britain and Spain. Spain disputes Britain's sovereignty over the southern tip of the Iberian Peninsula, a sovereignty that goes back to the 1713 Treaty of Utrecht. In 2006, Spain, Gibraltar and the UK started a process of tripartite negotiations to settle disputes related to air movements, customs procedures and telecommunications. But as the 2013 fishermen incident showed, the British-Spanish rivalry over Gibraltar is characterized by unilateral steps and retaliation.

While Spain claims sovereignty over Gibraltar, it is uncompromising about Spanish-controlled territories claimed by others. Indeed, the Spanish government refuses to negotiate with ETA, the Basque separatist movement. ETA hasn't used violence since October 2011, although it still has arms and explosives, but it won't forgo armed struggle indefinitely unless the Spanish government meets some of its demands. Spanish Prime Minister Mariano Rajoy, however, insists that he wants ETA to surrender unconditionally. Three of ETA's leaders, David Pla, Iratxe Sorzabal and Josu Ternera, are asking for a release of ETA prisoners in exchange for full disarmament. But the Spanish Government is adamant: freeing terrorists, it claims, would be an affront to justice and to the families whose dear ones were killed by ETA terrorists.

The Basque and Catalonian regions struggle for more political and cultural autonomy, but not necessarily for full independence. Other European-controlled territories, such as New Caledonia, unsuccessfully vie for full independence. Since 1986, the United Nations Committee on Decolonization has included New Caledonia on its list of non-self-governing territories. Following secessionist unrest and military repression, the French Government agreed in 1988 to hold a referendum on Caledonian independence within 10 years. In 1998, the French Government convinced the pro-independence Kanaks to push off the referendum by another 15 to 20 years. Since 1998 plus 15 equals 2013, Kanaks have been inquiring lately about their referendum. France's reply is that independence will mean the end of all economic aid –undoubtedly a powerful deterrent.

While Europeans lecture Israel on peaceful negotiations, on the liberation of terrorists for the sake of peace and on the universality of self-determination, they hardly apply those principles to themselves. The British are bullying the Spaniards in Gibraltar, the Spaniards refuse to liberate ETA prisoners and the French are procrastinating about New Caledonia's independence.

Europeans, of course, are entitled to their own policies, but their credibility is at stake when they ask Israel to make gestures which they themselves would never consider, even for the sake of peace.

European diplomats are keen to pride themselves of the EU model as a successful implementation of Kant's "democratic peace" theory. If the model worked in Europe, they typically argue, why can't it work elsewhere like in the Middle East for instance?

The answer to that question is twofold.

First, Europe ceased being a chronic battlefield only after US military power brought down a dictatorship and imposed democracy upon countries where democracy had existed before, even temporarily. Moreover, and paradoxically, the Hobbesian urge of surviving the Soviet threat is what made the Kantian ideal of supranational European governance a reality.

Second, Europe can hardly expect Middle Easterners to adopt principles that seem to be valid only as long as European interests are not affected. The fact that France and Britain dispatched their air forces to stop the civil war in oil-rich Libya while letting President Bashar al-Assad produce 100,000 victims in oil-bare Syria speaks volumes about what "humanitarian intervention" is really about.

The Middle East certainly has something to learn about Europe's transition from endemic wars to enduring peace. But to be influential, Europe must first be credible.

Chapter 81:

If Obama doesn't Act, Israel and Iran will draw their Conclusions

Foreign policy doctrines rarely survive the test of reality, but Barack Obama's 2009 Cairo speech has been cruelly challenged by Middle East events. One of the President's messages in Cairo was that America had humbly learned to tackle international problems with the help of others. With Russia hindering tougher sanctions on Iran, impending military action against President Bashar Assad in Syria, and China's threats to go to war with Japan over the disputed Sankaku islands, Obama's 2009 confession sounds embarrassingly out of touch with reality.

The US president admittedly has a choice of bad options in Syria, but he is the one who cornered himself in a catch-22 situation. Had he not dithered for so long about imposing no-fly zones in Syria and about arming moderate rebels, al-Qaeda backed radicals would not have become so dominant on the ground. Because of his hesitation, Obama now has to choose between tolerating mass murder with chemical weapons and empowering unsavory jihadists. And if the US President doesn't carry out his threat to intervene in Syria now that the "red line" of chemical weapons has almost certainly been crossed by Assad, Iran will rightly conclude that it can proceed with its nuclear program.

Barack Obama naively and arrogantly thought that being more sophisticated than George W. Bush would shield him from the tough dilemmas of foreign policy. In his Cairo speech, Obama dismissed what he called the "false choice" between national security and the constitution – hence his promise to close the Guantánamo prison. The fact that Guantánamo is still open goes to show that the choice between freedom and security is not that "false," after all. In his acceptance speech for the Nobel peace prize, Obama disingenuously claimed that there was no need to choose between realism and idealism in foreign policy. If only life were so simple. No leader is spared difficult trade-offs and dilemmas, no matter how uplifting his speeches. Barack Obama is learning this lesson the hard way in Syria. His hubris has created nemesis.

In 2012, Obama declared that "we have been very clear with the Assad regime: that a red line for us is if we start seeing a whole bunch of chemical weapons moving around or being utilized. That would change my calculus." If the use of chemical weapons by Assad is confirmed and if the US president fails to carry out his threat, the consequences will be far worse than getting buried in the Syrian quagmire.

President Obama must now intervene, for three reasons.

First, the use of chemical weapons is against the rules of war, and if these rules are to have any meaning, they must be enforced. Second, after 100,000 dead and some 7 million refugees, the human tragedy is far beyond the toll that justified humanitarian intervention in places such as Bosnia in 1995. Third, America's credibility and deterrence are at stake. The previous reported use of chemical weapons in Syria was ignored by the US president, and Assad is obviously testing Obama. If the "red lines" drawn in the sand by Barak Obama fade with the tide, Iran will take notice.

In retrospect, Obama's efforts to conquer the hearts and minds of the Arab world have been an abject failure. He is now loathed in the Arab world, especially in Egypt where he is alternately accused of having supported Muhammad Morsi's Islamist government and of backing the army's coup.

If the use of chemical weapons by Assad is confirmed and if President Obama fails to act, Iran and Syria will be empowered, while America will lose its credibility and deterrence. The lesson for Israel will be obvious: if Obama is not willing to intervene in Syria, he will likely not intervene in Iran.

The Middle East is at a crossroad and Obama can no longer dither. If America fails to act in Syria, Israel will have to draw conclusions and take responsibility.

Chapter 82:

Forget about the UN Charter, Listen to Churchill

Would a US and French military strike against Syria, in August 2013, have been illegal without a United Nations Security Council resolution?

Most international legal experts say so. Indeed, President Barack Obama himself has questioned the legality of a US strike without a Security Council resolution, though he has also defended its necessity.

Article 2 (4) of the UN Charter forbids the use of force except in cases of self-defense (Article 51) or for military actions authorized by the Security Council (Chapter VII). Clearly, for the use of force against Syria to be legal in the eyes of international law, a Security Council resolution is a must.

The problem, of course, is that the five permanent and veto-wielding members of the Security Council (the US, the UK, France, Russia and China) are neither academics nor judges pondering whether the use of force meets the requirements of jus as bellum. They are countries with different (sometimes conflicting) national interests and they think in terms of Realpolitik.

The UN Charter's requirement is largely unattainable in the real world, and that's why the Security Council was paralyzed during the Cold War. In the case of Syria, the Security Council is paralyzed by Russia's eagerness to preserve its last Middle East ally, and its obvious glee at poking America in the eye.

Are we to tolerate humanitarian tragedies in the name of legalistic purism?

The UN Charter's requirement for going to war is not only impractical because of the reality of power politics. It is also morally flawed, since it puts on equal footing countries that abide by the rule of law and countries that don't. It is morally abhorrent and aberrant that Russia should have the power to make a humanitarian intervention technically illegal by vetoing it at the Security Council, since Russia has no respect for the rule of law domestically and internationally (for the record, Russia attacked and occupied Georgia in 2008 without a Security Council resolution). And it is disingenuous for authoritarian regimes that trample the rule of law to lecture Western democracies on legality.

Winston Churchill accurately captured this inner contradiction of international law and even proposed a remedy. When it is blatantly obvious that tyrannical regimes disingenuously evoke legality only to undermine the very principles that the law is meant to protect, democracies should simply and temporarily ignore the letter of the law in order to protect its spirit. It is worth quoting what Churchill said on the matter: "The letter of the law must not in supreme emergency obstruct those who are charged with its protection and enforcement. It would not be right or rational that the aggressive power should gain one set of advantages by tearing up all laws, and another set by sheltering behind the innate respect for law of its opponents. Humanity, rather than legality, must be our guide."

This principle is what motivated NATO's intervention in Kosovo in 1999, when the Security Council was asked to act in response to the Serbian army's crimes against Kosovo's civilian population. The Council passed a resolution in September 1998, but the resolution only expressed "grave concern" at reports that more than 230,000 people had been displaced from their homes in Kosovo by the Serbian army. The Council did not approve the use of force against Serbia because Russia used its veto to shield its Slavic protégés. So, technically, NATO's military intervention was illegal. But the alternative was to let a humanitarian tragedy unfold. Even Michael Walzer, a liberal American thinker whose book *Just and Unjust Wars* was written to conceptually curtail America's "right" to go to war, expressed support for NATO's military intervention in Kosovo.

Just wars can be illegal, and unjust wars can be legal. The US-led invasion of Iraq in 2003, regarded by many as unjust, was legal according to both US and international law. The war was approved by Congress in 2002 with a wide majority, and it was authorized by UN Security Council resolutions. By failing to disarm and submit to weapons inspections, Saddam Hussein's Iraq was in violation of those two resolutions which allowed member states to use "all necessary means" to compel Iraq to disarm and accept weapons inspections.

If and when Barack Obama and François Hollande give the order to strike at Syrian military targets, their orders will technically be illegal. They will, however, be entirely justified in disregarding the UN Charter, because this document is cynically exploited by authoritarian regimes that actually believe that might is right. Faced with such cynicism, Western democracies must not be fooled and it is their duty to act according to Churchill's maxim: "Humanity, rather than legality, must be our guide."

Chapter 83:

Seriously AIPAC, You're not Helping

AIPAC's open and active campaign on Capitol Hill, in August 2013, to convince lawmakers to approve President Obama's military strike against Syria, has puzzled many Israelis. Obviously, AIPAC does not argue in the letter it drafted for Congressmen that a US strike against Syria would serve Israel's interest. Rather, AIPAC's central argument is that backing down at this point would be so harmful to America's credibility and deterrence that Iran would inevitably conclude that it can proceed with its nuclear program without fear of a US military attack. This argument makes sense, but AIPAC's initiative on its behalf doesn't. Indeed, this initiative will almost certainly backfire against Israel.

Whether or not a US military strike against Syria would serve Israel's interests is questionable at best. True, a US volte-face would likely convince Iran and Hezbollah that Obama's pledge never to let Iran go nuclear is an empty threat. But the fact that Iran may reach such a conclusion does not mean that it is correct. Assuming that Obama still means business with Iran (admittedly a generous assumption), convincing the Iranians that the US is chickening out would actually make a US military strike against Iran's nuclear plants less predictable and thus more lethal. But besides the psychology and the speculations, a US military strike in Syria would likely make Israel the target of Hezbollah's huge rocket arsenal. Assad's threat that he would retaliate against Israel with Iran's support might be hollow, but it cannot me dismissed. The fact that Israelis have nervously been waiting in line for the past three weeks to get gas masks makes one wonder if AIPAC would be so gung-ho were its leaders to share the same aggravation and were they exposed to the same dangers.

Make no mistake: I have made the case for a US military strike against Syria and I continue to support such a strike despite the fact that its immediate side effects on Israel would likely be painful. What I am disputing is not the potency of AIPAC's arguments, but the wisdom of AIPAC's initiative.

AIPAC defines itself as "America's Pro-Israel Lobby" and it is definitely perceived as such in America and in the world. Therefore, AIPAC is perceived as advocating a military strike in Syria on behalf of Israel. If America ends-up striking Syria (a big "if" at this point), and if the military operation goes awry, Israel will be blamed for dragging America into another fine mess. Indeed, this is precisely what happened after the 2003 invasion of Iraq started to look like a fiasco.

In 2006, when the US Army seemed to be sinking into a Vietnam-type of quagmire in Iraq, the "Iraq Study Group" published its report about the situation in Iraq with recommendations about an exit strategy. At that point, the war in Iraq had become highly unpopular in the US and had lost the support of most of its former backers. The report, among other things, described the Israeli-Palestinian conflict as a major source of instability in the Middle-East, and suggested tackling that conflict as part of the exit strategy in Iraq.

Around the same time, Professors John Mearsheimer and Stephen Walt published their paper "The Israel Lobby" in the *London Review of Books*. The paper was turned into a book published in 2007 under the title *The Israel Lobby and US Foreign Policy*, which argued that "The Israel Lobby" (especially AIPAC) mostly determines US foreign policy and, as a result, "Israel's enemies get weakened or overthrown, Israel gets a free hand with the Palestinians, and the United States does most of the fighting, dying, rebuilding, and paying." Basically, Mearsheimer and Walt implied that AIPAC had dragged America into the Iraqi mess to serve Israel's interests. It is time for US foreign policy, the authors argued, to act according to its own national interests and to stop being manipulated by AIPAC.

This argument was reminiscent of the one voiced by the Eisenhower Administration in the 1950s. Truman, the argument went, had been manipulated by the Jewish Lobby into recognizing Israel, thus alienating the Arab world and hampering US efforts to rein in Soviet influence in the Middle East. Then Secretary of State John Foster Dulles declared in Cairo on 11 May 1953: "The United States has, in the past, unduly favored the interests of Israel as a result of the pressure of certain lobbies. This Administration is committed to a more balanced position in the Middle-East." Already back then, the pro-Israel lobby was accused of acting against US national interests.

This argument, therefore, is not new. But as Israel finally recovers from the toxic effects of the "Iraq Study Group" and of the Walt & Mearsheimer book, AIPAC is about to provide fresh arguments to anti-Israel conspiracy theorists in Washington by giving the impression that "The Lobby" is trying to drag America into another Middle-East war to serve Israel's interests. This is the last thing Israel needs at this point.

On the Syrian crisis, AIPAC would be well-advised to ponder and apply the Jewish maxim of the Ethics of the Fathers: "Silence is the guardian of wisdom."

Chapter 84:

Will the US-Russia Agreement on Syria Lead to War?

The agreement struck between the US and Russia on Sept. 14, 2013, compels the Assad regime to submit a full inventory of chemical weapons within a week. The agreement also states that "in the event of non-compliance, including unauthorized transfer, or any use of chemical weapons by anyone in Syria, the UN Security Council should impose measures under Chapter VII of the UN Charter." On paper and in theory, Russia has agreed to approve the use of force against Syria if Assad fails to dismantle his chemical weapons. But Russian Foreign Minister Sergei Lavrov suggested the very opposite during his joint press conference with Secretary of State John Kerry: "There is nothing said about the use of force, nor about any automatic sanctions" he clarified.

Clearly, the Russians did not approve the use of force. Their agreement with the US only says the Security Council "should" (not "will") impose "measures." Indeed, when Kerry said the Security Council "will impose measures" if Assad doesn't cooperate, Lavrov interrupted him repeating twice: "Should, should." Moreover, Chapter VII does not necessarily mean the use of force. Russia will likely want to limit such measures to the sanctions listed in Article 41 of Chapter VII, i.e. "complete or partial interruption of economic relations and of rail, sea, air, postal, telegraphic, radio, and other means of communication, and the severance of diplomatic relations."

The Kerry-Lavrov agreement could have been credible and efficient had it made the use of force the automatic and unquestionable consequence of non-compliance by Assad. But that is not the case. Just as Saddam Hussein did in Iraq, Assad will play cat-and-mouse with UN inspectors, who will find it daunting to reach Syria's chemical sites while the civil war rages on. Russia can reasonably be expected to be complicit.

Paradoxically, Vladimir Putin provided Barack Obama with a face-saving exit. Obama cornered himself on military intervention in Syria with his red line declaration on the use of chemical weapons, but having been elected to extricate America from two Islamic civil wars, he was wary of getting involved in a third. Americans, who feel that they have no dog in that fight, are understandably in no mood to sacrifice their sons and spend their tax money in another failed state. Passing the buck to Congress was thus clever, except that the President seems to have underestimated the opposition of liberal Democrats, libertarian Republicans and conservatives. Putin saved Obama from a likely humiliating defeat in Congress.

While insincere and unworkable, the Kerry-Lavrov deal grants the main actors something they need: Assad is spared a US attack; Obama is able to back down from a war he never wanted; Putin can say that the post Cold War trauma of Russian irrelevance is over.

Russia's apparent diplomatic achievement, however, is both misleading and potentially dangerous.

It is misleading because Putin is mainly posturing and does not have the military and economic means to implement his punchy diplomacy. Russia is a petro-state whose revenues rely almost entirely on hydrocarbons. The Russian economy's dependence on gas and oil exports is a mixed blessing that is showing signs of exhaustion with the success of shale gas in the United States and the construction of alternative pipelines to Europe (such as the "Nabucco" pipeline). Russia, moreover, is in a state of endemic demographic decline with shrinking birthrates and high mortality rates. Russia is too vulnerable economically to credibly challenge US supremacy.

But Putin's diplomatic posturing is potentially dangerous because it emboldens Iran, while making Israel nervous. Right after the signature of the Kerry-Lavrov agreement, Putin declared that Iran was entitled to nuclear energy. As for Israel, it now has very good reasons to doubt Mr. Obama's reliability. This might convince Israel that the time for a preventive strike against Iran is now or never.

Such a scenario is reminiscent of the pre-Six Day war period. While Russia was encouraging the bellicosity of its Middle East allies in May 1967 (Egypt and Syria), President Lyndon Johnson remained non-committal, saying he had enough of a headache with the war in Vietnam. The Mideast war broke out precisely because Egypt thought it could rely on the Soviet Union and Israel thought it could not rely on the United States. Putin and Obama have managed to create a similar scenario.

Chapter 85:

The Israel-Iran Proxy War in Nairobi

The horrific attack perpetuated in September 2013 by *al-Shabab* in Nairobi is a painful reminder of the Islamist threat in Africa. It is also an opportunity for Israel to leverage its counter-terrorism expertise among African countries targeted by Islamist terror.

Al-Shabab (which means "youth" in Arabic) is an Islamist organization that was founded in 2005 in Somalia. Since the fall of Siad Barre's military rule in 1991, Somalia was left without an official government and central authority. The country sank into chaos with gangs and militias competing for power. By 2009, *al-Shabab* had about 5,000 fighters and had gained control over the southern half of the country (including the capital Mogadishu). It thus became the first al-Qaida ally to partially rule over a Muslim country. In 2011, *al-Shabab* lost Mogadishu to the troops of the Transitional Federal Government (TFG). Since then, *al-Shabab* has lost about two-thirds of the territory it used to control in southern Somalia, but it is lethally active in other parts of Africa – as tragically shown by the Nairobi terrorist attack.

Al-Shabab collaborates with AQIM (al-Qaida in the Islamic Maghreb) in the Sahel and with *Boko Haram* in Nigeria. AQIM operates from Mali and aims to overthrow the Algerian government and to replace it with an Islamic state. *Boko Haram* (whose meaning is "Western education is sinful") aims to establish Sharia law in Nigeria, as well as in Cameroon and Niger. The former chief of the US Africa Command, General Carter F. Ham, has repeatedly warned that *al-Shabab*, AQIM and *Boko Haram* collaborate throughout Africa in coordination with al-Qaida. Geographically, therefore, the three terrorist organizations span from East to West Africa via the Maghreb. This "Islamist Arc" goes through three countries that are of strategic importance to both Africa and the world economy: Mali is Africa's third largest gold producer (after South Africa and Ghana); Nigeria is Africa's top oil producer and has Africa's largest proven natural gas reserves; Somalia borders a major sea passage for international trade.

Africa's "Islamic Arc" involves Iran. In February 2013, UN monitors for the arms embargo in Somalia reported that *al-Shabab* was receiving arms from Iran and from Yemen. Iran is also an active supporter of its ally Hezbollah in Africa. The Nigerian government, in cooperation with Israel, recently uncovered a Hezbollah cell and arms cache in the city of Kano in northern Nigeria. The cooperation between Israel and Nigeria is part of a wider Israeli activity aimed at countering Hezbollah's presence in Western Africa. Israel has been offering security training and equipment to West African governments who oppose Hezbollah's activities on their territory.

But Nigeria's "Islamic problem" goes beyond Hezbollah and *Boko Haram*. It includes the Islamic Movement in Nigeria (IMN), an organization founded in the early 1980s with the financial and logistical support of Iran. In fact, IMN was started by Nigerian students from the Muslim

Student Society who were trained by the Islamic Republic of Iran after 1979 in order to produce an Iranian-style Islamic revolution in Nigeria. The founding leader of IMN was Ibrahim Zakzaky, who converted from Sunni to Shia Islam. Today, Zakzaky is the undisputed leader of the Shiites in Nigeria. When addressing his supporters, he typically sits under a portrait of Ayatollah Khomeini. His speeches are violently anti-Semitic. According to Abel Assadina, a former senior Iranian diplomat who defected in 2003, Iran is establishing local power bases in Africa with the purpose of influencing local governments and inducing them to act against Western interests. In November 2010, Iran's Foreign Minister openly declared that Iran's "African outreach" was a top priority.

The consequences of the Islamic infiltration in Africa have been lethal, starting with the 1997 al-Qaida terrorist attack against the US Embassy in Nairobi. Then came the 2002 al-Qaida terrorist attack against Israeli tourists in Mombasa. More recently, in May 2013, a Kenyan court convicted two Iranians for planning terrorist attacks against Western targets in Kenya. Israel had been involved in Kenya's counter-terrorist activities before the latest attack in Nairobi. The Iranian defendants convicted in May 2013 had been interrogated in a Kenyan prison by Israeli investigators.

Israel actively assisted the Kenyan Government against *al-Shabab* terrorists during the 2013 attack in Nairobi. This assistance is likely to increase, and not only in Kenya. In a way, a by-proxy war is being waged between Iran and Israel in Africa. Throughout the African continent, more and more countries are the victims of Islamic terrorism, but not all of them are ready to entirely forego the economic benefits of doing business with Iran. The US should actively compensate African states for abandoning their economic ties with Iran, and Israel should proactively assist African governments threatened by Islamic terrorism.

Israel and pro-Western African governments have a common interest in defeating Iran's "outreach" diplomacy, and the tragedy in Nairobi is a reminder of how urgent this task is.

Chapter 86:

Israel Must not Miss a Second Opportunity with China

In October 2013, the Israeli government approved an ambitious railway project that will connect the Red Sea port of Eilat to the Mediterranean port of Ashdod. The ultimate purpose of this railway is to become a "land bridge" for goods transported between Europe and Asia and thus to compete with the Suez Canal. The construction of the railway might be undertaken by a Chinese company, a prospect that has drawn criticism from former Mossad director Efraim Halevy, who claims that awarding the project to a Chinese company would be detrimental to Israel's relations with the United States and with Europe. Actually, the very opposite is true.

In January 2009, Israel's economy and international stature were transformed overnight when the Texan firm Noble Energy discovered gas in the Tamar field in the eastern Mediterranean. This field is estimated to contain 9.7 trillion cubic feet (TCF) of natural gas, which amount to over half of what the European Union's 28 nations consume annually. Two years later, in 2011, Noble Energy discovered a huge gas field, Leviathan, which is now estimated to contain 18 trillion TCF. Leviathan alone contains about as much gas as what Europe consumes annually.

Europe is facing a major gas supply crisis due to the spread of instability in Algeria and the rest of North Africa, and because it is eager to reduce its dependence on Russia's natural gas. About 20% of Europe's gas supplies come from collapsing states whose populations are reverting to tribalism and to Islamism. The revolts and instability in the Arab world and in Turkey in the past two years have reminded Europe of the potential unreliability of gas and oil supplies from the Middle East and from North Africa. This presents a golden opportunity for Israel to offer Europe an alternative natural gas supply.

Asia may also emerge as an export destination for Israel's gas.

The Israeli "land bridge" between the Red Sea and the Mediterranean will enable Israel to leverage the supply of marginally critical amounts of gas to both Europe and Asia. There are serious questions about the viability of the Suez Canal as a major European-Asian transit route because of growing political instability in Egypt.

A cross-Israel railway, as well as a cross-Israel natural gas pipeline, could transform Israel into a major trans-ocean passageway, connecting the Mediterranean and Red Seas and turning Israel into a major trade and transport route alternative to Suez. The new railway could also become a conduit for Liquefied Natural Gas (LNG), as Israel is contemplating the construction of LNG terminals at both ends of the Eilat-Ashkelon Pipeline.

Since China has become a huge energy consumer, Israeli natural gas would likely mitigate China's pro-Iranian policy, a policy dictated by Iran's natural gas resources. And since China would likely become a major consumer of future Israel gas exports, it does make sense to involve

China in the construction of the infrastructures that will deliver Israel's gas to Asia. Were China to become less supportive of Iran thanks to the diversification of its gas imports, the United States would only benefit. As opposed to Israeli arms sales to China, which did draw criticism from the United States in the past, involving China in Israel's energy revolution would not affect America's strategic interests.

The very idea that Israel shouldn't get too close to China for fear of crossing America caused great damage to Israel's strategic interests in Asia in the past. This mistake should not be repeated. In 1954, the government of Communist China offered to establish full diplomatic relations with Israel. But the Israeli government thought at the time that establishing full diplomatic relations with China would incur the ire of the United States, and so Israel rejected China's request. This was a miscalculation that cost Israel dearly. China embarked on a pro-Arab foreign policy.

The geopolitical context is admittedly different today. But the idea that Israel should forfeit its relations with China so as not to cross the United States is as wrong today as it was in 1954. Israel's emergence as an energy exporter will create some leverage on China's Middle East policy in a way that will serve both Israeli and American interests. The Israeli "land bridge" between the Red Sea and the Mediterranean will constitute a critical element of that strategy, especially if it is built by a Chinese company.

Chapter 87:

What is Good enough for the West is not Good enough for Israel

In his speech at the UN in October 2013, Prime Minister Netanyahu declared that "Iran wants to be in a position to rush forward to build nuclear bombs before the international community can detect it and much less prevent it" and that Iran wants to reach the point of "sufficient nuclear material and sufficient nuclear infrastructure to race to the bomb at a time it chooses to do so." This is why Netanyahu listed four conditions for the negotiations with Iran to succeed: 1. Cessation of all uranium enrichment; 2. Removal of the stockpiles of enriched uranium from Iran's territory; 3. Destruction of the infrastructure for nuclear breakout capability (including the underground facility at Qom and the advanced centrifuges in Natanz); 4. Cessation of all work at the heavy water reactor in Iraq aimed at the production of plutonium.

The negotiating powers are willing to settle for less than that –indeed for much less. They seem willing to reach an agreement in which Iran will commit not to produce nuclear weapons but will be allowed to produce a large amount of highly enriched uranium and plutonium –two ingredients that are required to build a nuclear weapon. The problem is that the development and manufacturing of nuclear weapon components are very hard to detect. So in the emerging trade-off between Iran and the negotiating powers, it will be nearly impossible to know if Iran actually has nuclear weapons. Iran would be able to keep its nuclear weapons a secret, and it could even replicate Israel's policy of "nuclear ambiguity."

If the US is willing to accept such an agreement, sanctions against Iran would be eased or even repealed. Iran might also demand, and likely obtain, a US commitment to prevent an Israeli attack and to stop supporting Iranian opposition groups. In such a scenario, the US would be able to claim that it technically prevented Iran from obtaining nuclear weapons. For Iran, such a deal would provide protection from an Israeli attack, it would weaken internal opposition, and it would ease or even repeal economic sanctions. Meanwhile, Iran would be able to secretly produce more bomb material. That would be an excellent deal for Iran but a terrible deal for Israel, since Israel would not be able to detect whether or not Iran is building a bomb, and therefore Israel would not be able to prevent Iran's "breakout capability."

Israel has good reasons to doubt the United States' ability (or willingness) to prevent Iran's "breakout capability," because no less than four countries obtained nuclear weapons under America's nose: Israel itself (in the 1960s), India (in 1974), Pakistan (in 1998), and North Korea (in 2006). The latter successfully bought time by fooling the international community. The only two countries that abandoned their nuclear programs are South Africa (in 1989) and Libya (in 2003). Western economic sanctions were critical in convincing South Africa to abandon its nuclear program. As for Libya, the 2003 US-led military intervention in Iraq convinced Kaddafi that he was next in line and that forgoing his nuclear program was the only way to prevent a US attack.

In other words, there is no precedent for successfully ending a nuclear program by diplomacy. On the other hand, crippling economic sanctions have worked in the case of South Africa, and military threat has worked in the case of Libya (as well as in the case of Syria's chemical weapons). Netanyahu, therefore, is correct to argue that for the current negotiations with Iran to succeed, sanctions must be maintained and even reinforced, and the military threat must be as credible as ever.

Israel's problem is not that the West doesn't agree with Netanyahu's undisputable argument. Rather, the problem is that what is good enough for the West is not good enough for Israel. The United States and Europe are likely to let Iran enrich uranium and plutonium as long as it doesn't actually build a bomb. But for Israel, that would mean giving Iran the option of building a bomb when it so decides.

Both Iran and the United States are seemingly willing to compromise on a mutually face-saving formula. If such is the case, Netanyahu will inevitably conclude that Israel stands alone. And as he said in his UN speech: "If Israel is forced to stand alone, Israel will stand alone."

Chapter 88:

If it Flogged Criminals, would Israel Get a UN Security Council Seat?

Much has been said and written about Saudi Arabia's bizarre rebuff (in October 2013) of the UN Security Council. What went nearly unnoticed is the fact that Israel announced at the same time that it was running for a Security Council seat (in 2019). This is Israel's first attempt since its admission to the UN in 1949 to join the organization's most powerful body. Unlike Saudi Arabia, however, Israel stands no chance of being accepted (and of declining). The fact that Israel's bid is hopeless provides an opportunity to understand what is wrong with the UN.

While declining Security Council membership, Saudi Arabia is applying for a seat on the United Nations Human Rights Council (UNHRC) - although its legal system practices flogging, amputations, and eye gouging. This is a country that lashes rape victims instead of punishing the perpetrators, publicly beheads homosexuals and, in February 2013, arrested 53 Christians for the "crime" of praying in a private home. It is one of the world's most horrendous human rights violators, but its bid for UNHRC membership will be successful because most members belong to the same league. Since its founding in 2006, the UNHRC has included countries such as China, Russia, Cuba, Pakistan, Mauritania (a country that practices slavery), Venezuela (under Chavez) and Gadhafi's Libya. Saudi Arabia will be in good company.

Unfortunately, the UNHRC is not the only UN body that makes a mockery of sanity and common sense. Earlier this month, Iran was elected to the General Assembly's Committee on Disarmament and International Security. A country that openly defies Security Council resolutions in its pursuit of nuclear weapons and support of terrorist organizations, is now entrusted by the General Assembly to monitor disarmament and international security.

Appointing pyromaniacs as firefighters is a UN tradition. In January 2003, Saddam Hussein's Iraq was selected to chair the UN's Disarmament Conference. At the time, Iraq was defying UN weapon inspectors. That same year, Syria was sitting on the Security Council (it was elected in 2002) to enforce international law and order, while serving as an active arms transit between Iran and Hezbollah.

Israel, by contrast, was never elected to the Security Council, to the UNHRC or to the Committee on Disarmament. Would Israel stand a better chance were it to promote international terrorism, to amputate thieves, or to produce chemical weapons? Hardly.

As UN Secretary General Ban Ki-moon declared in August 2013, Israel "has suffered from bias and sometimes even discrimination" at the UN. Not only is Israel excluded from the Security Council and from the UNHRC, it is also disproportionately condemned by the General Assembly and by the UNHRC for alleged human rights and international law violations. This, despite the fact its human rights record is by far superior to that of its accusers, and that actual human rights abusers are immune from General Assembly and UNHRC condemnations.

It wasn't always so. The United Nations was founded as the result of an alliance against Nazi Germany and the forces of hatred which led to the genocide of the Jewish people. More than one million Jews fought in the ranks of the Allied forces that eventually crushed the Axis powers and brought the UN into being. The Isaiah Wall across the street from the United Nations building on First Avenue in Manhattan proclaims the Jewish ideal of beating swords into plowshares. In November 1947, the General Assembly recommended the creation of a Jewish state. When Israel became a UN member state in 1949, Foreign Minister Moshe Sharett emotionally declared that the Jewish people had rejoined the family of nations.

Decolonization and Cold War polarization radically changed the makeup of the General Assembly, a makeup that was shrewdly exploited by the Arab world after the Yom Kippur war. Hence the 1975 General Assembly resolution declaring Zionism a form of racism, and hence the avalanche of ludicrous UN resolutions which prompted the late Israeli Ambassador Abba Eban to quip that the Arab world had a majority to declare the Earth flat. Despite the end of the Cold War and the Oslo process, the Arab world and the PLO never ceased activating the "automatic majority" they enjoy at the General Assembly in order to isolate and defame Israel.

It is the same "automatic majority" that blocks Israel's access to Security Council membership, since non-permanent members are elected by the General Assembly. So the only point of throwing Israel's hat into the ring is to publicly remind the free world that it has become a minority in the very organization it founded and which has since been hijacked.

Chapter 89:

Germany Plays a Double Game when it Comes to Israel and Human Rights

At Germany's behest, Israel renewed in October 2013 its cooperation with the United Nations Human Rights Council (UNHRC) after boycotting the controversial body for nearly two years. Israel's boycott was motivated by the UNHRC's threefold discriminatory policy toward Israel: singling it out for special discussion in every human rights conference; baring its election to the council by virtue of Israel not belonging to any regional grouping; and subjecting it to more condemnations than any other country.

Israel was guaranteed that this unfair treatment will end if it renews its cooperation with the UNHRC.

The UNHRC Charter has a special article (Article 7) which stipulates that any conference on human rights must hold a separate discussion on Israel. This stipulation applies only to Israel, and no other country in the world is subject to such treatment – not even actual and horrendous human rights abusers such as Syria, Saudi Arabia, China or Sudan. This "Israel-only" clause was adopted by the UNHRC in 2007. At the time it was criticized by UN Secretary General Ban Ki-moon, who publicly voiced disbelief at such bizarre treatment of a democracy given the range and scope of human rights violations throughout the world.

The second discriminatory policy has to do with the fact that Israel is the only country that does not belong to any regional group at the UNHRC, thus making it ineligible to be elected to UN bodies. Israel does not belong to the "Asia-Pacific Group," because this group includes the Middle East and because Arab countries refuse to accept Israel. At the UN in New York, Israel finally became a permanent member of the West European and Others Group (which includes Turkey) in 2004, but in Geneva, it is still excluded. This exclusion makes Israel the only country that is ineligible to the UNHRC. As former UN Secretary General Kofi Annan said, this exclusion is inconsistent with the basic principle of equality among UN members.

The third discrimination has to do with the disproportionate condemnation of Israel by the UNHRC. In its March 2013 session, for instance, the UNHRC adopted six resolutions against Israel, and only four for the rest of the world combined (the four other resolutions condemned Syria, Iran, Myanmar and Sri Lanka). There were no resolutions about the gross and systematic violations of human rights in countries such as Saudi Arabia, China, Cuba, or Zimbabwe. This disproportionate and discriminatory policy characterized the UNHRC way before Israel decided to pull out. But the fact that the UNHRC fails to condemn actual human rights offenders should come as no surprise, since many of these offenders are among the 47 elected members of the committee. Indeed, in two weeks, the UNHRC will welcome among its newly elected members China, Cuba, Russia, and Saudi Arabia.

So why did Israel decide to rejoin this tragi-comic fraud? Mostly because of pressure from Germany, which apparently committed to rectify the UNHRC's discriminatory policy toward Israel. But how can Germany reasonably claim to act against the fraudulent and cynical politicization of human rights by the UN and by NGOs, when German political parties contribute to that very farce by funding NGOs that defame Israel and advocate the dismembering of the Jewish state in the name of human rights?

It is ironic that German Foreign Minister Guido Westerwelle urged Israel to rejoin the UNHRC while acknowledging the shortcomings of this institution, when his own political party (the Free Democratic Party) donates money, via its Friedrich Naumann Foundation, to the Ramallah Center for Human Rights, a Palestinian NGO that propagated the slanderous claim of "Israeli massacres" in Jenin and Nablus during Operation Defensive Shield.

The Free Democratic Party is not the only German political party that donates money to political NGOs that disguise their anti-Israel activities with a human-rights agenda.

The Konrad Adenauer Foundation (affiliated to Angela Merkel's Christian Democratic Union), and the Böll Foundation (affiliated to the Green Party) provide significant funding to MIFTAH, a Palestinian NGO that accuses Israel of "massacres," of "cultural genocide," of "war crimes" and of "apartheid." The Christian Social Union Party gives money, via its Hans Seidel Foundation, to the I'lam Media Center for Arab Palestinians in Israel, which promotes demonization campaigns against Israel.

The German Left Party, via its Rosa Luxemburg Fundation, funds Zohrot, an NGO that advocates the "Palestinian right of return" whose implementation would turn Israel into a binational state with a Jewish minority.

The German political parties and their foundations are obviously entitled to give money to whomever they wish. But when that money goes to political NGOs that disingenuously use the "human rights" magic formula to disguise their actual agenda of demonizing Israel and of undoing Israel's Jewish majority, then the German government loses its credibility.

Germany cannot reasonably act against the cynical denaturation of human rights by the UNHRC and, simultaneously, finance NGOs that actively take part in this denaturation.

Chapter 90:

The Questionable Wisdom of Piping Israeli Gas through Turkey

The reported political obstacles to the construction of a natural gas pipeline between Israel and Turkey are but another confirmation that relations between the two countries are strained. This last Israel-Turkey row also provides an opportunity to ponder the wisdom of building an Israeli pipeline to Turkey, in the first place.

There are good reasons why Israel and Turkey are considering the construction of such a pipeline. Turkey is a natural gas importer, while Israel is about to become a natural gas exporter. Not only is Turkey trying to diversify its gas imports in order to reduce its dependency on Russia's expansive natural gas, but it also wants to solidify its key role as a transit country for energy flows: Turkey is strategically located at the crossroads of energy exporters (the Middle East and the Caucasus) and energy importers (European countries). As the EU will likely become an importer of Israel's natural gas, Turkey could provide a transit route for an Israeli gas pipeline to Europe.

However, relying on Turkey as a transit country for Israel's exports to Europe would constitute a long-term strategic mistake.

The infrastructure for the delivery of natural gas (either via pipelines or liquefaction) is complex and expensive, which is why exporting and importing countries are generally locked in long-term agreements. Hence the need to carefully understand the potential risks of the Turkish option.

Building an Israeli pipeline via Turkey would likely undermine the emerging energy partnership between Israel and Cyprus. Noble Energy, the company that discovered the Tamar field off Israel's coast, also discovered a field of comparable size (Aphrodite) off Cyprus. As a result, Israel and Cyprus control together about 40 billion cubic meters of natural gas – which represents two years' worth of the EU's natural gas consumption.

This is why an energy partnership between Israel and Cyprus is taking shape. Turkey, however, is opposed to such a partnership. Because of the Turkish occupation in northern Cyprus and because the tensions between Cyprus and Turkey, Israel cannot have it both ways and will eventually have to make a choice.

In January 2013, the Director General of Israel's Ministry of Energy, Shaul Tzemah, suggested the possibility of an energy partnership between Israel and Turkey. Right after that, Turkey's Deputy Energy Minister Murat Mercan retorted that Israel would first have to apologize for the Mavi Marmara incident, compensate the families of the victims, and end the military blockade of Gaza. Even if Israel were to meet these demands, Mercan added, it would have to end its energy cooperation with "Greek Cyprus."

The long-term trends clearly suggest that Israeli-Turkish ties will continue to deteriorate. The tension started way before the Mavi Marmara incident and is deeply rooted in President Erdogan's Islamist ideology and policy.

Edorgan's political mentor is Necmettin Erbakan, a former Turkish prime minister whose foreign policy was based on trans-Islamic solidarity and uncompromising opposition to Israel. As soon as he became premier in 2003, Ergodan's foreign policy followed the path of his mentor.

In March 2004, Erdogan called Israel a "terrorist state" following the assassination of Ahmed Yassin. In February 2006, he received Hamas leader Khaled Mashal in Ankara. In January 2009, Erdogan publicly humiliated Shimon Peres at the Davos conference. In October 2009, Turkish state television started airing a series showing Israeli soldiers murdering Palestinian children. In November 2009, Erdogan declared that he would rather meet Sudanese President Omar al-Bashir (who perpetuated a genocide in Darfur and in South Sudan) than Israeli Prime Minister Benjamin Netanyahu. In March 2010 Erdogan claimed that the Temple Mount, Hebron and Rachel's Tomb in Bethlehem were never Jewish sites. All of this happened before the Mavi Marmara incident.

In February 2013, Erdogan called Zionism a "crime against humanity" and in August 2013 he claimed that Israel was responsible for the military coup in Egypt. Obviously, Erdogan's hostility to Israel is irrational. It was not caused by the Mavi Marmara incident, it was not fixed by Israel's apology, and it will not be mended by international mediation between the two countries.

As long as Erdogan and his Islamist party are in power in Turkey, relations with Israel will continue to deteriorate. Therefore, relying on Turkey for Israel's gas exports to Europe would be a mistake. Israel should pursue its partnership with Cyprus, instead, and build any future gas pipeline to Europe via Greece.

Chapter 91:

Strange Bedfellows: Israeli Nationalism and French Socialism

Many commentators were puzzled by the fact that a French-Israel rapprochement took place under a Socialist President. *Le Figaro*, for instance, wrote that there was something awkward about the hugs and mutual praise between a French Socialist and the leader of Israel's right during French President François Hollande's visit to Israel in November 2013. This seeming awkwardness, however, only confirms that French Socialists are friendlier to Israel than their Gaullist counterparts.

When the Vichy regime replaced the Third Republic in July 1940, many in the French right rejoiced at what they dubbed "a divine surprise." Vichy was a revenge for the "Republic of the Jews and Free-masons" and a return to "authentic French values." Léon Blum, the French social-ist leader who became France's first Jewish Premier in 1936, was the very incarnation of what the French right hated about the Third Republic.

Blum was also a Zionist who used his power and influence to obtain France's 1947 vote in favor of the UN partition plan.

In fact, France led the international efforts for the partition of British Palestine and for a humanitarian solution to the tragedy of Holocaust survivors denied entry to Palestine by Britain. It was under Pierre Mendès-France, another Socialist premier (as well as a Jew), that France and Israel started developing a military relationship in the mid-1950s. This close relationship culminated in the Franco-Israeli military operation in Suez in 1956, when the Socialist Guy Mollet headed the French government.

When de Gaulle came back to power in 1958, he was determined to "correct the mistakes" of the Fourth Republic. While he himself never made anti-Semitic comments about "The Republic of the Jews and Free-Masons," the French right welcomed the end of the Socialist-dominated Fourth Republic. For de Gaulle, the Fourth Republic's decision to fight an Arab country together with Israel in 1956 was a terrible mistake, which ended in diplomatic humiliation. As soon as he came back to power, he significantly lowered the level of military cooperation with Israel.

With the end of the Algerian war in 1962, the underlying cause of the French-Israeli alliance (i.e. the two countries' common animosity towards Egyptian President Gamal Abdel Nasser) vanished. De Gaulle was determined to repair France's strained ties with the Arab world. This policy was incompatible with France's cooperation with Israel.

There was an additional reason for the widening gap between France and Israel under de Gaulle. While de Gaulle embarked on a confrontational foreign policy vis-à-vis the United States (a policy that culminated in France's departure from NATO's military command in 1966), the United States started reevaluating the pro-Arab policy of the Eisenhower Administration. With Nasser actively supporting anti-US forces in the Middle East, the US progressively ceased to consider Israel an impediment to its interests in the region. Hence, since de Gaulle's foreign policy had become so confrontational toward the US, it also became more confrontational toward Israel.

De Gaulle deeply resented "les Anglo-Saxons." Humiliated by Churchill and Roosevelt during WWII, his policy of restoring France's "grandeur" always had a flavor of revenge. Defying the United States became a central motto, and policy, of Gaullism.

De Gaulle's conservative successors, Georges Pompidou and Valéry Giscard d'Estaing, championed France's "Arab policy." During the Yom Kippur War, Pompidou refused to allow the US airlift to Israel to cross French airspace. Giscard d'Estaing freed Abu Daoud (the mastermind of the massacre of the Israeli athletes in Munich), and he condemned the Israel-Egypt Camp David Agreements for not including the PLO.

François Mitterrand, the first Socialist President of the Fifth Republic, put an end to this outrageous policy. He was the first French president to pay an official visit to Israel. Because Mitterrand was not a Gaullist, he was not anti-American. Indeed, in 1991 he joined the US-led coalition in the Gulf War.

But Mitterrand's Gaullist successor, Jacques Chirac, led an international anti-US diplomatic coalition during the 2003 Iraq war. Chirac vocally blamed Ehud Barak and absolved Yasser Arafat of the failure of the 2000 Camp David summit and the ensuing wave of terror. Chirac visited Arafat in hospital in Paris in 2004, and he had his coffin wrapped in a French flag. As for Nicolas Sarkozy, he was what French grammarians call "un faux ami." The warmth of his words was only matched by the hostility of his deeds.

As a French Socialist, François Hollande does not share the anti-Zionist and anti-American ideology of Gaullism and of the aristocratic Quai d'Orsay. But, mostly, he realizes that France's interests in the Middle East and Africa are threatened by Islamism and that the Obama administration is unwilling to confront that threat militarily. Hence Hollande's military intervention in Mali, hence his readiness (stopped by Obama) to intervene in Syria, and hence his unwillingness to appease Iran.

As opposed to John Kerry, François Hollande called upon both Israel and the Palestinians to make concessions for peace. While in Ramallah, he told Palestinian President Mahmoud Abbas to get real about the "right of return." Hollande called for a halt to Israeli settlements but, when pressed by a French journalist, he refused to call them "illegitimate" (as Kerry repeatedly does). In sum, France today is tougher on Iran and more impartial on the Israeli-Palestinian dispute than the United States.

The self-proclaimed "realism" of the US Administration today is affecting both Israel's security and French interests, just as it did in the 1950s. And, then as now, American miscalculations are creating strange bedfellows between Israeli nationalism and French socialism.

Chapter 92:

South Sudan: Israel's last Regional Bastion

South Sudan's descent into civil war is not only a tragedy for the South Sudanese and a disappointment to those who supported their independence after decades of abuse and massacres by the Khartoum regime. It also constitutes a blow to Israel's geopolitical interests.

South Sudan's independence in July 2011 was welcomed by Israel and was given a cold shoulder by Palestinian Authority Chairman Mahmoud Abbas. After the International Criminal Court (ICC) issued an arrest warrant in 2010 for Sudanese President Omar al-Bashir on charges of genocide, war crimes and crimes against humanity in the Darfur, Abbas declared (on 28 November 2010): "We lend complete support to Sudanese President Omar al-Bashir." Shortly after South Sudan freed itself from its genocidal northern neighbor, Abbas sent al-Bashir a letter (personally handed to him by Fatah Central Committee member Azzam al-Ahmad) which expressed support for the Sudanese leader in his efforts to prevent the independence of South Sudan. Abbas' bureau chief Tayeb al-Rahim claimed at the time that Sudan's breakup had been engineered by Israel to weaken the Arab world and to benefit from South Sudan's oil resources.

The conflicting interests and policies between Israel and the PA over South Sudan's independence are symptomatic of a less-known aspect of the Arab-Israeli conflict: the struggle over the non-Arab countries and minorities of the wider Middle East.

In the late 1950s, Israeli Prime Minister David Ben-Gurion initiated and implemented via the Mossad what came to be known as Israel's "periphery policy." The idea was to develop strategic ties with the non-Arab countries of the Middle East that shared Israel's animosity toward the Soviet Union, as well as toward Egyptian President Nasser because of his support for pro-Soviet rebellions throughout the Middle East. Israel successfully developed close intelligence and military ties with Iran, Turkey, and Ethiopia, as well as with minorities such as the Kurds in Northern Iraq and the Christians of Southern Sudan and Lebanon.

Ben-Gurion conceived the "periphery policy" in order to counter Israel's isolation in the Middle East, as well as on the world scene. With the demise of the Fourth Republic and the return of de Gaulle to power in 1958, the alliance with France was in jeopardy. In the United States, the Eisenhower Administration remained faithful to its policy of keeping its distances from Israel so as not to lose more Arab states to the Soviet Union (such as Egypt in 1955). So Ben-Gurion decided to counter the Soviet influence with Middle East countries that shared Israel's concerns. Closer ties with Eastern Africa were made possible by the opening of the Tiran Straits after the 1956 war.

Ben-Gurion succeeded in turning Iran, Turkey and Ethiopia into strategic allies (in the case of Iran this alliance had a major economic benefit because of its oil supplies to Israel). But the triangle of Israel's "periphery" eventually crumbled following regime change and revolutions: Ethiopia became communist in 1974 and Iran Islamist in 1979. As for Turkey, it actually strengthened its ties with Israel in the 1990s (both countries even signed a military accord in 1996). But with the electoral victory of Erdogan's Islamist party in 2002, Turkey was "lost" as well.

Israel, however, never completely abandoned its "periphery" strategy. The demise of Saddam Hussein in 2003 enabled the emergence of a semi-independent Kurdistan. The 2005 Cedar Revolution in Lebanon seemed for a while to undermine the power grip of the Assad family and of Hezbollah. Those hopes, however, were eventually shattered because Iran entrenched its influence in both Iraq and Lebanon.

The independence of South Sudan in 2011 was a blow to Iran. Ten years after Iran's 1979 Islamic Revolution, Sudan followed suit with Omar al-Bashir's military coup and subsequent Islamization. Sudan thus became Iran's closest ally in Africa. In October 2012, Iran dispatched a naval task force to Sudan only a few days after a reported Israeli airstrike against a missile base run by Tehran in Khartoum. It is no coincidence that both Israel and the United States welcomed the partial weakening and breakup of Sudan in 2011. With the recent outbreak of civil war in South Sudan, however, the country might switch international allegiances and even fall under the partial control of Sudan and Iran.

Hence the pro-Israel "periphery triangle" of the 1960s (Iran, Turkey, East Africa) has become a nightmarish triangle of Islamist regimes.

Ben-Gurion used to quip that, in Israel, the true realists are those who believe in miracles. No doubt about this: it would take no less than a miracle for the Middle East to revert to its pre-Islamist, Realpolitik days.

Chapter 93:

European Companies Should be Concerned by the BDS Campaign

On February 5, 2014, the Supreme Court of the United Kingdom rejected a third and final appeal by BDS (Boycott, Divestment, Sanctions) activists who were convicted of criminal trespass for chaining themselves to a concrete block outside the London shop of Ahava, an Israeli cosmetics company. The activists claimed that Ahava is guilty of "war crimes" because it has a factory beyond the 1949 Armistice Line. The Court ruled that Ahava should not be penalized for Israel's allegedly illegal occupation of the West Bank.

This is not the first time that BDS activists were dismissed by a European Court. On March 22, 2013 a French Court (the Appellate court of Versailles) rejected a lawsuit filed by the Palestine Liberation Organization (PLO) and a pro-Palestinian NGO against Alstom, a French energy and transportation conglomerate that built a tramway in

Jerusalem. The petitioners claimed that since part of the tramway's tracks, built by Alstom, run beyond the 1949 Armistice Line, Alstom violated, inter alia, the 1949 Geneva Convention and the Hague Conventions of 1907 and 1954.

The Versailles Court ruled that even if it were to be determined that the State of Israel had breached the above conventions by signing a contract with a private company for the construction of a tramway beyond the 1949 Armistice Line, the aforesaid company should not be penalized for undertaking a project for which it was hired by the Israeli Government. No less significantly, the court ruled that the State of Israel did not breach international law by signing a contract with Alstom, since the 1907 Hague Convention allows the occupying power to build infra-structures (including tramways) that enable the proper administration of the occupied territory.

According to these two court decisions, there is no legal ground for penalizing Israeli companies that operate beyond the 1949 Armistice Line – even though those decisions do assume that the State of Israel's partial control or sovereignty beyond that line is illegal, and that the 1949 Geneva Convention applies to the West Bank. This assumption, how-ever, is mistaken.

The so-called "Occupied Palestinian Territories" are neither Palestinian nor occupied. When the United Kingdom unilaterally with-drew from its Mandate in May 1948, it left a legal void that was filled by the newly declared (and borderless) State of Israel. There was no Arab declaration of independence on the territory that had been allocated to an Arab state by the UN partition plan of November 1947. That plan, in any case, was a non-binding recommendation (like all General Assembly resolutions) and it became moot the moment it was rejected by the Arabs. The British Mandate, by contrast, had been allocated to the Jewish people for self-determination by the 1920 Treaty of Sèvres and by the 1922 League of Nations Mandate.

When Transjordan conquered the West Bank in 1948 and annexed it in 1950, it did so on a territory that had been allocated to Jewish self-determination by post-World War I international treaties. Hence Jordan's sovereignty over the West Bank was never recognized by the international community (with the exception of Britain and Pakistan). When Israel conquered the West Bank in June 1967, it did so in a legitimate act of self-defense (as opposed to Jordan's military aggression in 1948). Israel did not cross an international border, but a temporary armistice line. It did not conquer a recognized sovereign territory, but one that had been allocated to the Jewish People by the League of Nations and that had been unlawfully controlled by Jordan for 19 years.

Therefore, many international lawyers dispute the assertion that the West Bank is an occupied territory and that the 1949 Geneva Convention applies to it. Article 49 of the convention, which prohibits the mass transfer of populations into occupied territories, was meant to prevent what was a common German practice during WWII, not the voluntary settlement of Jews in a land that was allocated to them for that very purpose by the League of Nations.

The actions brought against Israeli companies that operate beyond the 1949 Armistice Line are therefore legally groundless, even according to the disputable opinion that Israel's presence beyond that line is illegal. However, were other European courts to vindicate anti-Israeli boycotters in the future, then hundreds of European companies would be exposed to lawsuits because of their activities and investments in countries that occupy territories or that control disputed ones. The list includes, among others, China (over Tibet), Russia (over Abkhazia), Turkey (over Cyprus), and Morocco (over Western Sahara).

Although BDS activists do not have a case, they are potentially exposing hundreds of European companies operating in the above countries to liability. I say bring it on and give Europe a taste of its own medicine.

Chapter 94:

By its Silence on Ukraine, Israel has Chosen Dishonor to Please Putin

Remember the op-ed Vladimir Putin published in the *New York Times* in August 2013 after Barack Obama had threatened to punish Assad for his use of chemical weapons? In it, Putin explained that the use of force is legal only when authorized by the UN Security Council or in case of self-defense. Since there was no Security Council Resolution authorizing Russia to invade Ukraine's Crimean peninsula, Putin is evoking "self-defense" (the alleged need to protect Crimea's Russian population) to justify his military invasion.

It is the same peculiar Russian definition of "self-defense" that brought Russian tanks into Budapest in 1956, into Prague in 1968, into Afghanistan in 1979, into Poland in 1981, into Chechnya in 1999, and into Georgia in 2008.

Joseph Stalin used to say that, when dealing with the West, he knew until what point he could exaggerate. Similarly, Putin is testing the West's determination to contain his irredentist policies in the former Soviet Republics. Canada has bravely led the way by recalling its ambassador to Moscow. The US and the EU for their part can inflict economic pain on Russia. One is to hope that the Americans and Europeans will extract from Putin an economic price that will make his adventures too costly.

Israel, for its part, did not take a public stance on this issue. It should have.

Obviously, Prime Minister Netanyahu and Foreign Minister Lieberman figured that since Israel does not have a dog in that fight, it cannot afford to cross Vladimir Putin when his cooperation is otherwise needed to curtail Iran's nuclear program. This foreign policy decision, however, is morally wrong and strategically ill advised.

Morally, Israel should always make its voice heard loud and clear, together with other democracies, when thuggish leaders like Putin violate international law. Israel should emancipate itself from its "beaten wife syndrome." While Israel is far from irreproachable and often deserves to be criticized, it is also unfairly, disproportionately and disingenuously accused of violating human rights and international law. This does not mean that Israel should feel embarrassed to condemn countries and leaders who actually do violate international law and human rights. Israel made a moral mistake by not condemning Putin's bullying and total disdain for international law.

Strategically, Israel's silence is ill advised, as well. Its attempts to sweet-talk Putin into downgrading his nuclear cooperation with Iran have been completely fruitless. Putin will do whatever it takes to poke America in the eye and to fill Russia's coffers with the sale of hydrocarbons and nuclear technology. Israel's existential angst is simply not on Putin's list of concerns. Russia continues and will continue to vote with the Palestinians at the UN, to host Hamas leaders in Moscow, to help Iran with its nuclear program and to sell missiles to Syria (which happen to end up in the hands of Hezbollah). In 2008, Israel agreed to stop supplying weapons to Georgia because Putin promised, in return, not to sell an S-300 air-defense system to Iran. Instead, Putin sold the S-300 air-defense system to Syria.

Israel should remember the 1950 Korean precedent. When the Soviets and the Chinese invaded the Korean Peninsula, they clearly breached the UN Charter. Israel had recently been admitted to the UN. It had successfully fought its war of independence with weapons provided by the Soviet Union via Czechoslovakia. The Soviet Union had voted in favor of the 1947 UN partition plan and immediately recognized, in 1948, the newly declared State of Israel. Israel, therefore, wanted to stay neutral in the Cold War and tried to avoid condemning the Soviet invasion of Korea. Eventually, Israel added its voice to the UN condemnation of the Soviet Union and to the UN force that was sent to Korea. It was the right thing to do, as a matter of principle. But it was also the right thing to do in terms of Israel's interests, because once the Soviet Union achieved its goal of driving Britain out of Palestine, it had no more reason to be supportive of Israel, regardless of Israel's stance on Korea.

Israel's Soviet-born Foreign Minister, Avigdor Lieberman, is partly to be blamed for this morally and strategically flawed policy toward Russia. After the rigged Duma election in 2011, Lieberman was the first foreign politician to congratulate Putin on his party's "victory." This statement was an embarrassment, and it certainly did not make Putin more amenable to Israel's concerns over Iran.

Israel's foreign policy toward Russia today may be summarized by paraphrasing Winston Churchill: Israel has chosen dishonor to please Putin, but at the end Israel has both dishonor and Putin's middle finger.

Chapter 95:

Netanyahu's Finest Hour? On the Iranian Threat

In 2012, I was in lower Manhattan during the 9/11 commemorations. Eleven years had passed since that terrible morning, but America has thankfully killed Bin-Laden. From a historical perspective, however, Bin-Laden did achieve one of his objectives: to replace US-backed Arab regimes with Islamic ones.

Iran has played a major role, and continues to play a major role, in the Islamic takeover of the Middle-East and of North Africa. It also pursues nuclear weapons with the declared aim of wiping Israel off the map.

History has taught us that when Jew-haters threaten to kill Jews, they should be taken seriously. But history has also taught us that no country has ever abandoned its nuclear ambitions as a result of economic sanctions. The Reagan administration didn't want Pakistan to go nuclear, and the Bush junior administration didn't want North Korea to get the bomb either. Yet in spite of pressures and sanctions, both countries went ahead.

Iraq and Libya, on the other hand, did forego their nuclear programs only because they either suffered or feared a military strike. Saddam Hussein abandoned his nuclear ambitions after his French-built nuclear reactor was bombed by Israel in 1981. Muammar Gaddafi stopped his nuclear program right after the US and British invasion of Iraq in 2003, because he feared that he would be next in line. Even Iran temporarily suspended its nuclear program after the invasion of Iraq for fear of a US strike. As soon as it became clear that the Bush Administration had abandoned the idea of destroying Iran's nuclear plants, Iran renewed its nuclear program.

Not surprisingly, economic sanctions are not convincing Iran to stop its nuclear program. For a start, these sanctions are a sham because they are not enforced by China (which needs Iran's oil) and by Russia (which sees in Iran the last rampart against US hegemony in the Middle East). In addition, Iran and Egypt are now negotiating an oil deal to make up for Iran's lost sales to the European Union. Iran supported the 2011 uprising that brought Muhammad Morsi to power. Now it is ripping the economic benefits of having a new Islamic ally.

But even if sanctions were actually enforced against Iran, they would be powerless: a leadership that has declared its readiness to sacrifice millions of its own citizens for the sake of destroying Israel surely has no qualms about temporarily lowering the living standards of its future victims. So saying, as Hillary Clinton recently did, that sanctions are the best way to get Iran to abandon its nuclear ambitions is simply wrong.

Containment is not an option either. The threat of Mutually Assured Destruction (MAD) is what deterred both the United States and the Soviet Union from going to war. Such deterrence will not apply to

Islamists because they are suicidal. If anything, they believe that an Israeli nuclear strike will grant them a short-cut to heaven.

Nothing, bar a devastating military strike, will prevent Iran from getting the bomb.

America has the military capability to annihilate most of Iran's nuclear installations, but candidate Obama will not attack Iran while on the campaign trail. More worryingly for Israel, a re-elected President Obama will unlikely order a military strike. After all, the United States has already lost most of its Middle-East allies to Islamic regimes. So why contain and deter Iran when the latter has already achieved its goal of replacing US-backed Arab regimes with Islamic ones?

A nuclear-armed Iran could technically close the Straits of Hormuz (a major oil route) without fear of American retaliation. But such a move would be so harmful to Iran's economy that it wouldn't make sense. America was able to live with a nuclear Soviet Union, and it is able to live today with a nuclear Russia, a nuclear China, a nuclear Pakistan, and a nuclear North Korea.

A nuclear-armed Iran would further undermine US interests and power, but it would not constitute an unbearable threat to the United States. The Iranian bomb constitutes an existential threat to Israel, not to America. So Israel has good reasons to suspect that the current US administration is bluffing when it says that all options are on the table to prevent Iran from getting the bomb.

In September 2012, the International Atomic Energy Agency declared that Iran is moving its nuclear production underground by doubling the number of centrifuges it has installed at its facility near the city of Qom. While Iran is approaching the "immunity zone" that would make its underground nuclear fuel sites impregnable to attack, the US government isn't sending any ultimatum to the Mullahs.

So it looks like Israel is on its own with Iran. To add insult to injury, the Obama administration is now trying to hold us back. Prime Minister

Netanyahu's remark that "those in the international community who re-fuse to put red lines before Iran don't have a moral right to place a red light before Israel" was spot-on.

Israel is on its own today the same way that it was on its own when it declared its independence in 1948, when it grounded the Egyptian air force in 1967, and when it rescued Jewish hostages in Uganda in 1976. In all cases, the Jewish leadership made a tough decision that defied logic but that relied on what Israel's Declaration of Independence calls "The Rock of Israel."

Making hard decisions and taking calculated risks is what leadership is all about. The coming years will be decisive. May they be remembered as Netanyahu's finest hour.

Chapter 96:

In Iraq, the US must Choose between Legalism and Islamism

The Islamic State of Iraq and Syria (ISIS) symbolically bulldozed, in June 2014, a barrier on the Iraq-Syria border - a border drawn in 1916 by Sir Mark Sykes and François-Georges Picot on behalf of the British and French governments. This border was endorsed, with changes, by the San Remo Conference (April 1920), by the Treaty of Sèvres (August 1920), by the Treaty of Lausanne (July 1923), and by the League of Nations mandates on Palestine and Syria (September 1923). In a way, ISIS does have a point: those borders, drawn by the French and the British to serve their imperial interests, artificially divided the Arab nation. Why should they be immutable?

The answer is that most borders are artificial and arbitrary, and that they were generally drawn without the consent of locals. Moreover, one cannot challenge the borders of the states that replaced the Ottoman

Empire without challenging the borders of the states that replaced the Austro-Hungarian Empire (as Hitler did in the 1930s, thus bringing about the outbreak of World War II). True, the states that emerged from the ruins of the Austro-Hungarian Empire were nation-states, while, in the Middle East, one nation (the Arab nation) was divided into several states. That difference, however, is not a good enough reason to argue for the redrawing of borders in the Middle East but not in Eastern Europe.

This does not mean that borders cannot be redrawn. They often are. Territories switch sovereignties and allegiances, sometimes with the approval of local populations but generally without. Saarland decided to become part of Germany in 1935 (and again in 1955). In 1939, the Alexandretta (or Hatay) province voted to secede from French Syria and become part of Turkey. After World War II, Poland's territory was expanded westward, at the expense of Germany. In 1950, China took control of Tibet. In 1954, Soviet leader Nikita Khrushchev transferred Crimea from Russia to Ukraine. In 1974, Turkey conquered northern Cyprus. In 1976, Morocco took partial control of Western Sahara (Morocco extended its control to all of Western Sahara in 1979). The list goes on.

Precisely because borders can always be contested and often are, it is an accepted principle in international law that when new countries emerge from old ones, or from former colonies or mandates, the last official boundary is considered the international border. This principle, known as *uti possidetis* ("you possess by law"), has been endorsed by the International Court of Justice. According to that principle, the borders of the Middle East or of Eastern Europe cannot be contested, regardless of how unfair and arbitrary they might be (*uti possidetis*, of course, does not condone the conquest and occupation of sovereign countries, such as the occupation of Afghanistan by the Soviet Union in 1979 or the occupation of Kuwait by Iraq in 1990).

Contesting and erasing the Middle East's borders is precisely what Islamists are trying to do, with Iran leading the process. True, Iran is Shiite and ISIS is Sunni. But the rise of ISIS benefits Iran because it makes Iraqi Prime Minister Nouri al-Maliki more dependent on Iranian protection. Iran wants Iraq to become a subservient client state divided along Sunni, Shiite, and Kurdish sectarian lines. Some even claim that Iran contributed to the strength of ISIS. Back in February 2012, the US Department of the Treasury accused Iran of providing money and weapons to "al-Qaida in Iraq" —the radical Sunni group that became ISIS in April 2013. Abdul Rahman al-Rashid, a Saudi commentator for *Asharq Al-Awsat*, as well as director of the *Al Arabiya TV* channel, recently claimed that ISIS is a creation of Iranian and Syrian intelligence.

Faced with the ISIS and Iranian challenge, the United States has two choices. It can either acquiesce to the partition of Iraq, with Sunni Iraq uniting with those parts of Syria not controlled by Assad, and with Shiite Iraq becoming an Iranian protectorate. Or it can insist on the strict respect of borders and of *uti possidetis*.

In both cases, the idea of establishing a 23rd Arab state (a so-called Palestinian state) is at odds with reality.

If one accepts that islamization is superseding artificial Arab states, why establish another one of those? If one insists on the inviolability of the League of Nations borders, then Israel, and Israel only, is the legitimate and legal inheritor of the Mandatory borders under the *uti possidetis* principle (the occupation of parts of the former British Mandate by Egypt and Jordan between 1948 and 1967 did not legally change the borders that Israel inherited from the Mandate).

True, the Obama administration claims that creating a 23rd Arab state in Israel's midst would bring peace to the Middle East. But, then again, Barack Obama described Iraq, as the last American troops left the country, as "sovereign, stable, and self-reliant."

Chapter 97:

US Security Guarantees and Human Rights Preaching Sound Hollow

A standard and widespread comment on the July 2014 war between Israel and Hamas was that, at the end of the day, only a political settlement can spare us the recurrence of rocket firing and of retaliation. *The Economist*, for example, wrote in its 12 July 2014 edition that "lasting peace will come about only when the two sides reach a comprehensive settlement." President Obama declared that "the only path to true security is a just and lasting peace between Israelis and Palestinians." Such statements are tautological: obviously, there would be no war if there were peace. The question is not whether peace between Jews and Arabs is desirable, but whether it is possible.

President Obama says that he believes it is. The White House's Coordinator for the Middle East, Philip Gordon, came to address the "Israel Conference on Peace" in Tel-Aviv in July 2014. "How" Gordon asked "will [Israel] have peace if it is unwilling to delineate a border, end the occupation and allow for Palestinian sovereignty, security, and dignity?" This is a good question, but here is a better one: how will Israel have peace if it *is* willing to delineate a border, end the occupation and allow for Palestinian sovereignty, security, and dignity? Because Israel had no peace when there was such a border between 1949 and 1967, and because when Israel offered to re-delineate this border with minor changes in July 2000 and in May 2008 it was unable to obtain the peace that such a move was supposed to produce.

Experience, logics and deduction suggest that the West Bank would turn into a larger and more lethal version of the Gaza Strip after the Israeli withdrawal that Gordon is calling for. He is aware of that: "We know that many Israelis fear withdrawal from the West Bank due to the experience in Gaza, from which rockets continue to strike Israel, notwithstanding the full withdrawal of Israeli troops and settlement." The solution? An American security plan whose details "remain classified." Gordon uttered those words shortly after his audience had to be evacuated because of rockets being shot at Tel-Aviv from Gaza by the "technocrats" that recently joined the PA government (a government that US Secretary of State John Kerry was quick to endorse because PA Chairman Mahmoud Abbas had assured him that it was "committed to nonviolence").

Because the details of the American security plan for the West Bank "remain classified" Gordon asks us to trust him when he assures us that the fate of the West Bank will be different from that of Gaza after an Israeli withdrawal. With all due respect, we may not have access to the "classified security plan" but we do have access to the showcase of American-trained security forces in Iraq.

During the botched round of negotiations between Israel and the Palestinian Authority in 2013-2014, the Obama administration had proposed to eventually replace the IDF's presence in the Jordan Valley with

US-trained Palestinian forces. US-trained forces in Iraq were unable (or unwilling) to stop the advance of the Islamic State of Iraq and Syria (ISIS). If US-trained Iraqi soldiers weren't willing to fight ISIS to protect their own country, why would US-trained Palestinian soldiers be willing to fight fellow Arabs to protect Israel in the Jordan Valley? Indeed, the US-trained Iraqi forces were as inefficient at protecting their Shiite government as the US-trained soldiers in Gaza were inefficient, in 2007, at protecting the PLO government there. And since ISIS, which has a Palestinian contingent, is now threatening Jordan, would US-trained Palestinians shoot their brothers to protect Israel's borders?

Philip Gordon is also unconvincing when he calls upon Israel to allow for "Palestinian sovereignty, security, and dignity." Which country in the Arab world, I beg you, provides security and dignity to its citizens? And if the Obama administration is so concerned about the "sovereignty, security, and dignity" of Middle-East peoples, why does it deny those attributes from the Kurds?

In June 2014, John Kerry asked Kurdish President Massoud Barzani to put aside his aspirations for an independent Kurdish state. The Obama administration fears that an independent Kurdish state in Iraq would encourage Kurdish secessionism in Turkey in in Iran. Obama does not want to cross Iran in the midst of tough negotiations on the Ayatollahs' nuclear program, nor does he want to further alienate Turkey's temperamental Prime Minister. So Kurdish "sovereignty, security, and dignity" can wait.

Surely, the United States cannot be blamed for practicing Realpolitik. But it should at least have the decency of not insulting our intelligence.

Chapter 98:

All Victims are Equal, but some are more Equal than Others

David Hume's theory of "concentric circles" provides an explanation for people's selective empathy: the more pain affects you, the more you care —and vice versa. Adam Smith explains this selectiveness with a graphic example: if you were told that your finger will be cut off tomorrow, you would spend the night tossing and turning; but if you were told that hundreds of people will die tomorrow at the other end of the world due to a natural disaster, you would sleep soundly. Cable television and the Internet have mostly turned Hume's theory on its head, because we all see the world's tragedies all the time. The average New Yorker is still more likely to lose sleep over his investment portfolio than over the number of Yazidis killed in Iraq, but the world's tragedies are constantly displayed on our screens. And yet, people still have a selective way of relating to those tragedies. Hume's theory is still valid, but for different reasons. Selective empathy in the 21st century is less the result of distance than of substance –your chances of gaining sympathy are less affected by how far away you are than by who is harming you.

As *The Economist* wrote recently: "Though it has long been known that there is little correlation between the attention paid to conflicts and their levels of casualties, the disparity is depressing." In terms of Google searches, Ukraine gets far more intention than Syria, even though there have been 20 times more victims in Syria than in Ukraine since the beginning of the year. The thousands of deaths in Iraq went unnoticed until the United States announced its air strikes. Try googling "Central African Republic" and you get 30,000 results on the news section. Type "Israel Gaza War" and you get 3.5 million entries. And yet, more people (about 2,500) have died in the Central Africa conflict this year than in Gaza.

In 2009, Israel became the target of an orchestrated international campaign following Operation Cast Lead, a campaign that culminated in the Goldstone Report. At the same time, the Sri Lanka government brutally decimated the Tamil independence movement, killing at least 40,000 Tamils and producing hundreds of thousands of refugees. A UN human rights commission was set up but it has yet to compile a report (five years after the deeds); there were no massive demonstrations around the world, and the media barely covered this tragedy.

As British writer and comedian Pat Condell pointedly asked: "Where were you all progressive humanitarians when Assad was butchering thousands in Syria, or Bashir in Sudan? Where were the angry mass demonstrations for those people or for the victims of the butchery in Nigeria? Or for the thousands murdered in Iraq? But the Jews of Israel finally respond to being constantly attacked by Islamic terrorists, and the world goes insane." Or, as French writer and professor Pierre Jourde recently wrote: "One hundred lynched Christians in Pakistan are worth less, media-wise, than one dead Palestinian." The same goes for the non-Muslim victims of the Islamic State in Iraq and of Boko Haram in Nigeria.

One wonders, indeed, why Western media and the "progressive humanitarians" of the world have no time for the Tibetans, the Uighurs, the Tamils, the Kurds, the Chechens, the Georgians, the Sudanese Christians, the black slaves in Mauritania, the Tuaregs in Nigeria, the Indians in Guatemala, the Sahrawis in Morocco, the Yazidis, Christians, Turkmens, Shias, and Shabaks in Iraq, the Blacks in Darfur, or the Christian minorities around the Muslim world. And one wonders why the massacre of Muslims by Muslims is never a source of commotion.

One possible answer to that question was provided in August 2009 by then Turkish Prime Minister Recep Erdogan. Addressing the accusation of genocide in Sudan, Erdogan said that "A Muslim can never commit genocide. It's not possible." One is left wondering who committed the genocides against the Armenians and against the Black Sudanese. And who, exactly, killed over 100,000 Kurds in Iraq in 1988, 150,000 Algerians in 1991, and over 250,000 Syrians in the past three years?

Then there is cold Realpolitik. China gets away with oppressing and colonizing Tibet and Xinjiang because nobody (including the United States) can afford to mess with China. The Chinese government killed about 200 Muslim "rebels" in Xinjiang in 2009. It killed another 100 three weeks ago. Yet you will not hear a US call for a free Tibet or for a free Xingjian. The fact that the Chinese government holds $1.33 trillion of US Treasury Bonds might be part of the explanation.

My point is not that Israel should ignore the laws of war because of the hypocrisy and double standards of our critics. Israel should pride itself for not behaving like China, like Russia, or like Sri Lanka. But Israel's leaders must understand that this theater of the absurd will go on as long as they stay on the defensive instead of going on the offensive. Answering smears won't do it. Exposing the crimes of our enemies and publicly embarrassing them will.

Chapter 99:

What Israel and ISIS have in Common

As America commemorated the 13th anniversary of 9/11, a paradox emerged from the tragic opening act of the 21st century. On the one hand, Osama Bin-Laden was eliminated and al-Qaida is mostly on the run. On the other hand, Bin-Laden's dream of re-establishing the Caliphate is still alive and lethal – as recently proven by the progress and barbarism of ISIS (the Islamic State of Iraq and Syria). The fact that America is trying to build an international coalition to defeat ISIS is in itself a reminder that Bin-Laden has not been defeated.

Like his predecessor, George W. Bush, President Obama keeps repeating that America is not at war with Islam. Obama even added that ISIS "is not what Islam is about."

President Obama's attempts to distinguish between ISIS and Islam were recently challenged by Brother Rachid, a Moroccan Muslim who spent 20 years studying Islam and eventually converted to Christianity. Rebuking Obama's declaration that ISIS does not speak on behalf of Islam because its members behead American journalists, Rachid said: "Beheading is commanded in the Quran in Surah 47, verse 4 ... Ironically, this Surah is called the Surah of Mohamed." Telling Obama about his own Muslim education, Rachid explained: "We have been brainwashed to hate all of you ... and to make Islam the religion of the whole world, as the Quran says ... ISIS is just one symptom; if it disappears other ISISs will appear under a different name ... If Islam is not the problem, then why is it that there are millions of Christians in the Middle East, and yet none of them has ever blown himself up to become a martyr, even though they live under the same economic and political circumstances? Why have new converts to Islam become terrorists? I am imploring you to take a stand ... for the future of democracy: speak the truth about the real threat that is facing all of us."

The European converts to Islam mentioned by Brother Rachid enter Syria and Iraq via Turkey's "jihadist highway." Turkey is a member of NATO, the organization around which Obama is trying to build an anti-ISIS strategy. The irony does not end here.

ISIS's spin-off in Sinai calls itself "Ansar Bait al-Maqdis." Literally, this means "The Faithful of the [Jerusalem] Temple." "Bait al-Maqdis" is the Arabic pronunciation of the Hebrew "Beit Ha-Mikdash," whose meaning is "The Holy Temple [of Jerusalem]."

Jerusalem was conquered by Muslims in 638. The modern Arabic name of Jerusalem, al-Quds, can be traced to the 9th century, but it only became widely used in the 11th century. "Al-Quds" derives from "Bait al-Muqaddas" which is a different pronunciation of "Bait al-Maqdis." ISIS's branch in Sinai is using the original Arab word for Jerusalem, a word that in itself testified to the fact that the Arabs used to recognize Jerusalem as the site of Solomon's Temple. Indeed, after the Arab conquest of Jerusalem, Jews were allowed to pray freely on the Temple

Mount because the Arabs recognized that this is where their Temple once stood. A tourist guidebook published by the Supreme Muslim Council in 1924 says the Temple Mount "is among the oldest in the world. It is, beyond any doubt, where King Solomon's Temple once stood."

Today's denial of the Temple's very existence by Arab leaders is a recent phenomenon that does not reflect Islam's traditional stance. When Arafat shocked the Israeli and American delegations at the Camp David summit in July 2000 by saying that there had never been a Temple in Jerusalem, he was expressing a new Palestinian myth. This myth has been endorsed and repeated by Sheikh Ra'ed Salah (the head of the northern branch of the Islamic movement in Israel); by Arab MKs (and former MKs) Abdulmalik Dehamshe and Muhammad Barakeh; and by Shauki Khatib (chairman of the Israeli-Arab Follow-up Committee). "Temple denial" is truly a recent phenomenon. Even Araf al-Araf, a Palestinian historian close to Hadj Amin al-Husseini, wrote in his 1951 book Tariah al-Quds that "Al Aram Al Sharif [the Temple Mount] is on Mount Moriah, mentioned in the Book of Genesis ... It was bought by David to build the Temple, but it is Solomon who built it in 1007 BCE."

So Brother Rashid is right: ISIS does represent Islam – not least because it recognizes Jerusalem's Jewish past. In Israel, there is also a movement called "The Temple Mount Faithful," an organization that militates for Jewish freedom of worship on the Temple Mount – a freedom that is denied today by the Israeli government but that was respected in the 7th century by Muslim rulers. On the question of the Temple Mount, the gap is wider between Israel and the PLO than between Israel and ISIS. Too bad they would behead us before giving us a chance to explain this to them.

Chapter 100:

Scotland, Israel, and the Lessons for Europe

"In Western Europe, particularist nationalism is fading and the idea of 'citizen of the world' is taking hold," wrote Shimon Peres in his 1993 book *The New Middle East*. Peres wrote those words right after Czechoslovakia was dismembered into two separate nation-states, and as nationalism was tearing apart the former Yugoslavia. Two hundred years before that, in 1795, Immanuel Kant published an essay ("Towards Perpetual Peace") in which he argued that republican governments are intrinsically peaceful – even though the French republic had declared war on the British and Dutch monarchies in 1793. As Mark Twain said: "To succeed in life, you need two things: ignorance and confidence."

To be fair, the European Union (EU) somewhat fulfilled Kant's vision of a pacified Europe. But it took two world wars, the complete surrender of Nazi Germany, the Soviet threat and the Marshall Plan for the Europeans to abandon war, to embrace democracy, and to build a common future. Jean Monnet conceived the common market to subdue Germany's industrial power, and François Mitterrand devised the common currency to tie the newly reunified Germany to Europe. This is why the EU is a trompe-l'œil: it looks like a Kantian ideal, but it was built out of Hobbesian fear (and thanks to US nuclear deterrence).

The EU has not quelled nationalism. In fact, it has even revived it – for two reasons.

The first is that European integration has backfired. The powers of the European Commission are perceived by many Europeans as an undue infringement of a Kafkaesque bureaucracy upon elected and answerable national governments. As for the Euro and open borders, they are accused of worsening unemployment and of impeding economic growth. Hence the rise of populist and nationalist political parties that capitalize on the claim that "Brussels" is responsible for the erosion of national sovereignty and for the loss of jobs. The rise of nationalist parties was confirmed by the 2014 elections for the European Parliament. In September 2014, Sweden's far-right party obtained 13% of the vote in national elections.

The second reason is that the EU, paradoxically and unintentionally, encourages nationalist secessionism. Regardless of the result of Scotland's referendum, the fact that it was held in the first place is symptomatic of secessionist tendencies within the EU. Scotland is not alone. Catalonia is also demanding a referendum on independence from Spain. In Belgium, the New Flemish Alliance (which became Belgium's largest political party in the 2014 elections) officially advocates Flanders' secession.

The fact is that the EU makes it safe and affordable for small nations to secede.

Post-WWII Europe became the central field of the global power struggle between the United States and the Soviet Union, and European nation-states on both sides of the Iron Curtain had to be strong and united to face a common enemy. In Eastern Europe, artificial states that were kept together by the Communist iron fist fell apart with the end of the Cold War (tragically in the case of Yugoslavia, peacefully in the case of Czechoslovakia). In Western Europe, the then European Economic Community (EEC) became a European Union (EU) with a common currency and federal aspirations. Between 2004 and 2009, Europe's former Soviet satellites became EU members.

Within the EU, is it politically viable to be small: no country is in danger of being conquered by a larger neighbor (if anything, the Flemish would rather have France annex the Walloons and take over their subsidized economy). Being small, in the EU, is also a great deal economically thanks to lavish EU subsidies and to the Euro (spendthrift countries can chronically live beyond their means and count on Germany to pay their bills).

Hence the secessionist appetite of small European nations that would never have dreamed of independence two decades ago. It is telling that Alex Salmond, the leader of the Scottish National Party, has explained that his bid for independence is partly motivated by the aspiration of "playing a full part in the European Union, whose last big expansion in 2004 saw the admission of ten new states - six of them smaller than Scotland, and six of which had become independent since 1990."

So the patronizing European advice to Israel that it is time to follow Europe's example by relinquishing national sovereignty for a supra-national structure has become completely off the mark. Europe is reverting to nationalism. European peace and stability are once again threatened by Russian paranoia and expansionism. As for the Middle East, it is sinking into the most primitive and barbaric forms of Islamic fanaticism. The Middle East of 2014 is hardly a place and time to experiment with Kantian theory.

In fact, it is Europe that could learn an important lesson from Israel: that the future belongs to democratic and coherent nation-states that have a sense of purpose and that are resolute to fight for it.

Conclusion

In the wake of the Yom Kippur War, the Arab members of OPEC leveraged their oil exports to blackmail importing countries into isolating Israel. Between October 1973 and March 1974, they refused to sell oil to the United States and to other countries deemed "friendly" to Israel, such as Holland, Portugal, South Africa, and Rhodesia. Even countries that were not "punished" suffered from the oil shock of 1973 because Arab countries cut down on the production of oil, causing oil prices to quadruple within a few weeks from three dollars a barrel to twelve dollars a barrel.

Forty years later, the "oil weapon" is about to become inefficient.

In 1973, western economies, used to importing cheap oil, were taken by surprise and had to limit the costs of this sudden price surge. They tried to adapt by cutting on consumption, for example, with speed limits and daylight saving hours. Yet in spite of those measures, the US economy could not sustain the oil embargo. For the embargo to be lifted, however, America had to put pressure on Israel to withdraw from the territories it had conquered during the Six-Day War. It did. The United States convened the Geneva Conference after the Yom Kippur War, and it coerced Israel into withdrawing from a quarter of the Sinai Peninsula in 1975.

The oil weapon thus proved to be quite efficient, but it also boomeranged: it caused such a deep economic crisis in the West that the United

States and Europe started reforming their energy market so as not to be hit again.

The West could not just abandon its suppliers and shop somewhere else for its oil, however. Oil is concentrated in the Persian Gulf. There are, of course, large deposits of oil in Russia, Africa, South America, and even Norway. However, the Arab and Muslim countries of the Middle East and North Africa still control one third of the world's total oil production. Moreover, the world oil market is a cartel, and therefore there is no way for oil importers to shop around and turn competition to their advantage. OPEC controls 80 percent of the world's crude oil reserves and 40 percent of the world's production. In that cartel, Israel's biggest challenge today is Iran.

In 1973, Israel paid the diplomatic price for the West's dependence on Arab oil. Today it pays the diplomatic price for China and India's dependence on Iran's oil. China and India are two huge oil importers, and their oil consumption keeps growing. For geographic reasons, it makes sense for these two countries to import oil from Iran. There is a reason why China has been blocking tougher sanctions against Iran at the UN Security Council, and why India is not helping, either.

Israel, therefore, has an obvious interest in contributing to the progressive undoing of oil's monopoly over transportation, which is the main source of the world economy's dependence on oil. In January 2011, the Israeli government decided to launch an ambitious multiyear program whose goal is to promote "technologies to reduce the global use of oil in transportation." This program includes generous funding for scientific research, incentives for investment in local companies developing oil alternatives, a scheme for implementing these alternatives in Israel as a preliminary application site, and cooperation with multinational organizations and countries seeking to reduce oil dependency, such as China and India.

As opposed to countries like China, the United States, or Brazil, Israel cannot compete with the massive production of biofuels. Israel can theoretically produce biofuels in sub-Saharan Africa, but that remains a huge challenge in terms of logistics, distance, and funding. Rather, Israel's strength lies in its intellectual resources. Israel has world-renowned researchers who specialize in second-generation biofuels and other technologies that will eventually undo the monopoly of oil over transportation.

Israel's comparative advantage in developing new technologies still has to produce a technological breakthrough. Meanwhile, however, another breakthrough did happen in Israel's energy market with the discovery of natural gas. In January 2009, Israel's economy and international stature were transformed overnight when the Texan firm Noble Energy discovered gas in the Tamar field in the eastern Mediterranean. This field is estimated to contain 9.7 trillion cubic feet (TCF) of natural gas. Tamar represents over half of what the European Union's twenty-eight nations consume annually. Two years later, in 2011, Noble Energy discovered another huge gas field in the eastern Mediterranean, which is now estimated to contain 18 trillion TCF (trillion cubic feet). This second field was called Leviathan, and it alone contains about as much gas as what Europe consumes annually.

The discovery at the Tamar field came at the right time, since it happened just as the import of gas from Egypt was being constantly disrupted and just as the Mari-B field entered its last stages of production. Tamar averted what would have been a major breakdown in Israel's energy sector. Just when Israel found itself unable to continue the energy dependence that it had built with Egypt, Tamar has provided Israel with gas independence for the next two decades.

The flow of natural gas from Israel's Tamar reservoir in the Mediterranean to the Ashdod reception facility was inaugurated in March 2013. Besides providing Israel with enough natural gas for decades, the

Tamar deposit and the much larger Leviathan deposit could even transform the country into a major energy exporter. Leviathan and its estimated 18 trillion cubit feet of gas, is expected to go online in 2016.

In neighboring Cyprus, Noble Energy discovered another natural gas field, Aphrodite, comparable to Tamar in size. Israel and Cyprus together now sit atop at least 35 to 40 billion cubic meters of gas—roughly two years' worth of European consumption. Furthermore, in 2011 a team of geologists from MIT examined data from the Levant basin and concluded that Israel can expect at least six more 'Leviathans' in its territorial waters.

By the year 2010, gas supply from Egypt accounted for almost half of Israel's gas consumption, or 40 percent, and gas from the Mari-B supplied roughly the other half, or 60 percent. The two together transformed Israel into a country relying on gas for about 40 to 45 percent of its total electricity production in 2010. Israel is now on its way to becoming one of the most gas-reliant nations for electricity production in the industrialized world, with estimates ranging well over 60 percent reliance in the coming few years.

Given its geographic proximity, Europe would seem to be the natural export market for Israel's gas, especially considering that the continent is facing a major gas supply crisis both because of the spread of instability in Algeria and the rest of North Africa, and because Europe is eager to reduce its dependence on Russia's natural gas.

The Tamar and Leviathan discoveries will dramatically transform Israel's economy and international standing. Since its independence, Israel has operated under resource scarcity. Israel currently consumes about 7 billion cubic meters of gas every year, and is expected to consume over 15 billion cubic meters by 2030. So the Tamar field, with its 275 billion cubic meters of gas, meets Israel's needs for the next two decades.

Israel is about to go from energy importer to energy exporter. Not only will those exports save Israel tens of billions of dollars annually, but they will also enable Israel to finance large-scale desalination projects and thus to reach water independence as well. An Israel free of energy and water dependence will be a completely different geopolitical actor both regionally and globally.

For example, Israel can now leverage its gas exports vis-à-vis Jordan. Jordan imports 97 percent of its energy needs at a cost of 20 percent of its GDP, and 88 percent of the energy it consumes comes from natural gas. The fact that Jordan is energy-dependent and energy-desperate makes it a natural target for Iranian pressures. Israel can now afford, however, thanks to its new natural gas resources, to preempt this Iranian strategy. This is why Israel initiated talks with Jordan for the export of gas in February 2013. In September 2014, Israel and Jordan announced the signature of a $15 billion gas deal between the two countries.

Israel will also likely seek to leverage its strategic geographic position to service both Asia and Europe. Israel and Egypt both have direct access to Asia and Europe, which enables them to implement a dual export strategy. Hence the strategic importance of Israel's gas exports, considering the serious questions about the future and viability of the Suez Canal as a major European-Asian transit route because of growing political instability in Egypt. One possibility is that a cross-Israel natural gas pipeline can become an additional anchor for transforming Israel into a major transoceanic passageway connecting the Mediterranean and Red Seas, thus turning Israel into a major trade and transport route as an alternative to Suez. In fact, Israel is contemplating the construction of Liquefied Natural Gas (LNG) terminals anchored at either end of the Eilat-Ashkelon Pipeline, with terminals in Ashkelon, on the Mediterranean, facing Europe, and in Ramat Yotam, near Eilat, facing Asia.

Moreover, in October 2013, the Israeli government approved an ambitious railway project that will connect the Red Sea port of Eilat to the Mediterranean port of Ashdod. The ultimate, if not official, purpose of this railway is to become a "land bridge" for goods traveling between Europe and Asia, and thus to compete with the Suez Canal.

Forty years ago, right after the Yom Kippur War, countries had to keep their distance from Israel if they wanted affordable energy, especially oil. Today, however, the Arab world is falling apart and becoming more and more unreliable. The West is discovering new energy sources (especially thanks to the fracking technology for oil and natural gas), and Israel is about to become an energy exporter.

This geopolitical transformation will affect the political leverage of oil-exporting nations, and therefore it might also diminish the international pressure directed at Israel. Only world powers can defy international criticism and pressure. This is why there is no international pressure or even criticism over China's brutal occupation of Tibet, or over its merciless repression of Xinjiang's Muslims. This is also why Russia's partial occupation of Georgia has been forgotten. Even a regional and midsize power such as Turkey gets away with its occupation of Cyprus (an EU member) and with its refusal to grant national rights and political autonomy to the Kurds. By contrast, there is still massive international pressure on Israel to withdraw from Judea and Samaria (the West Bank).

After the Six-Day war of June 1967, Israel offered to return the Sinai Peninsula to Egypt and the Golan Heights to Syria in exchange for peace. There was something illogical in Israel's offer, since there had been no peace before Israel captured these territories: Egypt and Syria had attacked Israel with the purpose of destroying it, despite the fact that Egypt and Syria controlled those territories before the war. And, indeed, Egypt and Syria replied with a flat no at the August 1967 Khartoum Conference. As Abba Eban quipped at the time, the Six-Day War was the first war in history at the end of which the victor sued for peace, while the vanquished demanded unconditional surrender.

As for the West Bank, Israel decided not to annex it, mostly because it did not wish to significantly increase the proportion of its Arab citizens. "I prefer the dowry to the bride," said Levy Eshkol, Israel's prime minister at the time. Israel also feared international opprobrium.

Legally, however, there was a strong case for annexing Judea and Samaria, since this was part of the territory that had been allocated by the League of Nations for Jewish self-determination in 1922. This legally binding mandate had not been superseded nor canceled by the nonbinding recommendation of the UN General Assembly from November 29, 1949—a recommendation that anyway became moot the moment it was rejected by the Arab League. Historically, Judea and Samaria belong to the Jewish homeland. The patriarchs and matriarchs of the Jewish people are buried in Hebron and in Bethlehem. Joseph is buried in Shechem (Nablus). The Temple Mount in Jerusalem is the cornerstone of Jewish history and faith.

At the end, the Israeli government decided not to decide. At the time, however, no one in the international community called for the establishment of a separate and additional Arab state in Judea and Samaria. Even those who called for Israel's unconditional and full withdrawal meant only that Jordan should recuperate the territory it had lost in June 1967. Nobody spoke at the time of a "Palestinian state" or of a "Palestinian people." The 1947 UN partition plan called for the establishment of a Jewish state and of an Arab state. Had anyone ever heard of some "Palestinian people" at the time, the UN resolution would have said so. As for UN Security Resolution 242 (adopted in the aftermath of the Six-Day War), it did not call for the establishment of a "Palestinian state" either. It called for an Israeli withdrawal from territories (not from *the* territories) conquered by Israel in exchange for full peace and secure, recognized, and defensible borders.

Israelis who oppose the annexation of Judea and Samaria generally argue that annexation would turn Israel into a binational state. They claim that Arab birthrates are higher than Jewish birthrates, and therefore that time is not on Israel's side. But what about the actual demographic facts?

As I explain in this book in Part Two (Chapter 44: "The Two-State Religion" and Chapter 54: "Time Is on Israel's Side"), the "demographic time bomb" never went off and is not going off, simply because it is based on fraudulent demographic data. This is an important point that calls for some elaboration.

In 1997, the Palestinian Central Bureau of Statistics (PCBS) published a census that was described by its director, Hasan Abu Libdeh, as "a civil intifada." The purpose of this census was to scare Israeli public opinion about a so-called demographic ticking bomb that required Israel's withdrawal from Judea, Samaria, and the Gaza Strip. According to the PCBS census, Arabs were to outnumber Jews between the Mediterranean Sea and the Jordan River by 2015. It claimed that there were 2.86 million Arabs in Judea and Samaria in 1997, and that the figure would rise to 5.81 million by 2015. These figures did manage to panic many Israeli leaders, who referred to the "demographic ticking bomb" to justify the need to create a Palestinian state. And when reaching an agreement with the PLO proved impossible at Camp David in July 2000, the same Israeli politicians started advocating unilateral withdrawal in order to save Israel from demographic suicide. In December 2003, in fact, Ariel Sharon announced that he endorsed the unilateralist theory, and he carried out Israel's unilateral withdrawal from Gaza in August 2005.

That same year, however, the American-Israel Demographic Research Group (AIRDG) revealed that the 1997 PCBS census was fraudulent, having inflated the number of Arab residents by nearly 50 percent. The census had also inflated Arab birthrates and immigration rates, precisely as the Muslim world was entering a period of demographic contraction. For example, the census predicted 903,626 Arab births in Judea and Samaria between 1997 and 2003. In reality, according to the Palestinian Ministry of Health, there were 599,311 Arab births in Judea and Samaria over that period.

In fact, according to the US Census Bureau and the Israel Central Bureau of Statistics (ICBS), fertility rates have decreased for the past decade in the Muslim world in general and among Arabs in Israel and

Judea-Samaria in particular. Between 2001 and 2012, Arab fertility rates in Judea-Samaria dropped from 4.08 children per woman to 2.98, and from 4.33 children per woman to 3.11 among Israeli Arabs. Jewish fertility rates, by contrast, have increased from 2.53 children per woman in 2001 to 2.98 in 2011.

The census had also projected imaginary and unrealistic immigration rates. It claimed that 236,000 people would immigrate to the Palestinian Authority (PA) between 1997 and 2003. In reality, the PA experienced a negative annual net migration over that period, as reported by the Israeli border authorities: from 1994 to 2007, 322,000 Arab residents emigrated from Judea-Samaria alone. The figure reached 63,386 in 2008. Polls further show that large numbers of Arab residents of Judea and Samaria would emigrate if they could. Many of them apply for immigration visas. By contrast, Israel enjoys a high rate of aliyah: 241,673 immigrated to Israel between 2001 and 2011, and in the past three years, the immigration of European Jews (especially French Jews) has increased significantly, mostly because of economic recession and Muslim anti-Semitism in Europe.

The PCBS census claimed that the annual Arab population growth between 1997 and 2003 would be 4.4 percent for Judea and Samaria and 5.2 percent for Gaza. In reality, over that period, the annual Arab population growth has been 1.8 percent for Judea and Samaria and 2.9 percent for Gaza.

Furthermore, in 2013, Israel's Central Bureau of Statistics reported an Israeli population of 8,018,000 citizens, 20 percent (1,658,000) being Arabs. With an actual Arab population of 1.6 million in Judea and Samaria, there is a two-thirds Jewish majority in Israel and in Judea-Samaria combined. Demographic trends suggest that this demographic majority is stable and likely to grow. Since Israel's 2005 withdrawal from the Gaza Strip, that territory is out of Israel's demographic equation.

So while Israeli demographer Arnon Soffer has warned many times over the past three decades that Israel was about to become a binational state, he has consistently been wrong, because a million Jews immigrated to Israel from the Soviet Union in the 1990s, because Arab birthrates have been decreasing as Jewish birthrates have been increasing in the past two decades, and because Israel withdrew from Gaza in 2005.

With the rise of anti-Semitism in Europe, Israel is moreover seeing an influx of European Jews, especially from France. There are between 230,000 and 750,000 Israeli citizens outside of Israel who are not granted voting rights for elections to the Knesset. If they were, a stronger Jewish majority would emerge at the Knesset.

Clearly, there is no demographic time bomb. Does that mean that Israel should fully annex Judea and Samaria and that it can afford to grant Israeli citizenship to all its Arab residents, thus increasing its Arab minority from 25 percent to nearly 35 percent?

The annexationist option must be weighed against its alternatives. The so-called two-state solution has consistently failed since 1937. It was rejected in 2000 and in 2008 by the PLO because of the right of return issue. During the 2013–2014 negotiations, Mahmoud Abbas refused to even discuss the recognition of Israel as a Jewish state, because he understood that doing so would constitute a de facto renunciation of the right of return.

As explained in Chapter 65 ("Back to the Iron Wall"), unilateral withdrawal was meant to preserve Israel's Jewish majority in the absence of a peace agreement with the PLO. The consequences and side effects of unilateral withdrawal have proved to be so lethal, however, that the idea of repeating the experience to Judea and Samaria is a non-starter.

Admittedly, advocates of unilateral disengagement base their case not only on demographics but also on morality. The late professor Yeshayahu Leibowitz, who passed away two decades ago, claimed again and again that "the occupation" would eventually corrupt and even destroy Israeli society. He also predicted that concentration camps would be set up in Israel for people like him. There is no doubt that

Leibowitz's powerful intellect and unconventional ideas captivated many. But Leibowitz's argument about the moral weight of military occupation has been contradicted by reality. Firstly because Israeli society hasn't been corrupted or gone insane and secondly because the alternatives to military occupation have proved to be morally worse than occupation itself. Since Israel withdrew from Gaza, this territory has turned into a terrorist base that has dragged Israel into military operations every two years on average. Those military operations have killed thousands and caused large-scale destruction in Gaza. How is that more moral or more morally justifiable than the military government that was in place until 1994, or than Israel's partial military presence until 2005? Unilateral withdrawal, far from relieving Israel from a moral burden, has dragged Israel into unavoidable military operations whose human and material costs are far worse than those of running a military government over a foreign population.

This leaves Israel with two possible options: maintaining the status quo or formally annexing Judea and Samaria. These are bad options that must be weighed against each other. Full annexation would eventually be feasible only if the current demographic trends are confirmed, and if it excludes the Gaza Strip. Those demographic trends can be sustained by encouraging Arab emigration via economic incentives. To those who condemn such an idea as horribly illiberal, I ask the following question: Why is it acceptable to suggest the encouragement of Jewish emigration from Judea and Samaria (an idea promoted by the Israeli left) but unacceptable to suggest the very same idea for the Arab population?

There might also be unexpected events in the future that will change the demographic makeup between the Mediterranean Sea and the Jordan River. In that regard, I would like to quote Israeli historian Benny Morris. In his 2004 interview with Ari Shavit in *Haaretz*, Morris claimed that Ben-Gurion had committed a fatal mistake in 1948 by not completing the expulsion of the Arab population:

I do not identify with Ben-Gurion. I think he made a serious historical mistake in 1948. Even though he understood the demographic issue and the need to establish a Jewish state without a large Arab minority, he got cold feet during the war. In the end, he faltered. If he was already engaged in expulsion, maybe he should have done a complete job. I know that this stuns the Arabs and the liberals and the politically correct types. But my feeling is that this place would be quieter and know less suffering if the matter had been resolved once and for all. If Ben-Gurion had carried out a large expulsion and cleansed the whole country—the whole Land of Israel, as far as the Jordan River. It may yet turn out that this was his fatal mistake. If he had carried out a full expulsion—rather than a partial one—he would have stabilized the State of Israel for generations. If the end of the story turns out to be a gloomy one for the Jews, it will be because Ben-Gurion did not complete the transfer in 1948. Because he left a large and volatile demographic reserve in the West Bank and Gaza and within Israel itself…The non-completion of the transfer was a mistake.

So what must be done today? Again, Morris:

> If you are asking me whether I support the transfer and expulsion of the Arabs from the West Bank, Gaza and perhaps even from Galilee and the Triangle, I say not at this moment. I am not willing to be a partner to that act. In the present circumstances, it is neither moral nor realistic. The world would not allow it, the Arab world would not allow it, it would destroy the Jewish society from within. But I am ready to tell you that in other circumstances, apocalyptic ones, which are liable to be realized in five or ten years, I can see expulsions.

If we find ourselves with atomic weapons around us, or if there is a general Arab attack on us and a situation of warfare on the front with Arabs in the rear shooting at convoys on their way to the front, acts of expulsion will be entirely reasonable. They may even be essential...If the threat to Israel is existential, expulsion will be justified.

Morris gave another interview to *Haaretz* in September 2012. There, he said the following:

The Palestinian national movement has remained unchanged, throughout the different periods of the struggle, whether under the leadership of Hajj Amin al-Husseini or his successor, Yasser Arafat...It did not even change during the years of the Oslo process. In the end, both sides of the Palestinian movement—the fundamentalists led by Hamas and the secular bloc led by Fatah—are interested in Muslim rule over all of Palestine, with no Jewish state and no partition...Arafat, since the '70s, after Fatah's guerrilla warfare failed to yield results, concluded that the liberation of the homeland would be accomplished through a "policy of stages." The idea of the "struggle in stages" was meant to achieve the gradual elimination of Israel and a solution of a single Arab state. In other words, the Palestine Liberation Organization leaders continually put on a conciliatory face in order to please the West, but actually their goal was to eliminate Israel in stages, since they couldn't do it in one blow...The same staggered strategy, which sees the establishment of a state in the occupied territories as the first stage in the conquest of the entire land, was, in their view, better than a direct strategy of endless military confrontation. Abbas says it day in and day out, and continues to demand the right of return.

Benny Morris knows one or two things about the Arab-Israeli conflict, and he cannot be suspected of approaching it from a right-wing ideological stance. If the conflict cannot be solved, it must either be managed or won. So far, Zionism has been winning. Current demographic trends in Judea and Samaria, if confirmed and if encouraged by proactive Israeli policies, might eventually make the annexationist option a viable one. Until this happens, Israel should remember that, in the absence of a solution, settling with being a success story surrounded by failed states is not that terrible after all.

Made in the USA
San Bernardino, CA
27 January 2016